The Power of Dreams

27 years Off-grid in
a Wilderness Valley

Dave and Rosemary Neads

THE POWER
of DREAMS

*27 years
Off-grid in a
Wilderness
Valley*

Dave & Rosemary Neads

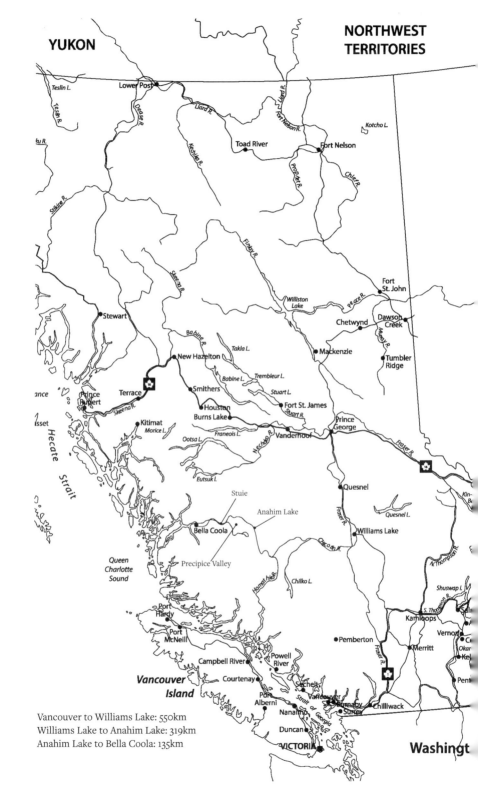

YUKON

NORTHWEST
TERRITORIES

Teslin L.

Lower Post

Teslin R.

u R.

Liard R.

Toad River

Kechika R.

Fort Nelson R.

Prophet R.

Fort Nelson

Kotcho L.

Chief R.

Stikine R.

Finlay R.

Williston
Lake

Peace R.

Fort
St. John

Stewart

Babine R.

Takla L.

Chetwynd

Dawson
Creek

Murray R.

Mackenzie

Tumbler
Ridge

New Hazelton

Babine L.

Trembleur L.

Terrace

Smithers

Stuart L.

Fort St. James

Prince
Rupert

Houston
Burns Lake

Stuart R.

Prince
George

ance

Skeena R.

Fraser R.

Kitimat

Morice L.

Ootsa L.

Franeois L.

Nechako R.

Vanderhoof

isset

Hecate Strait

Eutsuk I.

Quesnel

Kin-
Bo

Quesnel L.

Stuie

Anahim Lake

Bella Coola

Williams Lake

Chilcotin R.

N. Thompson R.

Precipice Valley

Queen
Charlotte
Sound

Homathko R.

Chilko L.

Shuswap L.

Chilko L.

S. Thompson R.

Kamloops

Vernon

Port
Hardy

C

Pemberton

Okar
Kel

Merritt

Port
McNeill

Campbell River

Powell
River

Fraser R.

Pen

Vancouver
Island

Courtenay

Sechelt

Chilliwack

Port
Alberni

Vancouver
Burnaby
Surrey

Nanaimo

Strait of Georgia

Duncan

VICTORIA

Washingt

Vancouver to Williams Lake: 550km
Williams Lake to Anahim Lake: 319km
Anahim Lake to Bella Coola: 135km

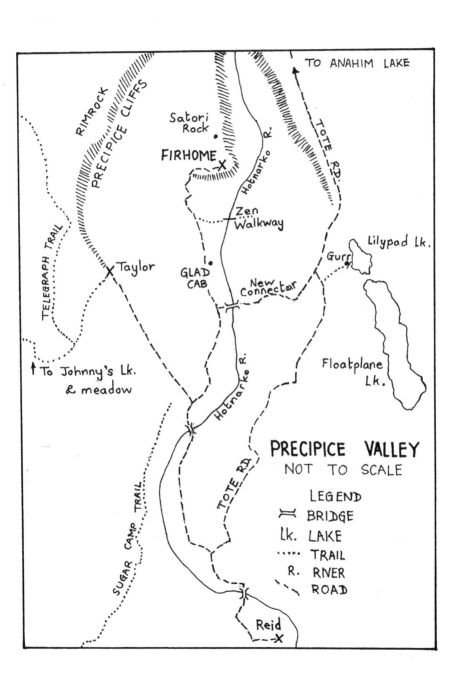

TO ANAHIM LAKE

RIMROCK
PRECIPICE CLIFFS

Satori
Rock

FIRHOME X

Hotnarko R.

TOTE RD.

TELEGRAPH TRAIL

Zen
Walkway

Lilypad Lk.

Gurr

X Taylor

GLAD
CAB

New
Connector

↑ To Johnny's Lk.
& meadow

Floatplane
Lk.

Hotnarko R.

SUGAR CAMP TRAIL

TOTE RD.

PRECIPICE VALLEY
NOT TO SCALE

LEGEND
⋈ BRIDGE
Lk. LAKE
..... TRAIL
R. RIVER
ROAD

Reid
X

hancock house

ISBN-13: 978-0-88839-718-8 [trade paperback]
ISBN-13: 978-0-88839-742-3 [epub]
Copyright © 2022 Dave & Rosemary Neads

Library and Archives Canada Cataloguing in Publication

Title: The power of dreams : 27 years off-grid in a wilderness valley / Dave and Rosemary Neads.
Other titles: 27 years off-grid in a wilderness valley | Twenty-seven years off-grid in a wilderness valley
Names: Neads, Dave, author. | Neads, Rosemary, author.
Identifiers: Canadiana (print) 20210285087 | Canadiana (ebook) 2021028563X | ISBN 9780888397188 (softcover) | ISBN 9780888397423 (EPUB)
Subjects: LCSH: Neads, Dave. | LCSH: Neads, Rosemary. | LCSH: Outdoor life—British Columbia—Chilcotin Plateau. | LCSH: Self-reliant living—British Columbia—Chilcotin Plateau. | LCSH: Chilcotin Plateau (B.C.)—Biography. | LCGFT: Autobiographies.
Classification: LCC GV191.52.N43 A3 2021 | DDC 796.5092—dc23

Editor: D. Martens
Production, Cover: J. Rade
Front cover: Photo by Rosemary Neads
Back cover: photo by Chris Harris
All other photos in the book are by the authors unless otherwise stated.

Printed in China

We acknowledge the financial support of the Government of Canada through the Canada Book Fund and the Canada Council for the Arts, and of the Province of British Columbia through the British Columbia Arts Council and the Book Publishing Tax Credit.

Hancock House gratefully acknowledges the Halkomelem Speaking Peoples whose unceded traditional territories our offices reside upon.

HANCOCK HOUSE PUBLISHERS LTD.
19313 Zero Avenue, Surrey, B.C. Canada V3Z 9R9
#104-4550 Birch Bay-Lynden Rd, Blaine, WA, U.S.A. 98230-9436
Phone (800) 938-1114 Fax (800) 983-2262
www.hancockhouse.com info@hancockhouse.com

ACKNOWLEDGMENTS

We wish to recognize the spirit and resourcefulness of the pioneers of the Chilcotin-Cariboo, both past and present, that inspired us to follow our dream to its fullest and were always there when we needed them.

A special thanks to Naomi Wakan for encouraging us to write our book, and to Harold Rhenisch for his guidance on organization and content. And of course to our friends and supporters, without whom we'd often have back-shelved our writing efforts!

TABLE OF CONTENTS

INTRODUCTION

I was standing on our ridge during a clear December midnight, stinging cold biting my cheeks. Overhead, stars sparkled with sharp blue light sent from far Arcturus, mirroring the diamond crystals scattered on the crusty snow before me. The silence was absolute. All I could hear was my heartbeat.

And then it came. At first I felt, rather than heard it: a mournful vibration, gathering volume, breaking the silence and raising hackles on the nape of my neck. From deep within the shadows of the ancient fir forest, this first solo was joined by more voices to become a full choir of wolf song bursting across the frozen meadow.

As if cut by a sharp knife, the chorus stopped in mid-phrase. After a beat, there came an explosion of yips, yowls and yelps, announcing a second choir on the ridge above. The coyotes had joined the concert. In this moment, the verses of wolf and coyote song became an orchestrated wilderness anthem. The magic of such a moment never leaves your heart.

Exceptional experiences like these may last for a just a few moments or for hours. They redefine our sense of reality, challenging our perceptions, shifting us into a sharper, clearer definition of ourselves and our place in the cosmos. These events are not planned or even expected; they arrive in their own way, following ancient patterns established over an immense span of time.

During our 27 years in the Precipice Valley, Rosemary and I often were challenged by these rhythms, reforming our image of ourselves and the world around us. Exhilarating, sometimes a little scary, this communion has opened many doorways, revealing new possibilities, giving us a more secure sense of being.

In this book we share our experiences with you; tales of events, places, practical solutions and ingenuity that filled our lives for nearly three decades. They may be philosophical, ethereal or humorous. Some are sad. We hope they will give you a feeling for life out in the wilderness. Perhaps they will inspire you to fulfill your own wilderness dream, carving a path through these challenging times when new ideas and understandings are so desperately needed.

THE POWER OF DREAMS

Dave & Rosemary dreaming on mountain top

Beginnings

Rosemary and I built a house in the wilderness of Precipice Valley, on the ancient trade route linking the Interior Plateau with the British Columbia coast. We lived there for twenty-seven years, much of it in near-total isolation. It was our dream. Dreams are powerful motivators, and they sustained us as we taught ourselves to work with wood, grow and store vegetables and plan supplies to last between our twice-annual shopping trips. We learned to share our lives with wildlife, manoeuver seasonal roads, use a chain saw, run snowmachines, and maintain the vehicles. We had optimism and belief in ourselves.

Like many of our generation, after we left high school Rosemary and I took time to work and travel instead of going straight to university. Even though we did not know each other at the time, in the early 1970s we were both in Mexico, living in Volkswagen vans that we had each camperized ourselves. We had travelled a lot, had a variety of jobs, done a lot of interesting things. We met at the University of British Columbia when we both went back to school in our thirties. By 1980, Rosemary had a B.Ed. and I had finished my first year on an M.A. in Urban and Social Geography.

In the spring of that year, fresh from university and undecided about our next stage of life but needing a break from our studies, we headed north up Highway 97 on our way to Haida Gwaii, but then detoured along Highway 20 to visit my old friend Tony and his wife, Diane, at his home in Hanceville in the east Chilcotin. Tony also owned a store in Alexis Creek, the next small stopping place west of Hanceville. The current lessors were leaving, he told us. He then persuaded us to check it out, with a view to taking over the lease. We didn't need much convincing. We were attracted to the country and the apparent freedom, so we agreed to Tony's proposal.

We continued on to Haida Gwaii, but that fall we returned to the hamlet of Alexis Creek, where we took over Tony's Alexis Creek store, called "Pigeon's" after the man who had started the business in the late '40s.

During our time at the store, we had made trips west from Alexis Creek to explore the country. The memory of our first trip on Highway 20 west of Alexis Creek is still crystal clear: Climbing up onto the plateau, we entered unbounded country under a big, open sky. There were no fences along the road, save for occasional stretches of old logs, and no hydro or telephone poles. The power grid stopped at Alexis Creek. There were few side roads, and Highway 20 was just a wandering, two-lane gravel road that headed west into unknown land. The little stopping places had no power, except for the odd generator. If it rained for a couple of days, the road would become impassable. One resourceful friend heading to Nimpo Lake with her 3 children simply camped in the car by the road until it dried up a bit! The feeling of freedom was intoxicating. It was easy to imagine riding through the wide open space, beyond the horizon. The Chilcotin had caught us. We were hooked on both the country and the vision.

Finding our Home

Although we loved the Chilcotin, neither of us were social creatures at heart, and we found the daily interactions at the store too restrictive. At the back of our minds was a shared but seldom-stated dream to live in an area that was totally wilderness. Through the two decades of working daily jobs, struggling with university as very mature students and then not at all sure how our degrees could be useful—we were agreed that we didn't want to live in a city--we hadn't pursued that wilderness dream actively. The Chilcotin reawakened that dream, but we saw no way to realize it.

As with many direction-changers, the Precipice Valley came into our life serendipitously. By then we were in our late thirties, an age when it is more usual to be throttling back and seeking life's comforts than to be carving a new, independent lifestyle far from civilization. One day, while still in Alexis Creek at Pigeon's, Rosemary was browsing the local paper, the *Williams Lake Tribune*, when a small, three-line ad for some property caught her eye. It offered remote living in a wilderness valley that had a mild coastal climate, good hay meadows and even fruit trees! The ad's simplicity and directness reached out to us, so we determined to investigate. We sent off a reply, but then, with the pressure of our business life, we almost forgot about it. Many weeks later, a letter came from the seller, David Gladden. It was written in faint pencil—more a scrawl than anything—giving directions so we could come and have a "look see." The note was irresistible.

Armed with the directions and lots of enthusiasm, I made the journey west to take a look at this dream property while Rosemary minded the store, which by then was open every day.

A few kilometres before the village of Nimpo Lake, I turned off Highway 20, onto a side road leading to Pine Point Resort at the east end of the lake, but instead of heading for the resort, I took a left fork in the road. It put me out onto a rarely used dirt air strip pointing southwest. Following instructions from the seller, David Gladden, I bounced to the end of the airstrip, found a track veering off the right, and started along it. I had no idea where I was going, but I was intrigued by the feel of it.

Then I began to know what a Chilcotin back road was really like. I was on the Tote Road, an access track pushed in by bulldozer in the late '40s to upgrade the original horse-and-foot trail down from the Chilcotin plateau through Precipice Valley to Bella Coola. For a variety of reasons, this shorter route to the coast was never built, and the present highway down the infamous, steeply dangerous "Hill" was completed in 1953. Still, the cat push into Precipice Valley was used sporadically over the years by Precipice residents and a few intrepid fishermen who wanted to fish Kappan Lake, located a short way in.

Tote Road to Precipice Valley

This was not a road in any formal sense. It was a rough track that wound through the trees, keeping to the high ground where possible and disappearing into beaver swamps when all else failed. There were no bridges, no culverts and no ditches, just the occasional place where rock and soil had been pushed aside to reveal some welcome volcanic hardpan

Talk about total immersion! This was beyond anything I had ever encountered, and I was thankful I was driving a 4x4. The first few kilometres alternated between hard-bottom swamp, rock gardens, basalt slabs, and eskers. Some of the puddles were so long and big that I got out, took a stick and walked alongside to see how deep they were and whether the bottom seemed solid. Then I'd ease into them, heart in my mouth, until my wheels found firm ground again. The farther into the bush I went, the greater the sense of adventure that grabbed me. Where was I going? How would I respond to it when I got there? What would I *do*?

After over three and a half hours along this remarkable track, I came to a faint junction where a small path led off the right. Here, nailed to a tree, was the promised rough cardboard sign saying "Gladden."

I parked the mud-spattered Nissan here and took off downhill on foot. Sloping steeply, the narrow path took me to the Hotnarko River. Since it was mid-June and the Hotnarko was still in freshet, I crossed on a huge, old, fallen cottonwood tree. David Gladden later told us he had felled it for this purpose several years earlier.

I will never forget my first views as I walked toward the log cabin: overhung porch, steeply pitched roof, horses in the meadow beyond, warm early summer breezes flowing through the cottonwoods, the smells of the earth, the river, the pungent air . . . I had never been in a place like this. These were real firsts. Under the rustle of the river, almost beneath the threshold of hearing, there was a stillness, a sense that normal time did not mean anything here.

My gaze was drawn up to the basalt cliffs on top of the steep, fir-covered hillside, rising a thousand feet into the clear air, with game trails snaking along the talus below them: gray and white streaks on a black canvas. As the scale of what I was looking at slowly seeped into my awareness, I began to feel the deep energy radiated by the river, the ten-million-year-old lava flows, and the strength and tenacity of gnarled, fire-scarred fir trees, whose history went back centuries before the arrival of Europeans on this coast.

Then David Gladden popped around the corner, his gold tooth gleaming in the sun. A faded grey ten-gallon hat was haystacked on his head. He was barefoot, wearing jeans held up with a piece of frayed rope, and had a smile so big I thought his face would split in two.

"Howdy," he said.

And we went from there. After meeting his two very shy pre-teen girls, I went for a walk around the property.

Magical Cottonwood Grove

That is when this magical valley spoke to me. I was walking amidst the great cottonwoods upriver from the cabin, reveling in this wild place, sensing energies that were new to me, when a voice in the back of my head, which I have never heard before or since, said in a very clear, commanding voice: "This is your home." Just a simple phrase, but it gave me direction. I had found that special spot on the Earth that called to me. Even though the so-called fruit trees were dead twigs barely one foot tall, badly bent and broken by bears and horses, the Precipice had cast its spell over me.

Three weeks later, Rosemary and I returned so she could see the valley. I was worried that she might not react to it as I did, that the spell I'd been under might not capture her. But in spite of the difficult access and even though the property wasn't as advertised—no fruit trees, not a coastal climate—she, too, fell in instant love. So, in 1984, we bought David Gladden out. It took over a year of awkward communication to complete the transaction and another to make the necessary arrangements for our transition into the wilderness, but in the spring of 1986 we moved into David Gladden's tiny log cabin, which we promptly dubbed the Glad Cab. We lived in it for five years while we established the basic structure of Firhome, our hand-built, two-story, 2,200-square-foot post-and-beam home.

Reality Strikes

The dream of moving into the bush, living off the land, free from the clutches of civilization, is just that, a naïve dream that disappears in the harsh morning light of dawn. Yes, I shot moose and deer and caught trout from our lake, and yes, Rosemary, through tenacity, much hard work and imagination, was able to grow root crops for storage, sprouts and summer greens. But what of salt, pepper, flour, and all the other staples? And what of clothes? Unless we made our own clothes out of moose hide, we had to buy those warm winter clothes and boots.

We needed propane, a stove, and a water heater. And, unless we wanted to walk everywhere, trucks, snowmachines, and ATVs. To keep warm, and to build anything, we needed chain saws, axes, all the rigging for getting firewood, and tools for the seemingly endless repairs on the equipment. On top of that, there was ongoing maintenance of equipment, gasoline, fuel, property taxes, medical and vehicle insurance, and so much more. The short of it was that to live in the harsh climate of the Chilcotin today, we needed a cash income far beyond what our small 15-hectare holding in a very cold climate could provide.

We were not alone. To supplement sparse income, almost everyone in the West Chilcotin "worked out." Some found work on a fencing crew, others joined firefighting crews in the summer, worked at the local sawmill, contracted to a guide outfitter in the fall, clerked in one of the stores at Anahim or Nimpo Lake, worked part-time at the post office, drove a school bus or maintained the local landfill. Others had a backhoe or a dump truck and did odd jobs here and there. If you were really lucky, you had a government job—janitorial services at the school or work driving a grader or a truck for Cariboo Road Services. Many men and women were independent contractors, driving logging trucks to the mills in Williams Lake, or worked in the bush as equipment operators. We were no different in our needs but a bit more limited because of the distances from our valley to the highway.

Ranger Dave waiting for plane pick-up

Rosemary says it best:

Many probably assumed we had inherited money, but we had no rich relatives. When we moved into Precipice we had enough saved to pay for the property and buy the basic building supplies, but even though we were supposedly mature and organized at our ages, we hadn't thought beyond that.

Then during our second year, the reality of having no income sank in. Fortunately, Jim Glenn, a former resident of the Precipice, intervened to help Dave get summer work as a park ranger based in Tweedsmuir Park, a 930,000-acre provincial park to the west of Precipice Valley. This was a wonderful experience for Dave. The downside was that he was gone for eight or ten days at a time, which meant that nothing got done on our house building. I couldn't really fill in for him. I could do a little carpentry, but not the real construction. I couldn't even begin to move the huge posts and beams we were using! It was frustrating to be making such slow progress with our house, but there seemed to be no choice, financially.

Dave was with B.C. Parks seasonally for five years. Occasionally I was able to join him when their working camp was too far out to bother running all the horses back to the holding corral near Highway 20, so either Dave or Jim would opt to stay in camp on the days off. Dave would meet me just off the highway with a saddle horse, and off we would go to yet another adventure.

People wondered if I got lonely with Dave away so much, but I seemed to be far too busy for that. I had the dogs, cats and horses to care for and for company, the demanding gardens to be maintained and new ones established at our building site, and later, when the main house construction was completed, the finishing work. If I ever ran out of things to do, I'd get a head start on some stained-glass commissions, although those were usually winter projects to very patient clients for delivery after spring breakup.

Truth is, income was often thin. For food, we largely lived off the land, especially at first. Then more permanent work found us by accident. During those first years in Precipice Valley, we were so intent on just basic survival that we hadn't given much thought to environmental issues, but when a

THE POWER OF DREAMS

serious threat came to the West Chilcotin—a company had massive plans to clear-cut deciduous trees for pulp chips, which could disastrously affect the water table—we somehow became involved.

This was before the internet, so Dave and I put out a little monthly newsletter, Chilconet, because so many people didn't have telephones and often were unaware of what was happening around them. It truly was a "cut and paste" operation, typing out our messages on our old selectric typewriter, pasting them in some sort of order and then making the long trip into Anahim Lake, where the Ulgatcho Band Office had a copy machine they generously let us use for the cause. We often worked far into the night, collating, stuffing, and addressing envelopes, and leaving them to be mailed, before heading home along the snowmachine trail, like travelling through a tunnel with diamonds sparkling in the frozen snow.

One thing led to another and, in spite of the difficulty of travel for us, we formed the West Chilcotin Resource Association and then the highly successful Anahim Round Table, which was part of the Cariboo Chilcotin Land Use planning. This was during the Mike Harcourt NDP government, when a lot of attention was being given to B.C.'s natural resources. We became busier and busier with conservation issues, learning to call ourselves "conservationists" rather than "environmentalists" because of the bad rep associated with that word during those years. The logging companies were moving into the Chilcotin Plateau and the situation had become dire for wildlife and tourism both.

A Vancouver-based company, B.C. Wild, heard about Dave's work and decided that he needed their support, so he became one of the very few funded conservationists working away from the Lower Mainland. He left B.C. Parks and then spent even more time away from house building as he travelled to meetings all around B.C., including meetings in Victoria with the Premier or his ministers.

B.C. Wild didn't last, but a new organization, B.C. Spaces for Nature, headed by Ric Careless and Dona Reel, took on the Chilcotin campaign and contracted Dave to organize the regional campaigns. He negotiated at both regional and provincial levels, often away from the valley for a week or more at a time.

In the twenty-seven years we were in Precipice, not only did we build Firhome and keep that lifestyle up and running, but Dave also ran successful campaigns for establishing protected areas. In one 18-month stretch he drove over 50,000 miles between Smithers and Clinton. Meeting with people in town halls, libraries, municipal offices, hotel conference rooms, home kitchens, and podiums, he covered a lot of territory. As well, there were the flights from Anahim Lake to Vancouver and Victoria for campaigning at a higher level.

After a long day in a meeting, strategizing or negotiating, when others went home to dinner and a hockey game, Dave went on the road. It became routine for him to drive two or three or more hours to the next meeting. With special high-intensity, long-range headlights installed so he could see a mile ahead, he liked driving at night on a deserted highway in the winter.

As he told me, "I felt I was moving through interstellar space, encapsulated in my single ship. I often arrived in town at night in preparation for a meeting the next day. After driving from Precipice along Highway 20 to the top of the hill down into Williams Lake, five to six hours in darkness, to see the town with its lights laid out below was a strange sight. I often thought that its yellow and orange glows looked like an omelet laid out on big black plate."

The Chilcotin Ark Campaign went on for twelve years before Dave felt he had wrung the last hectare out of the process. B.C. Spaces had wound down this part of their works after having achieved the protection of remarkable swaths of protected areas in the Chilcotin and other parts of B.C. Dave took various contracts, such as one with the forestry division of a local First Nation. By the time we left Firhome he was fully retired, although he still kept his hand in on various committees and advisory groups.

Over the years, Dave earned a good reputation with environmentalists and logging companies alike. He had a "let's work something out" attitude that gave combatants space to move without losing face. The Chilcotin has parks and protected areas now that would never have been created without the efforts of all these dedicated people.

FIRHOME

Firhome from the air

Building Firhome

When we say we built our own home, we mean just that. We had no access to, nor money for, contractors, building equipment or tradespeople. While still living in Alexis Creek we sketched numerous designs on graph paper, and in our ignorance our first ideas were totally unrealistic, such as an octagonal behemoth. I even made a scale model of that one! By 1985 we had finally settled on a traditional saltbox design: an efficient, well-proven use of space, and easier to construct for two inexperienced people without specialized equipment. The house was on two floors and had a 12-foot cathedral ceiling with open 4x6 rafters. We reversed the usual house layout, choosing instead to have the bedrooms on the bottom floor with the upper floor as the main living area. Rosemary planned the layout and I did the engineering. We had no internet in those days. All we had were a couple of books and a lot of determination.

We decided on our final building site, up on the ridge above the valley bottom, by selecting an area that had the fewest large trees on it, then driving Big Red (our 1969 wood truck) onto it. We placed boards across the back to get the right height and then sat up there to determine the exact orientation of our house. It was starting to feel very real to us.

We designed Firhome to take advantage of the exposure of the site. On the second floor the big south wall windows would be thigh-high to the top of the wall, giving us sunsets and plant-growing space. The kitchen window above the sink faced east for the morning sun, on the northwest side there was a large window over the piano, and on the northeast, under the eaves where the roof sloped steeply, there were no windows at all. Firhome had its back to the winter storms that roared down the valley from the high ridges behind.

The large entrance hall was on the bottom floor. We faced the master bedroom east, so the windows would catch the early morning light. It seemed to us quite luxurious, with its en suite plus a huge bathtub in an alcove across from the bed. A second bathroom and bedroom were originally planned for

Rosemary's mum, but she died before it was finished and it became an office and guest room. Rosemary's stained-glass studio, wood heater, laundry, cistern and batteries took up the rest of the space. Sleeping downstairs ensured we were cool at night, while upstairs we were warm with the sun during the day, or from the rising heat from our wood heater on the ground floor. I often wonder why more homes are not designed this way. Our dining room on the upper floor had a large deck and a walkway out to the ridge on our east side, giving us convenient access to the solar panels and a great view down to where the river curled around the snout of the esker, 50 metres below.

It had been simple enough to plan on paper, but little did we know the scale and scope of the task before us. While still in Alexis Creek the first building I had ever done had been a giant dog house for our Irish wolfhound, McGee, back in Alexis Creek. Admittedly, he was a big dog, and the commercial plans we used were definitely grandiose, but building a large home was another thing altogether. After our Precipice purchase was finalized, I realized I would need a workshop, so I found a local sawmill that supplied me with the large posts and beams I needed, and pre-assembled it behind our store in Alexis Creek. Then I loaded it all onto our long-suffering Nissan and trucked it into our new property. Stealing time from the store, I eventually got a building raised so I could start preparing the timbers for our house.

We had decided against using logs. For one thing, moving them around would be too difficult for just the two of us and no equipment. As well, a log house would have meant cutting down many more trees. The romantic in me wanted to build post and beam, or more accurately, timber frame. The difference between the two is that a timber frame has interlocking joinery and needs no fasteners, a system thousands of years old that uses dovetails, mortise and tenon, braces and wedges for holding the structure together. I wanted our home was to be a true representation of the time before the Industrial Revolution, when people built their own homes their own way. Living as remotely as we did, we had another advantage: We didn't have to follow the building codes for incorporated areas.

Rosemary spent long winter evenings coming up with floor plans and ideas of what needed to go where. She had very definite ideas about kitchen design, room layout and efficiency of space. While she was doing that, I dove into the world of timber frame joinery.

It was mid-June of 1987 when I started on the foundation. I was 41 years old. I built a 16x16x8-inch slip form, laid out the foundation lines, used a water hose for a level, and placed the first form. Using sharp sand and gravel I had dug out of old sandbars I had scouted out on the valley bottom, I mixed the cement using a gas-powered mixer I had borrowed from a friend in Nimpo Lake. The black flies were thick, the sun was hot, the day humid. I was sweating buckets, but I didn't mind at all. I was finally getting to the real work—I was building our dream house!

First foundation block, June 1987

THE POWER OF DREAMS

I carried each of my prepared beams over to the site and laid them across the newly poured foundation blocks. By the end of August I had a platform 30 feet wide, 40 feet deep, level and sound. As I stood on that finished platform, I felt an exhilaration that was beyond description. I was starting to believe I could really do this.

I reluctantly had to give up part of my dream. I realized that if I were to continue with the traditional mortice and tenon joinery, the project would take far too long to complete. So I compromised and adopted the "piece en piece" style. It was still an ancient style, but not as romantic as timber frame. Instead of interlocking joinery, the posts were set upright and braced with 2x6s; then a cross beam was laid across their tops. Steel pins were driven through them into the post below, then braces were affixed to the corners using 12-inch lag bolts, the holes pre-drilled and then screwed in using a large ratchet.

Once completed, it looked the same as timber frame. You had to look very closely to see any difference. But it got done.

The wood for Firhome was from centuries-old Douglas fir trees, horse logged on our property and milled for us by Lee Taylor in 1985. When we first bought our property Lee and his family were still in the Precipice full time with his family. He had a mobile-dimension sawmill, so even before we left Alexis Creek Lee and his friend Dennis from Washington worked up 30,000 board feet of lumber for us. It made quite a pile! All of it, from 1x8 to 14-foot-long 12x7 posts, was carefully stacked for air drying in piles at the foot of the driveway—more than a dozen stacks, all covered with blue tarps. It looked like the circus had come to town. Two years later, the wood was dried and ready. I could only hope I had measured correctly and that there would be enough material to build a house and the other buildings we needed.

Construction was simple but slow. I would stand a post up, Rosemary would balance it until I had it secured with braces, then we did another. Piece by piece, using homemade scaffolds and ladders, we gradually erected the frame, just the two of us: new creatures building their nest in the valley.

March 1988, framing progress

At one point during this process, we made another naïve decision—to cut off the west corner of the living/dining room. We thought that would give us even better views looking over to the Coast Mountains, and indeed it did. But it's a good thing we didn't have the internet then, because if we had checked this decision out, we would never have attempted it! The problems encountered with cutting odd angles evidently are myriad, and new builders are warned against it. But ignorance is bliss, and we were pleased in the end that we'd made that choice. I finally gave up trying to use mathematics to calculate the difficult angles for the braces and beams and simply eye-balled it, but I got lucky the first time, and we did a little jig of celebration.

Slowly, day by day, week by week, we got the first floor ceiling, which was the floor for the second storey, in place. All tied together, it was beginning to look like a structure. Next came the trickier part: Once a subfloor was laid on the second floor, the process of post and beam was repeated. This time, though, the middle of the wall was 12 feet high. Our scaffolding, which we christened the Siege Machine, morphed into a two-step affair, each platform four feet high: giant stair steps. We had to be super careful with this process. We were the only people in the valley. Sure, there was a phone in the Glad Cab if we had to call for medical help, but that phone line often wasn't working and in the winter, even if we did need help, it was at least four hours away, if at all. We were on our own.

Up and up Firhome went. It was eight metres from the ridgeline to the ground, yet finally the last rafter was laid in place, the last brace bolted across the last corner, and the skeleton of Firhome stood proud and true. Sitting on the ridge beam, Rosemary and I looked out across the meadow below and over to the mountains. It was a natural high that we will never forget.

That stage of the process took two years. One fine summer day, as I was nailing down the ceiling boards on top of the open-beam 5x7 rafters, I looked down into the meadow and saw a large black wolf sitting on his haunches, just watching the new kid on the block. I still remember that moment with awe.

Top floor in place

Bit by Bit

Now came the less exciting but still important work: metal roofing, closing in the building, insulation, wiring, plumbing, flooring, building the cabinets, window casements, dry-walling, glazing the windows, sanding, painting and staining, step by step.

Some things really stand out. Stairs were certainly a challenge, but building the chimney was formidable: 11 metres from the foundation block to the top tile. And I have a long, deep-seated fear of heights! Yet there was no choice, so I gritted my teeth and kept at it.

The thing was, though, I had never done anything remotely like this before. From a friend, I borrowed a book on masonry that had a chapter on chimneys. The opening sentence in the chapter read: "Don't attempt this unless you have experienced help. Chimneys are very difficult to do properly." Yeah, right. But I was doing it correctly: Nine-inch fire bricks, clay flue liner, the works. The chimney had to be absolutely vertical and straight.

Then came the day I seated the stovepipe from our wood heater into the chimney and carefully laid a small fire. When I watched the smoke rise out the top, with no leaks and drawing just fine, I had another moment of vibrant energy. I had done it!

Dave's chimney success

THE POWER OF DREAMS

All of this was accomplished at the end of a very long supply line. Materials had to be purchased in Williams Lake or even farther away, loaded onto a truck, driven to the trailhead of the Tote Road, then carefully packed for the rough trip into the Precipice, or loaded into skimmers to pull behind snowmachines if it was winter. We had to plan it carefully. If some essential piece of equipment or building material had not been purchased or was damaged, it could not be replaced until the following spring. The planning had to be meticulous.

Nevertheless, we had our share of disasters, like the time I was transporting two very large pieces of picture-window glass, a gift from Rosemary's brother who was remodelling their Tsawwassen home on the Lower Mainland. I had it vertically braced and fastened to two uprights. I was just a short half-hour from home when I hit a very large pothole and heard an ominous *snap!* I looked in the rearview mirror in time to see the glass shatter into small pieces. After some weeping and wailing, we simply redesigned our living and dining room windows to accommodate smaller, more easily transported glass.

As money was tight, I scrounged. In those days, the Arbutus neighbourhood of Vancouver was undergoing rapid redevelopment. Older homes were being torn down, to be replaced with behemoths. The developers saved on disposal fees by putting the contents and even the structure of these old homes up for sale: windows, doors, and furniture. After a few days, these open-house yard sales were done and the homes were abandoned until they could be knocked down.

I made several trips to Vancouver in our 1969 truck to take part in this last hurrah. I would cruise a neighbourhood, find these deserted homes, and remove doors, toilets, electrical panels, electrical plugs and other bits and pieces I needed for Firhome. It took a week of my time and an astonishing amount of gasoline, but it was the least expensive way I could obtain these components.

Moving In

In the fall of 1990, we were still living in the Glad Cab. But in early November we broke our vow to not move up to Firhome until everything was completed. Every day that particular cold fall we had hiked up from the cabin to light fires and warm up the building enough to work in it, so living there—even as rough as it was—seemed more logical. All that prep work had become just too time consuming. And after nearly five years in the Glad Cab, Rosemary was calling it "The Incredible Shrinking Cabin."

The house was still a work in progress, with plastic over the windows, no plumbing, and only one outside door accessible, up on the second floor, since there was lumber filling the downstairs entrance hall and no proper staircase. Shortly after we finished moving up there, we were rewarded by a snowfall of one and a half metres of snow in just 36 hours—on top of the half-metre we already had on the ground. At first it was very pretty, and we spent the evening sitting in front of our plastic-covered living room window drinking red wine and eating popcorn, congratulating ourselves on moving up in the world. But the next morning, our only door was buried up above the half-glass. Our dog Hobo was completely bewildered, while the cats just curled up and ignored the whole situation.

Did I mention the plumbing issue? The outhouse was over thirty metres away. Through very deep snow. After our first rather urgent expedition there, we trekked down to the cabin to collect our snowshoes because we weren't sure that our neighbour's caretaker, Mort (a 65-yr old who was recovering from a broken leg), would be able to feed the horses himself. The usual ten-minute walk took us more than two hours! The trip wasn't helped by Hobo, who was impatient with our slow progress and kept trying to leap ahead. He wouldn't give up, even though each time he was completely buried in the soft, fluffy snow and we had to dig him out.

We got to the valley bottom, and as we waded through the snow towards the cabin, we could see a strange bobbing ahead in Lee's big meadow off to our right. It was Mort's cowboy hat, with Mort under it, on top of his favourite horse, Diamond. His determined horse had to lunge to move through the deep snow, and Mort was simply hanging on.

Our finished living area on the 2nd floor

Among the three of us, we got the feeding taken care of and made snowshoe tracks back up the hill. Mort followed more easily on his horse, and we enjoyed a late but much-deserved hot breakfast in our new palace: plastic on the windows (Chilcotin thermopane), a ladder for stairs, old doors for counters, and bare subfloors. Plumbing was just a hope and a promise, with the deep snow complicating everything we tried to do. We just kept doing what we were doing, an attitude that helped us survive many times.

The Solar Story

Living in the bush was our dream but we weren't kids anymore, so part of that dream was to be comfortable doing it.

Our lights would be solar-powered, a central part of our plan to live off-grid but with some degree of comfort. Problem is, there were no "off the shelf" units available as there are today, and no internet. To piece it together, I read magazines, made phone calls, sent letters and money orders, and dealt with customs, all difficult propositions from where we were living.

The solar modules came from California, six of them, providing 30 amps at 12 volts. They were a far cry from today's standards, but back then they were the best you could buy. Each panel had 36 round black cells, set in a white background: unblinking eyes to stare at the sun.

Gridless in the Precipice

To produce the most power possible from these early modules, it was important that they faced the sun at a 90-degree angle. That meant they'd have to be moved during the day to face east in the morning, south at midday and west in the afternoon. What's more, because the sun is low in the sky in winter and high in summer, they'd also need to be tilted relative to the horizon on a seasonal basis. In short, the array would have to be moveable in two planes.

In Alexis Creek we had a satellite dish to receive TV and radio—a technology used for local cable stations to receive programs for distribution on their local cable networks. If you purchased a satellite dish of your own and bought a little black box to decode the signal, you could watch all the TV you wanted for free. You could also, I realized, use the satellite mount for dual-axis tracking of a solar array.

These early dishes were huge. Ours was ten feet in diameter, metal, with petal-shaped sections that had to be bolted together, but like all of them it could be rotated in both horizontal and vertical planes to pinpoint any particular satellite. You used a hand crank to move the dish on a swivel head, much like a giant camera tripod, on any arc, on any elevation. When I realized that the sun was like a satellite moving across the sky, I knew I had my solar panel mounts.

Cumbersome though it was, we moved our Alexis Creek dish into the Precipice. Once the satellite dish was installed I purchased a second mount and positioned it there also. I built a sturdy framework of 2x4s and 2x6s, attached it to the mount and then fastened the solar panels to it. Now we were able to move the modules twice daily for horizontal tracking and four times annually for vertical adjustments.

The original array was in the meadow, six metres in front of the Glad Cab, in the location that received the most sun throughout the year. Problem was, Cabin Meadow was also a grazing pasture for the horses, giving them the privilege of fertilizing their own winter feed. Horses and solar mounts, however, do not mix well: an 800-pound mare can decide to use the lower panels to scratch her derriere. So I had to build a fence out of logs to keep the panels in and the horses out. We did the same with our satellite dish.

I buried electrical wires from the array to the cabin, set up a generator to run a charger to top off the batteries when the sun couldn't do the job, added an inverter and meters, and threw the switch. Success! It was quite a thrill to have an electric light in the cabin, and it was fun to occasionally watch the evening news on TV—virtually our only contact with the outside world for months at a time during the long winters.

We used batteries to store the electricity from the panels. I knew they'd have to be large, as we did not get a lot of sun in the winter. My attention was drawn to stationary batteries used by telephone companies for backup. They changed them out every few years and kept new ones on standby. When I checked with BC Tel, I learned they were selling off a set in Prince George. Big ones. Really big ones. So off I went to Prince George, full of anticipation.

It was late October, the days were getting short and the evenings long, and it took a full 11 hours from the Precipice to Prince George, driving our Nissan 4x4. I arrived late in the evening and slept in the truck, scrunched up in the front seat. (Although the Nissan was a "king cab," it felt more like a "lackey cab" that night.)

Over to the warehouse bright and early to see my purchase. They were huge! Glass cases, 30 inches tall and 14 inches square. They weighed 400 pounds apiece and we need 6 of them.

Sure, the truck was only a half-ton, but hey, I had put in an extra leaf that spring. Things would be okay, even though I really hadn't counted on that much weight. The lift truck driver had to do some skilful manoeuvring as he loaded them; they filled the box completely.

As I drove away, I thought the steering felt a little odd, so I pulled over to take a look. Uh-oh. The weight in the back nearly lifted the front end off the ground! Still, everything was good. I still had enough traction to steer, although when I hit a bump the front tires literally left the road surface for an instant.

So, it was slow, slow down the highway from Prince George to Tony's place in Williams Lake. "You must be crazy" was his supportive observation. No argument from me.

The next day, the normal four-hour drive to Anahim Lake took more than six, so I overnighted again at a friend's place in Nimpo Lake. As a result, it wasn't until day four of the battery expedition that I started back in to the Precipice.

I could have walked that track faster than I drove. Over the boulders, into the puddles, in 4x4 low range, inching along like a caterpillar, ever so slow, but determined. A long six hours later and I was parked outside Glad Cab, proudly showing Rosemary our latest acquisition. I was wired but happy. I had made it.

Then it struck me. Six 400-pound glass containers filled with acid and lead had to be moved from the truck bed into the cabin. A problem to sleep on for sure!

By the next morning, I had devised a plan. First, I shovelled out the low bank between the driveway and the porch of the cabin. Then I carefully backed the truck up so that the bed of the box was (almost) level with the porch floor. Here, Gladden's rough building style was a bonus. He had simply cut logs in half and laid them, round-side down, to make the floor. Uneven to be sure, but very strong. I took several 2x4s and built a ramp from the truck bed to the porch.

Using a come-along attached to the far side of the porch, I laid a rope sling around the first one and ratcheted away—slow and steady, a couple of feet at a time. Then I reset the come-along, eventually manoeuvring the battery into its new home inside, in the northwest corner of the cabin. One down and five to go. By dusk that night, all were in place. Looking back at it now, it doesn't seem that hard a thing to do.

Those batteries took up a whole corner of our small cabin. They were a talkative bunch; while sucking up energy they would squeak, burble, gurgle and make other rude noises. After a few weeks of listening to the batteries, we named them Squeak, Bubble, Glug, Pop, Gurgle and Gargle. Snow White's dwarves had nothing on these guys.

When, four years later, we moved up the hill to Firhome, we wanted our home to have all the mod cons. So we purchased another, much larger, satellite dish mount and 16 more modules. I located both arrays on the edge of the ridge, with a clear, uninterrupted view of the southern sky. It was a perfect solar location.

I finished the system for Firhome with new batteries. These were from a supplier in Lone Butte, who was intrigued by our location and took on the task of delivering them right to our door. It was a far cry from my earlier Prince George trip for the first set of batteries. The new ones, which weighed a lot less, sat in the corner of the first, or ground, floor opposite the cistern, and came with a new inverter to change the DC battery charge into the AC current needed to run our appliances. I did wire Firhome for both DC and AC, to cover my bases. In those days it was more efficient to run 12-volt lighting instead of going through an inverter.

We had our generator and knew that during the two greyest months of winter we would have to use it for several hours a week to keep the batteries charged. Living at the other end of the Independent Power Producing (IPP) spectrum had given us a clear image of what electricity really is and how it fits into daily life. We had learned to respect it.

Living up on the ridge became a delight, with the openness and the great views. We used to look out the dining room window at Mt. Marvin in the Coast Range and say smugly, "Next stop, Japan."

Two or three times a day, depending on the season, we rotated the solar panels so their flat black cells could stare unblinkingly into the face of the sun. Sure, I could have made a remote-controlled device to move them, but as you learn when you run your own systems, the old adage "Keep It Simple Stupid" should be applied full force. Besides, there was nothing more bracing than going out on a -30 morning in mid-January and crunching through a fresh six-inch fluffy snowfall to tend the panels.

On morning like that, after a couple of cups of tea, with the early sun wanly peeking over the horizon, the walk to the panels became more of a ritual, announcing to the frozen land that you had made it through the night, that you were stirring to go about the business of living here, being part of the local fauna.

Because solar panels don't work well if covered in snow, we extended the handle of a brush so we could clear them off. One of the arrays was 2.5 metres high by 6 metres wide; the other, 2.5 by 4. They sat on the satellite mounts, so the tops were nearly four metres from the ground. To reach the top of the panels we had to stand quite close to the bottom edge—a dangerous place for the unwary because when the panels were touched, the smooth surface released the snow in the whoosh of a mini-avalanche. It really woke up the senses to have a face full—or worse, a boot full—of fresh powder at 30 degrees below freezing before breakfast.

Clearing snow from the solar panels

Wind was another issue for the array. The Ridge of the Dancing Firs, where we built Firhome, points directly west over the Coast Mountains. Wind blowing up the Bella Coola Valley and onto the plateau has an unobstructed fetch of a hundred miles. Until I got the hang of it, the panels were blown over a couple of times. There is no sorrier sight than to see your precious panels lying on their side partway down the steep hillside, jillpoked by a fir stump. Three were damaged (but incredibly, still producing at 80 percent!) before I reinforced the mounts. I was away that particular time, so Rosemary was without power for 10 days until I returned and rejigged the electrical cables.

"No big deal," she told me. "I used the propane stove for cooking and candles and kerosene for light." I realized I was fortunate to have such an unflappable partner!

After that, I placed a large steel base below each array, anchored with 1.5 cm aircraft cable secured to four 2.5 cm stainless-steel rods that I drove two metres into the ground. The steel base was weighed down with 450 kilograms of boulders I collected from around the place and stacked like a miniature pyramid around the central steel pole of the mount. There were no blow-overs after that.

On the power side, our electrical consumption was not as easy to control as you would think. Digital readouts gave us the state of the various inputs and outputs. Early on, we discovered that even when all appliances were turned off, all the lights were off, and apparently nothing running, the inverter was still sending out power. But how could that be, I wondered? Well, we discovered that because we live in a culture of instant-on, most of our toys, such as televisions, DVD and CD players, food processors, and computers have a small circuit built in so that there is no warm-up time when you turn them on. That means that even when off, these things use electricity. These "ghost" loads were a problem because they sucked power out of the batteries 24/7. Even though the current draw was small for each appliance, usually in the milliwatt range, they still added up to a lot of power in the course of a week. In the winter, especially, when conservation and wise use of electricity was mandatory, these phantom loads needed to be removed.

The solution I came up with was to have a deadman switch controlling the receptacles that these machines were plugged into. So when we turned off the unit, we didn't use the on/off button; we threw a switch that killed the plug, really turning these little bleeders off.

Electrical systems are fussy beasts at the best of times. The solar panels charged batteries, and a mystical device called an inverter changed the direct current of the battery to the alternating current, AC, which most appliances use. Inverters use very sophisticated electronics, of the type used in spacecraft. Like astronauts, we were very conscious of the amount of power we consumed. It was more than turning off the computer and the lights when we were not using them. We had to balance the loads to keep the demand down. For instance, we couldn't use the microwave when the washing machine was running, because of the big surge when the washer kicked into the spin cycle. Similarly, the microwave and the toaster couldn't be on at the same time. We couldn't afford power issues. If we burned a transformer or killed an inverter, it was a long and costly affair, not to mention the logistics of transporting sophisticated electronics 40 kilometres into the bush by snowmachine in the winter. Not a thing we wanted to do.

The Delights of Running Water

Our water system also was my own invention. The easy, logical building site was on the valley bottom, but we had chosen, perhaps shortsightedly, to build up on the ridge, mainly for the views and more sun. So Firhome sat 180 feet above the valley floor and 30 feet back from the edge of a steep embankment composed of rocks, boulders, gravel, bare sand, and rock covered with brown needles and some hardy shrubs. You could slide down and climb back up, but it was not easy. Digging a well up on the ridge was impossible, so the only way to get water was to do the same thing we had done in the Glad Cab—take it from the Hotnarko River. With no people or livestock living upriver, the water in the river was always pure and clean.

I had purchased a used forestry water pump used for fighting fires. It was a two-cycle centrifugal pump, capable of pumping several gallons a minute up to the house. I dug a little side pool along the bank of the river where the pickup hose could be located and built a 4x8x4-foot cistern inside Firhome and lined it with swimming pool liner. The roar from the little pump could be heard all over the valley. If anyone was in Precipice, they certainly knew when we were filling our cistern.

This worked fine in the summer. All Rosemary or I had to do was to prime the pump, pull the rip cord, and away it went. That is, as long as the choke was set correctly, the priming bulb had been pumped the correct number of times, and the gas mixture had no water in it. With me away so much, Rosemary became adept at working with the occasionally temperamental machine.

Winter was a whole different story. At -20 the pump was so cold that as soon as you poured water into it, ice would form, clogging the impeller. The solution was to fill a pail with hot water up at the house, balance it on your knees on the snowmachine, take it down to the pump site and prime the pump with it. You had to complete the operation before the water cooled so much that it would refreeze in the pump. If all went right, the engine fired up. If not, well, another trip up the driveway, and in some cases the whole apparatus needed to be hauled up to the house for thawing. You'd need to check that it would start, then take it back down the driveway and over to the river. Rosemary declined to do this on her own, preferring to melt snow rather than go through the whole, often frustrating experience.

A second pump in the cistern fed a standard pressure tank water supply for the house. In effect, the cistern was an in-house well. Water was heated with a propane demand water heater, so showers and laundry all worked as in any standard home. I was very proud of the pressurized hot and cold water we enjoyed in Firhome. It was certainly a far cry from the bucket brigade at the Glad Cab.

After a few years of the fire-pump method, we could afford to have a well dug. Now, "dug" is an operative term. Actually, a backhoe from Nimpo Lake bounced into the valley along the Tote Road, and I chose a spot at the base of the slope. "This looks good," I said, after trying to tap into that special consciousness that well witchers claim.

I was anxious, as the backhoe could dig down only 12 feet. But after about eight feet, the operator hit a large spring, and a bit further down, another one. At 12 feet, we hit more water yet, which quickly started to fill the cavity. Using a chain and lots of skill, the operator lowered three 4x3-foot well tiles into the hole and then backfilled around them.

I hooked up a deep well pump, connected the electricity, and attached it to the former water line. Now, when the cistern needed filling, all I had to do was to flip a switch and water would flow uphill and into the cistern. This was magic!

A Gardener's Perspective

Rosemary was challenged with devising her own adaptations to gardening in Precipice. Without her efforts and ingenuity, we would not have fared well at all in the realm of homegrown food. She remembers her earliest efforts very well:

Growing our own food was imperative. When we first moved into the Glad Cab the Gladdens' growing area was overgrown with weeds, but at least it wasn't totally raw and unworked, and being so close to the river there was a high water table and sandy soil. As soon as possible after we moved in, even though it was already late May, I started lots of vegetables—but inside our already crowded 15 x 18 cabin, because of the short growing season. My plan was to can or freeze as much as possible and have a root cellar for the storage vegetables. While the little guys grew, I started preparing the growing site while Dave continued working to make our cabin more livable.

Everything I planted that year was doing well and I was feeling a bit smug—until I had a rude awakening. On August 15, the temperature dropped to 15F. I rushed outside after midnight when the bright, starry night and rapidly dropping temperature inside the cabin alerted me that something was amiss, and threw all the extra bedding I had over my precious vegetables. It was too little too late, and we lost a lot of the more tender crops. That extreme drop in August never happened again, but, much the way our dog forever staked out a tree where years before he had seen a squirrel, forever after I covered everything on clear nights. Just in case.

As a result of that unwelcome freeze, during the rest of that first summer we had very few fresh vegetables. Dave made the torturous trip into Anahim Lake in September to buy some and discovered that the two small grocery stores there didn't have much to offer. Their own supplies had made a long trip west themselves and often were no longer very fresh.

That's when I got into sprouting in a big way. I ordered sprouting seeds through mail and grew seven different kinds, plus a few greens like black-oil sunflower seeds. Now those little four-inch greens are called "micro greens" and are even sold in stores and restaurants. But for us, they were simply a bit of crispness in our salads.

Something we hadn't considered when we were making plans to move into Precipice Valley—one of the many things—was how we would manage the shopping. When we first settled in, the road to the highway in the drier months took us three and a half bone-shaking, vehicle-punishing hours. Obviously, we weren't going to be making quick trips to the stores. It became clear fairly soon that we would have just two major shopping trips a year, before winter set in and after breakup in the spring.

You know the game where you try to imagine what you would want to have if you were stranded on a desert island? We were on that island! I spent weeks making up that first shopping list, trying to calculate how much we needed of basic essentials for the next seven months. This was a challenge in itself—how many people know how much toilet paper or eggs they use a month? Aside from the workshop, we'd never built anything larger than an outhouse, so how many nails would be needed for a full house? What size? After a lot of conferences with Dave I ended up with a shopping list of six typed pages, single-spaced, with two columns on each page.

It already was quite cold, so once in town that first year in late October we stocked up on a lot of insulated coolers to keep the vegetables from freezing in the SUV on the way home. I bought as much as possible from the bulk food sections of the grocery stores and had planned our trip to coincide with case-lot sales. All the perishables and vulnerable food—like eggs, avocadoes, and bananas (a very special, rare treat in our new lifestyle, we soon came to understand)—had to be packed very carefully for the final 40 kilometres of rocky road. Of course, by then we really were craving fresh fruits and vegetables, so that first year I bought far too many things that wouldn't last long enough for us to eat them before they added to my compost pile. But oh my, they tasted wonderful!

We now ran into a problem we hadn't quite thought through: where do you store seven months' worth of groceries when you're living in a 15x18-foot cabin, with a sleeping loft? Anything that could take some freezing, such as dry dog food, flours, pastas, etc., went outside in totes. We soon learned, to our dismay, that the heavy plastic totes were no deterrent to pack rats. So we checked them daily, setting a pack rat trap whenever we found new gnaw holes. The canned goods joined some of our less-used dishes and pots in the loft under the eaves. The bulk of our possessions were stored in an old cabin a couple of kilometers away. We had a large chest freezer we ran with solar, and after we moved to the new house added a second one.

We were very happy when a weasel moved under the cabin, because the pack rats steered clear of it, and the mice kept "Herman the Ermine" (he was white in the winter) well fed. Whenever we ate something with bones, we'd drop them down through the cracks in the floor boards of the porch, just to make sure Herman stayed around. The cats and dogs evidently didn't bother him, since he was still living nearby when we moved up to the new house.

Once winter arrived in Precipice Valley, it was there for five or six months. It was very unusual to have any melting before mid-April. I would order our vegetable and flower seeds by mail early in January (poring through the seed catalogues became a New Year's Day treat), starting them in our tiny cabin as soon as they arrived. By March, we'd be overwhelmed with all the seedlings. Most of these got planted out, under layers of agricultural fleece or plastic for protection, in mid- to late May. I hadn't done much gardening in my life (and neither had Dave), so it was a steep learning curve. Sure, we had six frost-free weeks each year, but the big problem was that those weeks weren't consecutive! We could usually count on July as "safe," but that window was very restrictive, and even with all of the cold frames we built and row covers I carefully laid out on top of the little guys, frost was an ever-present danger. I also grew a wide variety of flowers. As I often said, "We need the vegetables for our stomachs and the flowers for our souls."

While living at the cabin, for the warmer months Dave had built a wooden shower stall outside, behind the old Gladden tack shed. Dave would use that well into fall but I wasn't happy showering outside when it was that cold, so we set up a system in the cabin for the winter. It was based on our hiking and camping days--simply a bag of water hanging from the upper roof over the loft opening, while we stood in a large round canner on the bottom floor. A 12-volt pump moved the water to the loft from the cistern, and a propane flash heater gave us hot water. What a joy!

The learning went on. Since we were responsible for our own road maintenance, we didn't want to make ruts. After the snow was gone and before the road had dried up, if we went out of the valley it was by ATV. As you can imagine, by early spring we were anxiously checking the road out of the valley to see if it was dried up enough for our truck. We were

THE POWER OF DREAMS

really eager to make that first shopping trip after the long winter. We hadn't run out of any critical staples, but we were getting pretty tired of the supplies we had on hand. The early spring nettles were wonderful, but we worried about getting too much oxalic acid. So that late May, in addition to a lot of fresh fruits and vegetables, our shopping list included more interesting items: pizza ingredients, such as olives, anchovies, and artichoke hearts, and a variety of nuts and dried fruits.

After four and a half years, just when I thought I had a handle on when and how to grow things, we moved up to our new house, with its totally different microclimate, away from the river's immediate influence and sandy soil. I'd been working at creating gardens up there on the ridge, but it was totally raw land and mostly clay, rocks and non-edible weeds, especially the incredibly invasive quack grass, with its sneaky underground rhizomes.

We hauled sand from the sand bar we'd found that also gave Dave material for the cement house foundations, and we found some peaty soil on the valley bottom. Our horses provided manure, and slowly I was able to build up the soil. To escape some of the weeds, we built raised beds and rototilled the hard clay on the bottom to loosen it, adding ash and covering it with cardboard before adding the soil ingredients we'd collected from around the valley. Surrounded as we were by wilderness, though, keeping out the weeds was virtually impossible. I was constantly battling them.

 The worst was when tiny slugs arrived. We never figured out where they came from, unless birds dropped them. Wherever their origin, each morning I lifted my trap boards and (wearing gloves) squeamishly picked a couple of litres of the little devils, tossing them over the side of the berm. The birds had a feast every day and often hung around waiting for me! We did eventually have excellent vegetables and flowers, but it was tough going.

Our garden on the ridge

Things looked up after a few years in the new house when, at my urging, Dave added a large post-and-beam greenhouse. It was attached to the south wall of the house and accessed from the downstairs area, near the wood heater. The greenhouse itself was unheated, since putting a wood heater in it would mean someone would have to keep it stoked all night long. Neither of us was prepared to do that, so it wasn't until May that I could move flats of hardier seedlings into the greenhouse. They'd stay there until the temperatures rose enough for planting outside. Then I'd move the more tender plants such as tomatoes and peppers down from our upstairs sunny windows. We left the door to the greenhouse and a large window open to the main house at night so they could get some benefit from our wood stove heat. We reversed the process in the fall, to keep the tomatoes, herbs, peppers and summer squashes alive a few weeks longer. It did mean more wood had to be cut for our wood

THE POWER OF DREAMS

heater, though. This was a sore point for the chief woodcutter. Many volatile discussions were held each spring and fall over just when this need for more wood would begin and end. Each year, I'd reluctantly agree to closing the greenhouse off from the main house in late October. I picked all the green tomatoes then and put them into a cool cupboard in the entrance hall. They ripened very slowly there, and so every year we had enough for Christmas and New Year's dinners. I also learned that tomatoes the size of ping pong balls froze beautifully, without blanching, and that bell peppers could be sliced and frozen the same way. The frozen tomatoes eventually became sauce, while the peppers graced many a pizza.

Greenhouse and eager plants

When we became so involved with the conservation issues and then Dave became a full-time paid environmentalist, he often had business trips to "town" (Williams Lake). In the early fall, before the main stocking-up trip, he would bring back anything really bulky, such as dog food, but especially bales of peat and perlite I'd need for making up my soil mixes. Sometimes this became an issue for me, since there were few places in the Cariboo that sold garden materials that late in the year. I had to start my gardening in late winter, long before any garden centres were open, or my crops wouldn't mature before we had heavy frosts.

I remember one fall when I'd planned some extra time during my semi-annual shopping to visit an ailing friend on the Olympic Peninsula in Washington. I'd bought a bale of peat, which I needed for my potting mix, at a large gardening store aong the highway outside of Vancouver, then went down to the States through the truck border crossing to save time. Five long hours later, I was still at the border crossing! I still had the bale of peat moss but had learned that it was an important ingredient for pot growers, and since I naively had explained how remotely we lived, I had become highly suspect. I'll never forget being confined in that tiny holding area, watching through a Plexiglas barrier as a border agent frantically typed away on her computer, checking out my claim that the bare root aloe vera intended for my friend wasn't actually a psychedelic drug of some sort. They even put dog sniffers through our Suburban. (Evidently, driving a big old vehicle was another strike against me.)

When they finally passed me through, they looked very disappointed that they hadn't been able to find anything. The joke was that in all their searches they completely missed some real "contraband"—two pears I'd forgotten about, sitting openly in the console.

Windows and Skiffs

As Rosemary said, she started seeds in January or February, then nursed them through to late May or early June, hoping that, in spite of summer-long cold nights, with a good head start the flowers and crops would reach maturity before killing frosts in August. We set up tables along the south-facing windows to accommodate all these hopeful seedlings, all thrown together in the sunbath along the window sills. On cold mornings, Jack Frost sketched his intricate designs and some of the "little guys" got their new leaves frozen onto the glass. Instant sub-zero death was a few millimeters away, yet there they sat, unconcerned, their translucent green leaves arching toward the morning sun, licking at the frost: -30, another sunny March morning in the Precipice, and spring planting was underway.

So each year we had a two-month-long "breakfast with the plants," giving us the feeling that we were in the tropics, all thanks to our windows. The word *window* is actually a corruption of the phrase "wind doors," from the time when structures had openings in the walls to let in light—and the wind—but no glass. They were just open holes. We had come a long way since then.

The plants didn't care. They just did their thing, growing like mad in the burgeoning early spring sunshine, gulping photons and spreading their foliage wings. During the course of the day, we actually saw some long, slender stems twist as the tops followed the sun: humble supplicants bowing forward to Amen Ra, the greatest god of all.

When we first moved to Precipice, Rosemary had decided that if she were to meticulously record the daily weather—things like temperature, amount of rain or snow, what flowers came into bloom when, all the events that happened in the ecosystem around us—she would eventually be able find a pattern so she could plan the garden better. Even though no predictable pattern ever emerged, the effort at accuracy led to some heated discussions. As we sat sipping our morning tea, for example, we saw there had been a bit of snow overnight. Rosemary wanted to record the amount. But how much had fallen? A dusting? A skiff? It wasn't really enough to measure. And so the topic of discussion around the table one morning was "How many dustings does it take to make a skiff?"

Bushed? The term is often used to describe people who have lived too long out of the context of a larger society. They take on odd mannerisms, ideas and ways of doing things, and often discuss and talk about things that don't make sense to "city" folk. Some might say our morning exchanges fell into this category, but when you lived where we did, such discussion was generated by the reality of the events taking place outside the window.

Think of a chocolate cake, where the merest amount of icing sugar has been sifted across its surface. You can see the bumps and lumps of the cake beneath the white powder, yet the covering is still there, in a transparent sort of way. That is what a dusting of snow does. It gives a delightful, scant coating over everything: heavier than a thick frost, yet still semitransparent, so you can see the gold of the old grasses, the rusty green leaves of the ground-hugging kinnikinnick coveted by florists for their arrangements, and the darker soil surface beneath, suspended in time and space, waiting for the morning sun to free them.

"It's more than a dusting," declared Rosemary.

"But not much more," I argued. "It's more like a skiff."

Okay, so what's a skiff? We finally agreed that it was less than a centimetre. *Definitely* not see-through, though. Really, it just gives a white coating to the ground and the trees, and adds to the solidity of the existing snow areas.

"But what about when I total the snowfall for the season?" queried my precise wife.

"Does it really matter?" I countered.

After another pot of tea, we concluded that at least four heavy dustings might make up a skiff, but we might have to alter our assessment with the next frosting of snow.

Pass the tea please.

The First Time

Life is full of firsts. The thing is that you don't know when the first time will be before it becomes the first time. First times generate memories that are vivid, deeply etched into the strata of the mind. Living on the edge of the wilderness opened a portal into first experiences Rosemary and I could not have visualized in our most fertile imaginations.

In the early years, the firsts came tumbling into our lives on a daily basis, often strung together, linked to each other in a chain of entirely unforeseen events, catching us by surprise. There were the really challenging ones, such as that first snowmobile run using a borrowed machine that stalled every time it headed down slope, causing fear and near panic. Then there was the thrill of netting the first flashy rainbow into the canoe, its silver body caught in the green mesh of the net as it settled onto the gray aluminum hull; the first scary, exhilarating ride in a Beaver float plane as it clawed its way into the sky, an adrenalin rush in the extreme; shivering on the cabin deck in the stillness of -40 as we listened to the staccato explosions of fir trees surrendering to ice; a beaver slipping and sliding down the ice-covered Hotnarko River, searching for a new home, the river itself a furry snake against a white backdrop; discovering an 80-foot-high waterfall, hidden in the dense thickets across the river on the far side of one of our meadows, heard but unseen for many years; the delight of the first dive into the Hotnarko river on a hot August day, feeling like a kid splashing and laughing the afternoon away; sitting at the breakfast table, sipping hot tea, realizing that we were the only two human beings in several thousand square kilometres of wilderness on that frosty January morning; the first time I was bucked off a horse.

That one was serious. I landed on my right hip on a rock—not so bad, maybe, but the buck knife I was wearing came between my body and the top of the rock. It gave me quite a bruise, and I was black and blue for several weeks. What I didn't know at the time was that the impact had ruptured the bursa (a fluid-filled sac that lubricates the joint), so the hip was no longer being greased, as it were. Over the years, this hip became painful and sore to the point that I went to a physiotherapist, who just shook her head and told me to get an X-ray. My doctor informed me I needed a replacement! I was truly shocked, as I had no arthritis anywhere in my body. So, in early 2011, fully 20 years after the incident, I had a total hip replacement. All this proves the old cowboy saying, "A horse may not kill you, but it sure can mess you up some."

There was the year while I was working as a park ranger. My crew and I flew into Ptarmigan Lake, at timberline, to do some trail work. Close by was "Living Room Peak"—so named because we could see it from our living room, unreachable directly because there was a deep gorge between Precipice Valley and the mountain. So, of course we just had to climb that mountain. It was pretty steep, covered with lots of large rocks. There was the usual traditional rock cairn on the summit, but as we got close the rocks seemed to undulate—the whole cairn was covered with a huge swarm of flying ants. It made no sense, but there they were, at 7,000 feet on the top of the mountain, literally covering the rocks in a rippling, silent mass. We turned and fled back down the mountain, ants following us. When we returned a couple of days later, the ants were gone, but the mystery remained.

There was our first forest fire. It was the spring of 1987, our first full one in Precipice. One afternoon Rosemary called to me—there were ashes falling from the sky. Then, upriver, we saw some thick smoke coiling. We rushed up the ridge to get a better view, and sure enough, a kilometre or so away we could see flames dancing along the valley wall, headed our way. When I close my eyes, I can still see that fire heading for us. We called the Forest Service, who told us that by evening the winds would die down and that they'd be in the next morning at first light. We spent a very nervous, sleepless night.

As promised, a helicopter came over just after dawn. After checking out the fire, they figured it was serious and quickly moved in a large firefighting crew to back up the water-bombing. It took two weeks to finally put it out completely.

One good thing that came out of it was some much-needed cash. Rosemary fed the large fire crew, fetching compliments and money, and for two weeks after the firefighters left, my horse and I were under contract to the forest service, at $25 a day, to ride up along the fire's lower edge, looking for hot spots. Some of the firefighters still recall sitting out in front of the Glad Cab during the Stanley Cup hockey playoffs, watching the game

THE POWER OF DREAMS

on the TV I'd put out on the porch, and eating pizzas that Rosemary had somehow created from our dwindling spring food supplies.

Another momentous first for me was the first big tree I felled. Yes, I had cut some trees in Alexis Creek for firewood, but this was a whole different ballgame. We had chosen our building site because there were few trees on it, but one very big fir had to be removed. This was the real deal. I read and re-read my faller's and bucker's manual, stalked the tree from all directions, thought about wedges, angles, depth of notch, and how to make the back cut, which had to be done in a special way as the girth of the tree was wider than the length of my 24-bar. I slept on it. Then, early the next morning, I took a deep breath and fired up the saw. I took my time. But all went as planned, and the big old Ent crashed to the ground exactly where I wanted it. This was a thrill. I was able to do this! I cut four 16-inch high rounds from the bottom of the trunk—seats for our campfire. Those rounds are still in use 30 years later. Things decay slowly in the dry Interior.

I remember the first time I threw the breaker and our electrical system was energized. From solar cells to batteries, to inverter, to sockets and lights, all worked perfectly. I can't tell you the satisfaction that coursed through me. A fully powered home in the wilderness! I was very proud. I had done it.

There was our first night run on the snowmachines across the plateau to Jim's place at little Goose Lake. It was very dark, quite warm, barely below freezing, and snowing hard. The snow was enchanting: huge flakes, their crystal lattices sparkling in the beams of the headlights as they drifted lazily to the ground. They reminded me of the plankton showers in the deep ocean when they are lit by searchlights. Otherworldly! We were transported into another dimension.

Rosemary remembers that trip from another perspective, as well—she had packed up a stained-glass panel, a commission intended as a Christmas present for Jim's wife, and it was carefully padded and tied to the back of my larger machine. She was ahead of me on the trail, and waited at an agreed-upon junction.

When I pulled up beside her she nearly freaked. "Where's the box?" she exclaimed, frantically looking behind me.

It was gone, fallen off somewhere on the trail. I got the Skidoo turned around and worked slowly back, with just the Skidoo headlight illuminating the dark in the tunnel of trees, fearful that I would run over it. I found it in about ten minutes and returned to where Rosemary anxiously waited. We debated whether to check the glass but decided not to unpack the box. So it wasn't until the box was opened and the panel had been delivered that we truly relaxed. Incredibly, it had survived the fall intact.

There was the first time we travelled by Skidoo through moonlit snow to a New Year's Eve party out to a friend's log cabin, lit with kerosene lamps, their warm glow mingling with the orange-yellow light coming from the huge bonfire outside.

There was our first Precipice dinner of food completely from the valley: venison, potatoes, carrots, peas, salad greens, including kale and parsley and leaf lettuce. Our beverage was homemade rhubarb wine, and dessert was wild strawberries, freshly picked. We repeated it many times over the years.

There was the first Skype call. A young woman from Germany who was wwoofing (World Wide Opportunities on Organic Farms) for us told us her mother was going to call at 6 p.m., our time. No problem; we received overseas calls quite often from wwoofer's families. As we sat down to dinner, her computer, which was sitting on the sideboard, rang. Huh? A computer that rings? The wonders increased as she opened the laptop, and there, full screen, was her mother, very delighted to talk to her daughter. I sat back and marvelled. Here in the wilderness, halfway around the globe, two people were talking face to face. It's stuff not even thought twice about today, but back then, for me, it was the stuff of science fiction, and it was happening right there in Precipice at our dining table.

CONNECTIVITY

Dave making telephone repairs

Sugar and Grease

Much of a story of wilderness in the age of information is of maintaining connections, of getting out and getting in. We were at the end of the road, on the edge of the Chilcotin Plateau. When you live on the edge, you're at the centre of things and at the intersection of many trails. Some are in the mind and some are on the land. The name Precipice first appears on maps from the mid-1800s. The name comes from the steep drop over pentagonal basalt columns that form the valley's northern flank and which bear witness to the eruptions of the nearby Rainbow volcano approximately 12 million years ago. These sheer basalt cliffs run for several kilometres and are the reason the valley was named "Precipice," as they are approximately 300 metres high. The top 30 metres or so are the columns themselves. The talus slopes away from the lower edge of the columns at a very steep angle, 270 metres down to the valley floor. These slopes are chunky in places, covered in fir forest in others, where they are prime winter range for mule deer.

Three major "grease" trails connecting the Interior to the Coast meet in Precipice Valley, where they become the Sugar Camp Trail and drop down at the west end to follow the Hotnarko River as it cuts through the Coast Mountains down to the Atnarko River. Now mostly abandoned because of rotted bridges and rock slides, this route between the plateau and the coast was used by First Nations for millennia to transport goods, especially Oolichan grease (fermented smelt fat), a delicacy and a necessary dietary staple used when making pemmican, as well as being burned for lighting. The route got the name "Sugar Camp" from the stopping point at the base of the cliffs where the trail begins a 1500-foot climb out of the Atnarko Valley on its way to Precipice. At this bottom camp, sugar and other trade goods were unpacked from the backs of horses and repacked onto the backs of men, to be carried up to the Chilcotin Plateau by foot. By the 1880s this trail had been improved enough that pack horses and mules could traverse it.

It was a link to many worlds. The sugar and other trade goods carried on it came around the Horn from distant European ports on Hudson's Bay Company ships, which unloaded their cargo onto timber plank wharves jutting into South Bentinck Arm from Bella Coola. By the turn of the last century, this pack trail had become the major trading link to the central coast, with several pack trains moving daily up and down its steep twists and turns. Another trail farther to the north was created to ease the congestion and for moving cattle up to the summer ranges in the Precipice Valley. Bob Cohen, a Chilcotin old-timer, told us that by the 1940s the traffic was so heavy that groups had to wait their turn, having dinner and overnighting in the Precipice—and sometimes the next morning, finding it easier after a night of socializing, the packers would simply send their loaded packhorses off down the trail on their own. Later that morning, the recovered packers would catch up with them on saddle horses.

Before 1953, this was the route people had to use when travelling between the Bella Coola Valley and the Chilcotin Plateau. But in 1953, when some people in both areas had vehicles, the desire for a "real" road became realized. Having unsuccessfully lobbied government for a highway link, the enterprising residents took matters into their own hands. With just a couple of large bulldozers and some dynamite and working from both ends—top and bottom—they extended Highway 20 from the Chilcotin Plateau down "the Hill" to the Bella Coola Valley. The two bulldozers met roughly in the middle of the steep cliffs—incredibly, just 10 centimetres apart.

But until a few decades ago, the old trail was still used by local ranchers, driving cattle from winter grounds in the Bella Coola Valley to spring range in the Precipice and the high country beyond. We also used it. It was our "back door" in the spring. When other routes were still blocked with snow, we could go by horseback down the Sugar Camp Trail, making a dramatic trip down from winter into the spring of the Bella Coola Valley. The trail is still passable today, although overgrown in many areas and sometimes nearly obliterated by blow-downs.

Before it drops in a series of falls and rapids to the Atnarko River, the Hotnarko River winds at a leisurely pace through Precipice Valley, following the courses of its massive post-glacial flows. Sometimes, during spring floods, when ice jams cause it to flood the valley bottom, we got a sense of what it might have been like all those years ago. Most of the time, though, its peaty, dark waters meander through meadows and old beaver ponds. Along its banks flourish groves of giant northern black cottonwoods. Its twists and turns provide food and shelter for black bears, grizzly bears, moose, beaver, wolves, coyotes, a host of birds and the occasional cougar.

The Tote Road

In winter, which could set in as early as the first week in November, travel on the Tote Road was possible only by snowmobile, and often only under challenging and difficult conditions. A "run to town" took on a whole new meaning when the thermometer dipped to 30 below. To get the mail at Anahim Lake could take all day.

In the early years we often came and went on horseback, in true backwoods style. During our time in the valley we also had flown in and out of Precipice by helicopter and floatplane and had hiked and ridden the various trails, both down to the Atnarko Valley and up to Anahim Lake, following the footsteps of the first people. Arrowheads found in northern California which came from Obsidian Peak, located just northeast of Anahim Lake, are evidence of how widespread these trade networks were. It is easy to conjure up the image of early people walking these trails with all manner of trade goods, part of a flourishing coastal economy that existed millennia before Europeans came to this place.

Originally, the Tote Road stayed on the south sidewall of the valley, finally dropping to the bottom at the old Glenn homestead, which near the end of our time there became Fred and Monika's home. Even though the west end of the valley was only five kilometres from Firhome, a trip there took more than half an hour. Gates had to be opened and closed, rough sections driven slowly, and the constant change of scenery absorbed. Coming home from the Tote Road, we would turn east from the west junction and backtrack up the valley to Firhome, adding another half hour and more bad road to a town trip.

Sisyphus facing yet another rock on the Tote Road

The Bridge Solution

In the mid-'90s we went through the permitting process and built a bypass driveway, installing a new bridge so we could go directly to our property instead of travelling that last half hour, which seemed to take forever after the bone-jarring trip from the highway.

It was all very well to have the permits, but the "how" was slow coming. As I was thinking about this project, I bumped into the forester in charge of the logging operations for West Chilcotin Forest Products. As one of his responsibilities within the company was bridge design, I asked him about design and construction. He told me of a bridge that was being removed from a logging road in the East Chilcotin. "It's no longer needed," he said. This "bridge" was actually two 20-metre-long B.C. Rail flatcars laid together side by side. It was strong enough to carry loaded rock trucks.

This sounded very promising. Right away, I looked into the specs for B.C. Rail flat-deck cars. Ah, they would do. Each was designed to carry two tanks if they had to—something like 30 metric tonnes. That obviously was more than a pickup truck would weigh, or even a loaded cattle truck, so I investigated further.

I discovered that the two railcars were sitting in a rancher's barn in Williams Lake. I called the rancher and, sight unseen, said I would like to purchase one of them and have it delivered to Anahim Lake.

The rancher called back the next day and said it would cost us $2,500 to have it delivered to the local sawmill in Anahim Lake. Done deal. I got down to preparing some 4-inch x 8-inch x 12-foot bridge timbers at the site. I was excited.

A few weeks later we got a call from the mill saying, "Your bridge is here." That was great—but now what? I had already scoped out a narrow channel where the Hotnarko emerged from a small rock bluff. The river was only 12 metres wide and had high banks and a straight channel. In other words, it was a stable part of the river, unlikely to shift for many years to come. So that was no problem. The problem (there is always a problem) was that the flat car was at the mill and the bridge site was in Precipice.

As is usual in small communities, almost everybody in the West Chilcotin knows everything about everybody. I called a local rancher who had a lot of equipment, including a very large backhoe, and explained what we needed to do. A few days later he called back and said he had a plan. It involved one of his buddies who had a self-loading log truck—that is, with a large grapple built on the back end, used to lift bunches of logs onto the deck. The plan was simple: We would use the backhoe to lift one end of the rail car and the grapple the other. Then he and his buddy would slowly drive into the Precipice, inching along, caterpillar-like, with the rail car swinging between them like a hammock.

"Sounds like a good plan," I said, trusting in their expertise with equipment.

Hauling bridge deck plus a hay bale hitchhiker into the valley

It was several days before all the people involved got together to make this move. The process took a full day and involved several backup vehicles. Not one of us was surprised that it had worked...and they even collected a large round bale of hay that had fallen from Lee's truck!

The next morning, the backhoe pulled the bridge across the river and set it in place, a skillful operation that was accomplished very quickly. Then we had a bridge party to celebrate, with everyone congratulating one another.

Over the next week I laid the deck. I reckoned that those timbers would last at least 25 years and the bridge itself many, many decades for sure. Plus, not only would this bridge hold any weight we would ever need to transport, it was good to look at.

The best part of all this was that when I asked the rancher what I owed him and his buddy for doing the job, he replied, "It was a fun thing to do. Christmas whiskey should do it."

That's Chilcotin.

Zen Walkway

I had another bridge building challenge—what we like to call the Zen Walkway, my last major project in the Precipice. I'd been thinking about it for a while but hadn't followed through because our property seemed to be sold. But the buyer wasn't able to complete, so I suddenly gained enthusiasm for the project and decided to work out what I'd need and select a suitable crossing.

This project was bittersweet for me, as it brought back memories of that first day I came to Precipice, crossing on David Gladden's old cottonwood log downriver by the Glad Cab. My hope was that this little walkway across the river would last even longer, allowing many people the opportunity to sit over the middle of the river, letting their consciousness float down into the mists of the universe.

The bridge was necessary because the big spring flood of 2011 had carried away a small log that had served us for many years as a crossing over the Hotnarko when the river was too high or icy for the ATV, making the meadows and waterfall on the other side inaccessible, from Cottonwood meadow to Spruce and Waterfall meadows to the east.

It almost too late in the season, with frozen ground and then snow, but I was determined and finally got to it early in the winter of 2012. We'd already made our last town trip for the winter, but our neighbour Fred had to go to Williams Lake to collect some volunteer workers, so he picked up the cables, clamps and U-bolts I needed. The rest of the material, including the 80 2x6s for decking, I already had on hand. I found a good crossing site and decided to put in a suspended walkway between two sturdy young cottonwoods, on a straight, level stretch of the river, about twenty metres wide. The cottonwoods I chose were young, probably about 30 to 40 years old. Their bark was starting to wrinkle, and they were about 15 metres tall and 50 centimetres in diameter. They would last for many, many decades.

The site I chose had high banks on each side, and the river sluiced straight through there, with an overflow channel upstream. These banks survived the huge floods of 2011 nicely, so I figured they would be stable for many more years.

Of course, the river owned the valley bottom, so all I could do was play the odds and hope that Hotnarko waited for a while before she decided to move across the valley floor again. From up on the rimrock, you could look down and see the remains of old channels snaking across the bottom from one side to the other. There is no safe ground when it comes to the power of running water. But while a hundred years is a long time for us, it is but a moment in the life of the river. For over 100 centuries, Hotnarko has been roaming this valley bottom, constantly renovating her home here in the Precipice. In the short term, though, I reckoned the chances of my little bridge surviving were good.

I used 3/8-inch galvanized wire rope for the support cables, tensioned them with a come-along and clamped the ends in place, allowing enough tail so that the cables could be loosened over the years as the trees grew in size. The deck was 2x6 rough-cut lumber, strapped along the sides and fastened to the supports with good old fencing wire. It was a foot crossing only, no machines.

When it was completed in March 2012, we all loved it. Even Chilko got accustomed to it, although the springiness of the bridge took him a while to overcome. It was also a great place to stand or sit and watch the river, providing a very different perspective than looking out from the bank on either side. A Zen seat, hovering over the timeless flow of water.

Dave on his Zen Walkway across the Hotnarko River

Lightning and Phones

Before the fall of 2002, our phone system consisted of 25 miles of wire strung on poles, trees and fence lines. This meant, in effect, that our telephone was connected to a large antenna 50 miles long, as the phone line consisted of two strands of wire strung side by side, forming a huge loop strung through the wilderness around us.

Rosemary discovered just what an antenna can do. To set the scene: the heating of Firhome was simple. Around the south perimeter of the upstairs floor, I installed long, narrow vents, which allowed warm air to rise from the heater below. The stairs, located in the middle of the house, acted as the cold air return. This system worked well, with no cold spots, no noisy furnace fans, and no ducting—just simple, even, and quiet heating.

I was away on one of my many environmental trips when a particularly angry June storm swept into the Precipice from the east, above our phone lines to Anahim Lake. Rosemary was sitting at the dining table, prudently working on the laptop on battery, all power turned off, aware of the inherent danger of working with electricity during a lightning storm. But she hadn't reckoned with the phone line, which ran from the junction box downstairs up beside where she sat. Suddenly, there was a blue streak of flame coming up the phone line through the vent, momentarily blinding her with its intensity, as the thunder crashed so violently it shook the house to its foundations. Rosemary was dazed at first, having no idea what had just happened.

Once she recovered enough to realize she was not hurt in any way, she checked to see what the damage was. When she went downstairs and over to the electrical area, there not only was the acrid smell of burnt wiring but also a big black smudge on the front of the inverter. The inverter had been burned out, so there were no working lights. The phone was out, too. Her main worry was how we would deal with the loss of the inverter. She hoped that I might be able to repair it but knew that was very unlikely given the electronics involved.

I was in Williams Lake attending a series of meetings and would not be home for three days. I was not too worried when I could not reach her by phone. I figured the phone had "gone out" again as it often did in those days either from wildlife or falling trees, so I suspected it was something like that. Little did I know!

When I arrived home a few days later and heard the bad news, it soon became clear we had a real problem. The inverter was completely blown and the transformers that changed the battery power into house current were burned black. Lightning had struck the phone line somewhere "on top," sending a huge surge of high voltage along the wires and into our home, where it had arced to ground, causing the flash that Rosemary had experienced and burning out the expensive inverter and, of course, the phone. The surge was so powerful that it destroyed the cone of the woofer in one of our floor speakers across the room.

Fortunately we had a spare phone on hand. When I hooked it up, I got a dial tone. It took several phone calls and a few days to find an electronics repair shop that could repair the inverter. The shop was in Victoria, so the process of packing up the inverter, which weighed about 90 pounds, shipping it to Victoria, getting it back and reinstalling it took nearly three weeks. It was one of the few times in our 27 years that we were without power—a better ratio than most homes on the Lower Mainland can claim!

Precipice Gold Rush

Every time the phone rang in the Precipice, it made me think of the nuggets found on Bonanza Creek in 1896, which led to the great Klondike Gold Rush of 1898 and the establishment of Dawson City. To facilitate communications between Dawson and the rest of the Dominion, the government ordered the construction of a telegraph line from Ashcroft, BC, to Dawson. Much of the route followed an older route, called the Collins Overland route. It had been built to connect the continental US through Alaska and across Russia to Europe.

That dream ended with the laying of the trans-Atlantic cable in 1866. The route was abandoned. Later it was partially resurrected as the Yukon Telegraph Line, which eventually pushed through from Ashcroft to Dawson in 1901.

Here's where it gets interesting. In 1901, Bella Coola was a growing trade centre and was under consideration as a terminus for a railhead on the mid-Coast. In preparation, a branch of the Yukon Telegraph Line was run from Bella Coola on the coast to 150 Mile House in the Cariboo. Completed in 1912, the line went from salt water along the Bella Coola valley, up through the Precipice and on to the main regional centre on the plateau. A large line cabin was constructed in the Precipice as the supply point for repairs on the line between the Atnarko Valley and Anahim Lake.

In the end, the rail line was never laid, but the Dominion Telegraph Company ran the line until 1936. Then the provincial telephone company (which eventually became BC Tel) took over the line, upgrading it to voice in 1941 because of the perceived threat of a possible Japanese attack during the Second World War. In the early '60s the stretch between Precipice and Bella Coola was abandoned, as communication then went to Bella Coola by microwave. The Precipice literally was at the end of the line. In fact, BC Tel told us that the Precipice phone service was the last open-wire party line in western Canada — a dubious distinction at best. Over the years, even during long periods when no one lived in Precipice, various property owners who had phones always paid the bill (very small, in those early days), so the service was kept open. When we purchased our property in 1984, there was a working telephone line to the Precipice Valley. At that time, there were two phones in the valley. We became the third, still hooked to that original line.

My original training was in Ontario as a telephone lineman for Bell Canada, way back in the '60s. In the Precipice I drew on that experience to maintain the line. The poles were starting to rot and fall over, and in places the line was down on the ground. If a moose happened to rub his antlers on a pole, for instance, down it would come. It was a challenge. Sometimes I even used ropes to tie poles to trees. All the while, Rosemary and I kept asking for general repairs on the line, but to no avail. As for an additional line to us from the centre of the valley, we could forget it. The Glad Cab was just over a mile to the east of the line cabin, and BC Tel would have charged a fortune to extend the line—if they would have even bothered. The connection was up to me.

Undaunted, I purchased several thousand feet of speaker wire and ran it along fence lines, hung it through trees, and over the driveway to the cabin. Odd things happened to that wire. There was the time a coyote discovered the line, bit into it, received a shock and was thrown back a few feet, as told by its tracks in the snow. Mr. Coyote must have enjoyed this, though, as he returned several times! In the process, though, the line would break apart. Sometimes a bear would rip it apart, too, perhaps drawn by the salt from our hands when we handled the wires. Moose and horses both would break through, too, probably not even noticing the wires.

Of course, these minor disasters frequently happened when I was away. It's just the way of things. Rosemary became adept at tracking down the trouble herself, using an old telephone test set that a lineman had passed on to us to check the many connections and isolate the problem, then splicing the wire back together.

That was the Glad Cab line. When we moved up to Firhome, I replaced this rudimentary line with proper telephone drop wire and ran it up the hill, seven thousand feet of very expensive wire. Coyote's fun was over.

Here, though, the phone story took an unexpected twist. When Telus merged with BC Tel in 1989, it applied for a rate increase. The provincial government gave its approval, with the condition that every existing customer had to be upgraded to a private line within a decade. This, of course, included the Precipice. All those years when the old-timers had faithfully paid to keep the service alive were going to pay off.

For the time being, nothing happened. As the years ticked by, I continued my lineman's role. In winter, when most problems occurred, I would follow the line along the telephone trail on snowmachine, and then on snowshoes whenever it took off into the bush. Dealing with beaver dams, swamps, mosquitos, black flies—even replacing glass insulators that the odd hunter thought good targets—all were part of the job.

When the conversion crews arrived in the Chilcotin in 1998 to change over the services from party lines to private lines, we kept waiting for them to come to Precipice. By the fall of 1999, they were finished in Anahim Lake but had still not come to the valley. I began to ask the local crews about a service date, but they never had any information for me. Over several weeks, I gradually went up the ladder, with the same answer each time. Finally, I reached the regional manager. He said he would call back. When he failed to keep his promise, I left several messages.

At first, he didn't return any of my calls. I kept at it. Finally, he did call—to tell me that Telus was not going to upgrade the Precipice line. It was too expensive. Within a year, he told me, they were going to decommission the line. In other words, tear it down. No phone for the Precipice anymore.

We were was shocked by this new information. Remove service from the Precipice, which had been in place since 1941? A service that had always been paid for, even when no one was living there, a service that was often our only connection to the outside world? A service that they were bound by a legal agreement to upgrade? This was not going happen.

I went to the provincial government. They weren't willing to do anything: Telus was a large, multi-provincial company, a big corporate citizen; the ministry was in no position to tell them what they needed to do, and so on.

"But there is a contract," I insisted, to no avail.

I was told my option was to take Telus to court. As if that was even a remote possibility! I felt truly bullied and steamrolled by a big company that refused to spend money in order to live up to its contractual obligations. The more I thought about it, the madder I became.

But what to do? I finally realized that since Telus operated in different provinces, it was probably under federal jurisdiction, not provincial, so Rosemary and I put together a letter, complete with pictures of rotting, falling posts, downed wires, and descriptions of how remotely we lived, how crucial phone communication was to us, the history of the line, the broken contract, the way Telus was behaving in direct opposition to the advertising campaign of how they cared and the future was bright with them, including boasts of how friendly they were, how the quality of service was being improved, and their slogan that, indeed, the future was "Friendly." At the same time, I mentioned, I was being told we were going to be disconnected because Telus didn't want to spend money and honour its contract.

We packaged all this up and sent it to the Canadian Radio and Television Commission, the CRTC, pleading for their intervention on our behalf, to help us fight this corporate bully. Then we waited.

Several weeks later, we received a letter from one of the commissioners, asking for more information. He was interested in our problem. A door had opened! We sent more material and answered his questions. Finally, we received a letter informing us that Telus had "deemed it in their best interests" to honour the contract to upgrade our service. We will be forever grateful for this person who took up our cause. He was truly a knight in shining armour.

A few months later, Telus started to negotiate. Why didn't the residents of Precipice buy the phone line, become their own telecommunications company, and maintain the service? This proposal was so outrageous we just laughed. Their next gambit was to replace the land line but only to the connection in the central line cabin, no further—and it would *still* be a party line.

We held our ground. Finally, by the fall of 2001, Telus had realized that we not only were holding firm, we had the strong backing of the CRTC. They announced a plan to install a microwave tower on the rimrock above us and beam the signal to each of the properties. We would have a receiver in Firhome hooked to our private line.

I reminded them that we were all solar-powered and the new unit would draw power, unlike a regular phone would do, so in order to fulfill the agreement they would have to supply us each with three additional solar panels to produce the extra electricity needed. By now I guess they were weary of us, so they agreed, without creating further problems.

Almost a year later, in September 2002, we stood in Lee's Big Meadow, the ground vibrating beneath our feet, as the *whap! whap! whap!* of helicopter blades blurred into a solid wall of sound, assaulting the quiet autumn meadow. The tower, the hut, the batteries and all the components had arrived by road into the valley the previous day and were piled below the rimrock. The road up the steep hill had proven too rough for the trucks hauling the equipment, though, and it had to be airlifted to the site up on the rimrock.

Have dish, will travel

Slowly, the main tower rose from the ground, dangling below the machine, its spider web structure glinting silver in the fresh morning sun. Gathering momentum as they rose, helicopter and microwave tower were silhouetted against the deep black of the basalt columns guarding Precipice's northern flanks as they slid from view. Soon the chopper was back for more equipment.

"Have dish, will travel," quipped Rosemary as she snapped a picture of the satellite dish swinging dramatically from the helicopter. We were finally being upgraded to a private line service. .

It took a month or so to work out the bugs, but by October we were up and running. The transition from noisy, often unreliable phone service to the new private line was pure joy. And the best part? It only cost Telus $250,000 to do the job. Such a bargain: our own little Precipice gold rush.

The Computer Age

In 1991, the spring after we moved into Firhome, we were starting to hear about home computers. In spite of having chosen to live so remotely, we became intrigued. Rosemary and I decided she should go to Vancouver for the next supply trip, visit family and friends, and snag one of these new machines. She tells the story of that particular adventure:

A friend recommended a computer shop that advertised "complete units assembled here." It was a step up from when we bought our early solar system and had to collect the components from a variety of sources, but still a long way from the ease of buying a computer today. Another friend had given me some floppies (those 3x5-inch precursors to CDs) with a WP word processing program. I made the deal at the shop and he told me to return in a day. I gave him the WP floppies and he said he'd load them for me.

We were both pretty excited when I arrived home. We set up the computer in the only available space in our unfinished house, which was near the wood heater. Whenever the heater door needed to be opened, we'd pull a blanket over our new and still mysterious machine.

When we finally were ready to boot up, I obediently typed in *C://Dos/ WP* as instructed. That was supposed to get things happening. It said so right in the manual.

It didn't. I simply couldn't get beyond that blinking cursor. I phoned the computer guy in Vancouver and explained the problem, but he quickly got very frustrated and testy. Eventually we hashed it out—we'd been talking at cross-purposes. He had loaded *Word* onto the computer. Not *Word Perfect*, which were the floppies that I had given him. Of course, we hadn't any idea that there were two different programs. We'd been typing the wrong thing at the DOS prompt. This was long before Windows.

There was no Google. We had to check out floppies from our mail-service library based in Williams Lake. I was delighted to find a UBC gardening site, run by a SYSOP (system operator) at the Coast, and Dave got a kick out of a series on the Chaos Theory. Our download speed averaged 1 kb/second over our ancient phone line, so if we tried to get anything other than simple text, the connection would just time out.

Two years later, we got Windows 3. Things were looking up. We added a second memory card in the motherboard, which ramped us up to 1MB memory. It wasn't until 2005 that we really got into the Internet. A satellite system called Xplornet changed everything for us. Download speeds were now measured in megabytes per second, bandwidth in hundreds of megabytes. Now we were talking.

Literally. The biggest benefit of the system was that if the phone lines were down, I not only could contact Dave when he was away from the Valley, but if there was a trouble on the main line that he couldn't repair, we could report it to BC Tel by email. Often they were able to fix the problem simply by accessing the control computer in the hut up on the rimrock by their solar panels.

And so it goes. There was not a year that passed when we didn't learn more about inverters, loads and spikes, about how solar panels, fluorescent ballasts, controllers, satellite Internet power sources and Mother Nature interact with each other.

The speed with which this communication revolution happened still amazes us. But then, as Dave comments often, it's still a bit of a thrill to be able to flick a switch and have electricity, after growing up without it.

Satellites and Time Travel

Keeping in touch with the outside world was difficult, especially in the early years. Before we got internet and then a satellite dish, all we had for communication was 45 kilometres of open wire strung on poles and trees from Anahim Lake. Think of pictures you have seen of poles and wires along the railway in the 1890s. This line was like that, although it was built in 1941, at the end of that age. It was in need of some serious repair.

When we moved into the Precipice the phone line only went as far as an old cabin a couple of kilometres from us. We spanned the gap to our cabin ourselves, using speaker wire. The result was the last multiparty phone line in Western Canada—when it worked—and the phone would be out for weeks at a time until we could repair it ourselves. When we purchased that first computer in 1991, it not only was slow, but the modem often dropped off and the line was noisy.

The satellite dish was a treat: Suddenly, we had broadband access. The new technologies had issues, though. I had to be tenacious when fighting the various battles of our situation.

Several months after gaining this wonderful access, we had a strange situation regarding time zones to deal with. My first step was to call tech support. "I'm sorry, sir, that is not possible," said the young woman's voice. Although she was being polite, I could feel her exasperation filling the empty space in the line between us.

It may seem like that," I said, "but I assure you it is and I can prove it."

"Well sir, there is nothing more I can do!"

I hung on for about twenty seconds listening to the tinny mutterings of electrons banging around in the open circuit, thinking of the 73,000 kilometres or so between the technician in Moncton, New Brunswick, and my wireless handheld phone in Precipice Valley.

Our words were being sent 35,370 kilometres up to a satellite, then beamed 35,370 kilometres back to Earth, where they travelled a few hundred more kilometres on a late 19th-century technology of wires and poles, finally to be encoded into microwaves beamed into the Precipice from a tower located on the rimrock 400 metres above my head. All this was connecting me to an unknown person sitting in a heated cubicle on the other side of the continent. Talk about a time travel fantasy.

THE POWER OF DREAMS

This was the third time in as many weeks I had tried to get the trouble-shooters for my internet service provider to take my problem seriously. This last attempt at least had gotten me through to the level two people, the ones who were supposed to solve any and every problem that satellite service could encounter.

Satellite tower on rimrock above Precipice Valley

I finally said "thank you for your time" and hung up. I could tell that this was as far as I was going to get with tech support. After all, they were trained to follow a decision tree, test this, test that, and if the sequence failed, well, then they had nowhere to go. It was especially true in the matter of time zones. Time is time, and that is all there is to it.

Well, not quite. Our satellite internet service was designed to give us the ability to receive a certain amount of information in each 24-hour period: 200 megabytes each day, to be exact. If we exceeded that we were subjected to a closure of our service for 24 hours, rendering internet usage impossible. This was cleverly called the Fair Access Policy, or FAP. It was supposed to guarantee all customers fair access to the service by ensuring that no single user hogged all the capacity. At least, that was the PR spin. In reality, if you paid a few hundred dollars per month you could get almost as much bandwidth as you wanted. The more you paid, the less the company was concerned about Fair Access for the other users.

However, even high-end users, especially businesses, often need more bandwidth than they can buy. Updates for software programs and hardware, as well as major data downloads for computer sharing, will exceed even the largest available service packages. This is where knowledge of time zones helps. The North American satellite networks are keyed to major business centres on the east coast. All networks operate on Eastern Time. From 2 a.m. to 7 a.m. Eastern Time, when eastern seaboard traffic is low, there is a period when the free access policy is relaxed. This means large downloads can take place during this time frame without affecting the amount of bandwidth you are paying for. I needed this window once or twice a month to download updates and large files without penalty.

Now, as every grade school student knows and the frustrated tech was telling me, there is a three-hour difference between Pacific Time and Eastern Time, so when I called and said that was not happening, that my connection registered a different time, it was as if I told them water ran uphill or that the Queen of England chewed tobacco and played late-night poker in the back room of a London strip club. Impossible.

Not exactly impossible. There is a diagnostic menu I could access on my modem which records things like the time I log on to the network. It

THE POWER OF DREAMS

should have been synchronized to network time, which was ET. But when I checked this out by going online at 11 p.m. PST, the satellite showed me as booting up, not at 2 a.m. EST, but, get this, at 8 p.m. the *next day*. So if was 11 p.m. on a Monday night, the log on record showed me as coming online Tuesday at 8 p.m.

This started to get confusing. When you think about it, the satellite orbiting at 91 degrees west longitude doesn't care where the signal originates; it just records the time it receives it. Yet there I was, looking at the readout. The proof of the matter was confirmed when I went online at 11:15 p.m., downloaded a large series of updates, and was cut off, subject to the fair access policy restriction, because my bandwidth had been exceeded outside of the free period.

I was thoroughly bewildered at this point. If my access hadn't been cut off, I would have assumed there was a glitch in my program, but it was the satellite program itself that had cut me off, so it must have been incorrect in the time stamp it was recording. But, as I kept being told, this was not possible. This was a Hughes communications network bird, the same as the ones the US military used as their backbone of intelligence. If it was wrong, well, I didn't want to think about that—but at the same time, I knew something was fouled up.

Over the next several weeks, I created an Excel spreadsheet which recorded the local times the modem went on the internet and off again, and the times shown by the modem date stamp as per the satellite program. It was consistent: the satellite thought I lived in the Chatham Islands, west of New Zealand, east of the International Dateline. I was a time traveller.

Finally, in desperation, I sent a short but carefully worded email to the president of the satellite company. He assured me that the matter would be looked into.

Two weeks went by, but nothing happened. I sent another (still polite) email, offering to provide my Excel spreadsheets and other documentation to the parent company. All these satellite internet providers are owned by bigger fish, part of communications conglomerates covering the globe.

The next day, I received a phone call from the company's head engineer, who started out suggesting that perhaps my records were amiss, that after all this was a highly technical, highly sophisticated business that launched satellites and ran a North American-wide communications net. After several patient minutes, though, he became convinced that I was not some West Coast hippie breathing too much salt air; that there might be a problem here. He took all my information, relevant codes, numbers and my shoe size, then committed to call me back.

Which he did a couple of days later. Et voilà. There *was* a technical issue—a very large one. As soon as the chief engineer logged on to my modem, he could see that I was being transported by satellite into tomorrow, halfway across the planet.

The email chain he started internally went viral internationally. My modem was "the time traveller" in the subject line of the emails, copied to me, in a lengthy discussion followed over the next 36 hours by Hughes engineers in both the US and Europe. People were very, very disturbed that this could happen. Frantic investigations ensued, which finally found the problem. It seems the last time a software update had been done on the satellite there had been a glitch in the program that recorded a large group of modem network times incorrectly, mine being one of them.

Several days later, on the first of the next month during the overnight period, a new program was uploaded to the satellite, correcting the software problem and pulling my modem back into the present. The president sent me a personal thank-you for bringing this situation to the attention of the company and, as a token of appreciation, gave us free service for the next month.

I'm sure my modem felt good to be back home in Today, and I was very pleased to know that once again when it was 11 p.m. here, it was 2 a.m. Eastern Time. It was not nice to mess with time zones. It was hard on the psyche. I did wonder, though: does the Queen really smoke cigars and play late-night poker in the back room of a London strip club?

IMAGES OF NATURE

Rosemary meditating in front of the mountains we called the Camels

Thoughts of Wild Places

The concept of wilderness is the creation of an agrarian mindset. Agricultural communities define lands that cannot be fenced, ploughed, or tamed to service the needs of man as useless, even threatening areas. They are viewed as unfriendly, dangerous, and to be avoided.

If these landscapes are to be used at all, they must first be defanged. Wolves are killed; other predators poisoned, shot and disposed of. Shepherds armed with the best technologies must accompany any domestic animals; sometimes dogs and horses are used as allies to keep the raw nature of the feared lands at bay.

This idea that parts of the Earth where undisturbed systems interact fully are threats to our way of life is a very new idea, spawned just a few thousand years ago when agricultural societies became the prevalent culture for our ways and means of survival.

Taken in the context of the last few million years of human experience and evolution, this new thought is but a few seconds old. It is a grand experiment with technology, a leap into unknown territory much wilder and more dangerous than any landscape that has ever existed. We are now beginning to experience the realities of living in this new wilderness that we have created. Polluted water, smog alerts, declining agricultural production, dwindling food stocks in the oceans, and species extinctions are occurring at a rate and scale unprecedented. The world as modified by human intervention is not looking very good these days. In fact, it is becoming an increasingly difficult habitat to live in.

So the question arises: What is wilderness? Surely if we apply the definition of being a dangerous, inhospitable place to survive, then the current human landscape fits that definition far better than anything found in the parts of the Earth where humanity has not yet made its mark.

For untold millennia, the entirety of this planet was unmolded by human activity. Humans evolved in this wild landscape. We are natural hunter-gathers, making our homes in climates from the frozen arctic to the torrid equatorial forests. No matter where we roamed, the water was clean and pure, the air fresh and sweet-smelling to breathe. Yes, life could be dangerous, defence was needed against all manner of animals that saw us as dinner; but at the same time, we spent several million years fitting into that scheme of life, making our way down the evolutionary path.

Satori Rock, Dave with Hobo

We are now at the fork in the road. The philosophies and principles that brought us to this juncture no longer serve us well. Domination, alteration on a massive scale, dumping all manner of wastes, both physical and intellectual, into the global commons is beginning to fracture our societies, forcing a restructuring of the very roots of our existence.

The rules of life here on Earth are part of a much larger, ancient life force that we have lost touch with. All life is interdependent. Time exists in a different reference. Even as things change, there is a harmony, a vibration of energy connecting all things, from billion-year-old mountain ranges to the emerging petals of a fragile blue flower shyly posing on an ancient grey mat of lichens.

It is these feelings that drove us to live in the middle of a great wilderness and why I chose to work for its protection, using Firhome as a base, a source of renewed energy that kept me going.

The Lure of the Mountains

Humans always seem to need more of what they enjoy, and that certainly was true with us. Yes, we lived in a remote little valley in the midst of wilderness. But from our windows we looked out over the Coast Mountains and were constantly drawn to them. During Dave's years as a park ranger, we experienced many of the lakes in those ranges and had some great hikes and horse pack trips. In spite of all that, we longed for more intimate times with just us and those mighty peaks.

The Coast Mountains are wild. Older, geologically, than the Rockies or the lesser mountain ranges in eastern BC, they also are virtually undeveloped. Other than at the southern end, in the lower mainland in B.C. where there is access for skiing and tourism, only a few trappers' trails wind their way up their closest steep slopes, but to get to anywhere exciting and as remote as we wished would mean a minimum six-day hike, hoping to carry enough food and camping supplies for the three or four weeks we wanted to spend in there.

This was not an option for us. A few decades of heavy scuba diving had damaged my lower spine, and I no longer could hike with a heavy backpack or, in fact, anything heavier than my camera. We'd already done many years of minimalist camping, surviving with boring freeze-dried food and a stripped-down version of a camp. We even talked of making a pack for our dog, but three weeks of dog food would be more than even a large dog could carry comfortably. So hiking with a camp on our backs wasn't going to work, and we needed to find a way around that.

Beaver taking off over Bussel Lake

Our solution was to fly. By the mid-'90s, Dave with his ranger work and I, as his occasional companion, were familiar with the joys of floatplane travel. There is a rule of thumb in the mountains—float planes need 5,000 feet of lake at 5,000 feet altitude. Oh, they can certainly land on a shorter lake—but taking off again safely isn't possible. So during our long winters Dave would pore over topographical maps, seeking out yet another lake for us to explore. Then, when we could manage it in the summer, in we would fly for three weeks; the three of us—Dave, I and our dog. Since we were governed by weight rather than volume, we opted for comfort and flew in to our chosen lake with a large camp. We had a mesh cookshack, for the food and for protection against the ever-present bugs. We took a sleeping tent with air mattresses and cozy sleeping bags. I included interesting meals, preferring to leave memories of freeze-dried packets of limited nourishment and even less satisfaction where memories belong: in the past. Just before each trip, I would cook a lot of food such as a roasted turkey (yes, with gravy and cranberry sauce!) and a pot of chili. We'd pack bottles of wine and, from our garden, a cooler full of fresh vegetables. We were always quite high up, where it still stayed cold at night, so storage of food wasn't a problem. We also took the usual canned and dry foods, cheeses, sausages, etc. We lived well on our trips into those mountains!

I think my most favourite trips were the ones we made into Bussell Lake, southeast of Precipice Valley, about 40 minutes by air from the floatplane base at Nimpo Lake. When we decided to go there the first time in 2001, the pilots hadn't flown into that lake before—and knew no one who had—but after checking it out on Google Earth and doing a couple of low and slow flybys, they were game for it.

Bussell is a glorious lake, rimmed by red sand on one side, warm enough for a quick swim, and surrounded by meadows, smaller lakes, wildflowers, streams and always, the high mountains. None of them had names, so we gave them our own, such as the Camels, a series of camel-like humps. Egyptian Ridge looked like the edge of a pyramid. Radio Ridge was a stiff climb but the only place where we had reception on our hand-held radio. Diamond Lakes are a couple of gems in a small valley below Radio Ridge. We'd reach Satori Lake after hiking for a few hours, and there we'd strip off our hiking boots to cool our feet. Further up we came to Satori bench, a remarkable sitting rock overlooking the Kleena Kleene valley. There was Hobo Peak, named because Hobo was so amazing as he struggled up those steep mountain sides where dogs wouldn't normally walk. We were surprised, on that hike, to find a large boletes mushroom at 8,200 feet! And yes, we ate it.

We had promised our newest neighbours in the Precipice Valley, Fred and Monika, that we would show them this idyllic area, and so, near the end of our time in the Precipice, we planned a trip. It was memorable in many ways, sharing this special place with special friends, but even more memorable was the grizzly affair. We had assured them there were no bears up there since we'd never seen one, nor any bear scat. But we were proved wrong one day as we were prowling around at the far end of the lake from our camp. A large grizzly with two cubs appeared across a large meadow from us. She didn't see us, and we simply changed our route a bit.

That evening, nestled up against the krumholz (thick stands of stunted trees), we sat around our campfire after dinner sharing the day's experiences and were startled when Chilko suddenly leapt up and charged through the trees. Of course, we (perhaps foolishly?) followed, much less easily.

Scratched and cursing the sharp branches, we broke out on the other side—just in time to see that same grizzly sow and her cubs racing away from us—and from Chilko, who was in hot pursuit. Satisfied he had removed any danger from our camp, Chilko watched them go over a low hill and we all returned to our campfire.

Dave, Fred, Monika drying out hiking gear at Bussel Lake

"No bears, huh?" commented Fred. We decided the bears were on their way down to the coast, covering territory that would make the most determined mountain man give up. But they were long gone, and we slept that night unconcerned. After all, we had a big bad dog watching over us! During our time in the Chilcotin we had come to realize that bears, even though outweighing any of our dogs by hundreds of pounds, didn't know they could out-fight them. Chilko, especially, looked like a large, off-white wolf, so perhaps the ancestral fear of wolf packs lingers in today's bears.

For our 25th anniversary, Dave gave me a helicopter trip "to wherever." We both love helicopter flights, but they are very expensive, so this was a real indulgence. It took another couple of summers before we found the perfect place. It had to be inaccessible by floatplanes, with a few lakes, mountain peaks, and so far from trails and roads that hikers may never have been there. Of course, we called it "Anniversary Lakes," and a mountain we climbed that became ours after I built a cairn at 8,600 feet was dubbed "Anniversary Peak." We'd had Chilko then for just a year and weren't too sure how he would be in the mountains, but he was game for most things.

We had loaded up the helicopter with all our gear, leaving a tiny place for me in the back seat, then realized we hadn't made room for our 110-pound dog! But nothing fazed Chilko. He simply jumped in, crawled up on top of the pile of goods and flattened himself under the roof, peering out the window and ready for the next adventure.

We landed on a large plateau, and once we'd set up camp we went exploring. Chilko was always watching us, staying close. Then one day we came off a mountain peak and dropped down over a ledge—and found ourselves face to face with a young caribou. I don't know who was more startled, but the caribou reacted first and took off running. Chilko went after him, full out. We were near panic; if he had gone down off our plateau into the deep forest, filled with gullies and sheer drops, we feared we might not see him again. But twenty minutes later, our intrepid dog caught up

THE POWER OF DREAMS

to us, panting but looking very proud of himself. He had protected us and chased away the intruder.

When we originally checked out that location on Google Earth, we had seen a good-sized lake at the bottom of a glacier. When we hiked over to it, we discovered the water was a deep glacial green-blue, surrounded by rocks and alpine fireweed. Beautiful. But sadly, when we revisited it on Google Earth ten years later, the renewed image showed that the glacier had almost completely disappeared and the lake had shrunk.

These disappearing glaciers are the rule now, with climate change, although the Coast Mountains will probably be the last to lose them completely. Even when the Rockies have lost their Columbia ice fields, these remote glaciers of the Coast Mountains will still be providing fresh water to the rivers flowing from the Homathko and Waddington ice fields.

We feel very blessed to have had these times in this mountain wilderness. It is a rare privilege that few ever experience.

Spring Green

Moving to the Precipice Valley involved a lot more than the physical move itself. We soon learned that one of the important adaptations involved the weather. It was no longer a matter of whether to take an umbrella to work or wear an overcoat; daily awareness of the weather became one of our foremost concerns.

At first, living so close to nature was wonderful, but our first winter in the tiny Glad Cab seemed endless. Those darker months of November, December, and January weighed on us very heavily, and we began to wonder how many more days we could take of a monotone world of eggshell-white snow, charcoal tree trunks, bare brown alder branches, short, shadowy days and long, black nights.

But then we started looking more closely at our environment. Colour was subtle, but the golds of old grasses poked through the snow, and each tree had its own green.

We soon came to learn that green is part of every season. In winter, it sticks its audacious head above the deepest snow and smiles back at the cruelest wind and ice, keeping the promise of new life alive. The green of summer is more mature, marching along in stately fashion, in full control of the palette, eating photons, laughing and drinking fine nectar; enjoying the full feast of summer.

As the last courses are served, the green of autumn retires to the lounge, where it snoozes in the low light of afternoon, coyly rearranging its gowns, exposing gold petticoats, flirting with the winds, waving goodbye to the less hardy souls who are beating a hasty retreat to the southern reaches of the realm.

But, more than any other, it is the glory of spring green in the Precipice that is universal. Bursting with energy, joyful, exuberant, dancing and singing with the sheer force of manifestation, spring green is unstoppable, life's clarion messenger announcing that the miracle is still being reborn each and every season.

Late April has those special green mornings. Green is everywhere, from the river's blue-green sheen to the black-mottled green on the hummingbird's back as she perches on the feeder, calmly waiting for her next battle. These greens are not just a colour; these greens are the vibrations of life, tuned to the myriad energy flows emanating from the cauldron of spring.

From the slick, glassy, shiny green sliding along the blades of grass, mingled with the thick, quilted green that lies deeply dark on the leaves of shrubs and bushes, to the cottonwood leaves flashing white-green in the morning sun 150 feet above the forest bed, this green is magical. These high-flying cottonwood leaves are a sure sign that the benediction of spring has been received.

Nearby, the fuzzy yellow-green of the pine needles smiles at the squirrel, declaring that there are new, succulent buds for breakfast. Along the riverbank, willows glow in the shadows, their lantern green beckoning to the moths and butterflies to stop by for a tasty snack.

There is the green of the frog's leg, mottled, yellow-streaked, pulsing over the taut muscles. This is the green of camouflage, the green that hides the predator in the grass, the green that is part of the transforming of life from insect to frog's dinner.

More subtle is the pale, translucent, alabaster green of the ferns bathed by the morning light filtering down to the forest floor, where their delicate new whorls are unfolding in the magic spiral of life.

It is no accident that green symbolizes peace, energy, hope, and healing. Green is the colour that promises the ongoing mystery. We are told that the Earth is the "blue planet," but from the perspective of our own reality, it is truly the green planet, where the oasis of spring green flourishes in the blackness of space.

Satori Bench

During the huge melt of the last glaciation, the Hotnarko was a river orders of magnitude larger than it is now. With its huge back eddies, whirlpools and giant rapids, the ancestral Hotnarko would not be recognizable today. As it scoured the valley bottom, it left behind big gravel beds and large circular formations sculpting the valley walls, but its true scale is shown by its creation of a long ridge as it sluiced through crevasse systems in the melting ice. This esker runs from the valley floor to a height of 275 metres against the north slope of the valley, bearing witness to the immense forces at work in its creation, rising in a series of benches each a half hectare or so in size.

We built Firhome on the first step of this ridge and called it Dancing Firs, in honour of the magnificent, ever-moving ancient fir trees. On the second flat up the ridge above Firhome was a special spot we called Satori Bench.

Being there, perched on the brink of a steep slope, was like standing in the cockpit of a commercial airliner, with the valley and the mountains beyond laid out in all their grandeur. A global energy node, Satori Bench became our refuge. We used it for meditation, absorbing the view, philosophizing or to just to enjoy it together, like one winter when we saw a vertical rainbow created by the sun lurking behind a sky of billowing ice crystals: green, goldenrod yellow, giving way to a fiery orange, and bleeding into a deep, iron red, our very own Pollock canvas.

There was a mid-April morning, after a night of -10, when the grouse were booming, sounding like distant drum majors in a far-off parade, and the knife-sharp morning light was cutting through the new yellow-green needles of the firs and pines. As I crunched along, it was easy to imagine wearing crampons, clawing my way up a steep slope on a mountain ridge in the high Blanca of Peru, but this wasn't Peru. This was here. I climbed higher and higher up the ridge, gaining a wider and wider scope of the mountains piercing the blue spring sky: phalanx after phalanx disappearing into the gray-blue haze of the far horizon.

Soon the river was 90 metres below, swirling and dodging over, under and around chunks of ice that were still clogging the channel. It sounded like someone scrunching up a newspaper before they shoved it into the firebox, which is what I'd had to do at six that morning, one of the colder nights since spring had first made an appearance.

On the other hand, the confused Canada geese that arrived the day before and which were down in the meadow, far below me, had no such luxury. The flock was huddled in small groups on unexpected ice, wondering where the water was, honking and flapping their huge wings. Their presence seemed out of place in this late winter landscape, yet there they were, trying to make the best of an unusual situation. Maybe by two or three that afternoon, when the heat of the sun had melted a few puddles, they would be able to get some new sprouts and a drink of water, a foretaste of the lush feast that would be theirs in a few weeks as the fields exploded with tender, tasty new grass, slugs, worms, grubs and all manner of delicious morsels. But for now these big birds hunkered down, toughed it out, focused on keeping warm and scrounging what little food there was.

Sex was rampant, even on that cold morning. The grouse was booming out his "Here I am" message. The squirrels were finishing their frantic and noisy mating rituals. The redwing blackbirds were huskily throating their calls for territory and mates. The most sensuous of these mating songs was the ubiquitous chickadee. Its descending three-note call, "Oh poor me," lent itself to all kinds of bawdy phrasing in the mind's eye. Then there was the telephone bird, the one whose second long trill sounds uncannily like the phone ringing. Many a time I have rushed over to the workshop phone just to answer a dial tone, and realize that that bird, (which we never did identify) had caught me again.

He was not to be confused with Ladder Bird, who usually started his drumming at first light on the aluminum ladder pitched against the back roof, right behind our bedroom. This woodpecker loved the punk sound he smashed out on the rungs of that battered old ladder. It worked much better than the nearby fir snag that all the other guys used. I wondered if he got better or worse mates, and decided it depended on their tastes: trashy, edgy or traditional.

The exercise of climbing the ridge warmed the soul and the body. As I climbed higher, more and more of the Coast Mountains thrust into view. Such scale and perspective was difficult to fathom. It was much easier to settle the eye on the dusky blue berries of a juniper, clustered on the branch ends, with their promise of new life displayed for all to see, the whole universe enfolded in each detail. The pools of frozen mud that would be released by mid-afternoon, to flow for a couple of hours before freezing again, were part of the same process that had raised mountains in liquid form from the planetary deeps, only to freeze them into the rocks and cones I climbed upon, and which, too, would melt into flowing, viscous liquid in the next afternoon of geologic time, the seeming continuity dissolved into smaller and smaller elements, each a portal to the whole.

Moon with sunrise reflected on Mt. Marvin in the south

Spring Sunrise

By design, the living and dining room windows of Firhome looked southwest, into the throat of the Coast Mountains. Before starting to build Firhome we spent many days on the site, determining which angles had the best sight lines, where we wanted to eat and sleep or just sit and enjoy the view.

We chose well. One example was a March when we witnessed the most enthralling sunrise I have ever seen. It was one of those crystal clear mornings when the mountains seemed so close I could reach out and touch them. Their presence was a real force. The sky was lightly overcast, with a puffy ceiling of clouds—close overhead, yet filled with ragged holes, letting the eye wander to the deep black-blue sky above.

Ever so slowly, just inside the range of perception, the light began to shift, at first diffuse, then beginning to focus, the way a spot does on a stage. Suddenly, the peaks of the Coast Range came into stark relief, thrusting into

THE POWER OF DREAMS

the clouds. Slowly the spotlight faded, then remerged closer on the flanks of the nearest mountains, bathing the wind-sculpted curves in a creamy white glow, soft and sensuous.

Then the real light show began. The spotlights languidly shifted from ridge to mound to peak to headwall to serrated edge and back again. The blue holes in the ceiling shifted from light turquoise over the mountains to purples and violets overhead.

The lotus petals of this sunrise opened slowly, releasing warm light and melting the cold morning sky. I felt like I was sitting in the first balcony, watching the house lights gradually bring a stage to life, yet I was not looking east at the rising sun. I was looking southwest into the mountains, watching them as they were animated by the light coming from behind me.

So it was that I experienced this remarkable sunrise by turning my back to it, by absorbing its energy and beauty from the canvas of the mountains. I wonder how often I have missed the best moments because I have focused on the spectacular, rather than the softer, more subtle energies flowing around me. Not that day.

Soft

Although work on Firhome and my work, first as a back country ranger and then in conservation, were an ongoing affair, we tried to take time off, time to explore the mysteries in Precipice. This is the memory of a very special walk, just minutes away from Firhome.

There were several large spruce trees at the end of our cabin meadow where the driveway from the cabin started up the ridge to Firhome. This was a sheltered, wet area, and these trees were very special. At their feet were squirrel middens a metre deep. Nests of all manner were protected in this sanctuary. Yet even these thick branches, which shielded rain to the point that I had never seen the toes of these great trees wet, could not filter out ... well, softness.

I had thought I knew what soft was: the electric feel of a cat's fine fur, the sensuous caress of diaphanous silk, the smoothness of soft skin in secret places ... all these experiences were my definition of softness, until one grey winter day. It was one of those days where I felt more like hunkering down beside the heater, finishing a good book, and letting the world slide by into the black hole of the past, as I was used to doing, even after so long in the valley. Yet, somehow, I roused my spirit, knowing that I would feel more alive walking, experiencing the physical inputs of my body, not just relying on my mind to carry me along.

I took my time, pulling on my trusty green rubber felt packs, snugging the old red toque to my head, donning my well-worn blue down parka, all part of getting into a different flow of time and action. Part way down the icy, twisting driveway it began to snow. Well, not snow, really. I'm not sure what to call it. More like a frozen mist, rolling across the meadow, through cottonwood ghosts starkly black in their skeletal outline, advancing slowly, gently, a dull white shroud descending upon the universe.

On impulse I walked over to a thicket dominated by a large, centuries-old spruce, with branches spreading from her metre-wide girth, wide and low over the end of the meadow. As I ducked under this cloistered canopy I heard the river rustling and chuckling as it moved on toward its final destiny in the Atnarko, and beyond to the ocean. Somehow the little amphitheater I was in magnified those stream voices, making me more aware than I have ever been of how the river talks to the world around it.

I crouched down in this secret place, the needle crust give under my weight as my heels slowly sank into the duff. I felt exquisitely cosseted and sheltered, the way I imagine a deer and her fawn would feel tucked into this vaulted room under the big spruce: safe, able to see and hear any danger coming or going, yet invisible behind the needle-green curtain, backed by the scaly, slate-grey bark.

It was then, as I turned my face upward to visually explore the innermost secrets of this magic place, that it happened: the softest, most sensual caress

I have ever experienced. Filtering down through the great spruce's canopy were the smallest, most perfect snowflakes imaginable. No bigger than the head of a straight pin, they seemed to descend through another medium, like a plankton shower in the ocean. More ice crystals than flakes, these miniature emissaries from the skies above settled gently upon my cheeks. Such a feeling: not only the magic of the moment but the contrast of a cold, silent touch on warm skin, bringing my skin and senses fully alive. I was exhilarated.

Now I knew that *soft* was a mental awareness, not a sense; much more than a physical sensation, such as a tingling or a feather-light touch. Soft is really a mental state, one that translates sensory inputs into an emotional feeling. This is what comes of being intimately caressed by tiny snowflakes, of being emotionally and mentally alive in a moment.

The Old Ones

Mountains are what made Firhome and Precipice Valley exceptional. Whether it was the Rainbow, Hotnarko, Kappan, Trumpeter or Talchako range, no matter where we looked or ventured, either on horseback or on foot, the mountains were there. They had an elemental force, an unstoppable energy that transmitted itself across the valley and speared our hearts. We were caught by the power of a mountain . . . but what *is* that? Is it the energy captured by its head, thrust into the clouds? Is it the mountain's stance, anchored like a martial arts master in the crust of the earth? Is it the web of life forms supported by the mountains' chemical being?

To me, it is all of these things and many more—the spanning of time, a bridge from now to then. Folded, melted, crushed and ripped apart, the mountain carries the story of all the earth's toils and troubles around us forever, an emotional record of being a planet in the vast emptiness of space. A mountain is the Rosetta stone allowing us to decipher a language we intuitively understand but rarely speak, the original protolanguage of hardened basalt shattered by time and water, and the cracking of grey granite.

Mountain power

Although the mountains surrounding Precipice all speak the same tongue, there are dozens of dialects. In the lowlands, below timberline, the sibilant chorus of stream and birdsong mingles with the whispering, breathy susurrations of wind in the forest, and merges into alpine flowers. Higher up, the mountain snaps short, testy epithets as the rocks crack and shatter, splitting apart the mountain's very skin. Higher still, you can hear the throaty growl of the glaciers as they grind their way down, telling of reshaping the universe from solid rock into grains of sand in the ocean depths. At the mountains' heights there is the slow, barely audible speech of the peaks, where time seems to stand still and then suddenly is obliterated by shrieking winds screaming far into the night, filling the interface of earth and sky with relentless motion: fluid scraping against solid.

Every day spent among mountains brings their language a little closer, although it is far from well understood by the human mind. We do get glimpses now and then, though, when we are in the right tuning, and sometimes get a full moment of story, like children sitting around a late-night campfire listening to the elders speak their wisdom.

On dark, silent nights, you can listen to the stillness of eternity. As you stand on a high ridge, you can even hear the reedy song of the wind as it blows and pushes its way over the rocks and the secret hollows, and as you sit in a flower-filled meadow on a sunny afternoon you can feel the warmth and energy of a few quadrillion photons, as they caress the heads of humans and flowers alike. Then, as you kneel beside a liquid silver stream, your knees sinking into the cool, earthy peat, you are transported into the realm of all living beings on the mountain, from marmots to thousand-pound silverback grizzly bears—all of you stretching your necks, united in the simple pleasure of reaching down to drink your fill. As you rise and inhale the sharp, spicy smell of skunk cabbage or the thick, sweet scent of moss, bog and dancing flowers mingled in an exotic aroma that only wilderness can provide, you begin to get a sense of the continuum of a mountain. You begin to know that it is more than a possibility. It is real. Later, crouching along a red sandy beach, your eyes explore the garnet smoothness stretching before you as you search for the boundary where it melds with ghost mists on the far shore, a peace flows around and over you, locking your soul into its patterns.

This and much more is the true power of a mountain. It is the power to tell stories to us, to transport ourselves into other realms, and to impart wisdom older than our species—a wisdom tested and proven on the twin anvils of time and space. Living in the Precipice allowed privileged glimpses of this mystical universe.

In biology, edges are where the most interaction in any system takes place, where the connection between different energy flows creates new possibility, new ideas and new patterns. For 27 years, our edge was the Precipice Valley, on the western edge of the Chilcotin, a plateau the size of

Switzerland holding fewer than 5,000 people, on the edge of civilization on one side and on the other the eastern edge of the Coast Range, a 100-kilometre-wide band of mountains rising 4000 metres from the rocky edge of the Pacific to the edge of space. Among all these edges, the Precipice was the continental verge, the edge connecting the cold, dry semi-desert of the Interior to warm, wet coastal forests.

This dual-edged nature gave the Precipice Valley a unique exchange of climates, flora, fauna and human cultures, all rich in diversity. To this mix, Rosemary and I brought another edge: we were New Age pioneers, solar-powered off-gridders carving out a new life on the edge of untrammeled wild land.

The final edge, the one that united them all for us, was our house, Firhome. It stood on the snout of an esker rising 60 metres above the Hotnarko River, with a stunning, panoramic view of mountain wilderness as far as the eye could see. We owned just 15 hectares of it. But past the edges of those hectares we were surrounded by thousands of square kilometres of undeveloped, unroaded Crown land. We were truly living in the middle of pristine nature.

Some edges, we realized, can be in the middle of things.

Sustainability

One late winter day, when solid darkness dropped over the land around 5 p.m. and I was settled by the heater after a difficult day, my mind wandered into the larger realm of the human condition. That afternoon a fine crystalline snow had been falling, the temperature outside was minus 13, a wind was rippling the fir boughs and I'd just let Chilko out. He was the rescue dog we got after Hobo died at age 15, our Maremma/Shepherd cross: 48 kilos of great dog, constant companion who seldom barked but was a real talker. That is how I knew he wanted out. He came over and woofed quietly, then walked to the door.

I began to think about that. He had been splayed out by the wood heater, soaking up the infrared as only dogs can do, then he simply got up and walked outside into the cold, the snow and the wind. He didn't have to put on a parka, mitts, toque and felt packs. He didn't have to make any adjustments at all. He just went outside.

That is sustainability: To be perfectly adapted, to be able to live in the surrounding environment without external inputs foreign to the habitat you live in. But that wasn't me.

For the human species, three variables interact to allow sustainability. They are population, level of technology and expectations. In this climate the energy inputs needed to maintain my lifestyle were not sustainable. Sure, I was solar-powered, but I still needed gasoline to come and go, I still needed warm clothes, I still needed food that I couldn't produce myself and a host of things that this environment could not provide. To survive in this climate as aboriginal peoples had for millennia, population levels would need to be supported by the amount of food and energy local technologies could provide. That would mean no solar panels made in California and shipped by truck to the Precipice, no fresh fruit in January, and no gas for the chainsaw. It would mean gathering and moving wood by hand, not with a skookum one-ton truck. It would mean a shift to a much lower level of technology. The aboriginal people who survived here used stone age technologies. No bullets, horses, pickup trucks, guns or electricity. We fool ourselves if we think using more efficient wood heaters or passive solar design will solve these fundamental problems. Only a massive shift back to previous technologies or to some new, as yet uninvented means of clothing and feeding ourselves, will allow for continued survival in this climate. Sure, in the end, it may be possible for a few people to continue to live here under radically different conditions, but I think that in general human populations will slowly retreat to the tropics and sub-tropics, where the energy inputs needed to stay warm are manageable. After all, when the sun warms the air around you, you don't need to live in a controlled spaceship like Firhome to keep from freezing to death.

Every species has its natural range. Every range provides for natural technologies, such as caribou skins for warmth, local plants and animals for food, and no expectation to eat the same food in winter as in summer.

The complexity of the web of life on this planet ensures that imbalance cannot continue. There are too many connections, too many feedback loops, too many entanglements created over the billion years that life has evolved. To survive, we need to respect those first principles, not just in concept but in reality. Until we can live in a local environment as easily as our dog, until the inputs and outputs of our living processes are in balance with the niche we live in, on *all* scales, we will not, *cannot*, be sustainable, not in the long run.

What will a sustainable, post-carbon civilization be like? What will its philosophy be? What does the transition look like? Is such a life even possible? These are the questions we need to be asking, if there is to be another few thousand or few million years of human development on Earth.

Precipice Time Machine

Because the Precipice is the lowest, widest pass through the Coast Mountains between Vancouver and Prince Rupert, it is not surprising that when Lieutenant Palmer was commissioned in the 1860s to find a rail route to the coast, he chose to explore this ancient passage as a possible commercial link. I often pictured him as I walked the ridge, placing my feet on the very trail he trod. And who knows, I may even have actually stood in his footsteps in this slow-changing land. Each time, I felt I was travelling back in time to the mid-19th century. Of course I could go back several thousand years or a dozen, but this particular distance has special relevance.

One route in particular through the Precipice interests me because it crosses over the ridge above our home. This path goes by various names, but the usual one now is the Lunas Trail, used as an access route from Bella Coola to the Chilcotin plateau in the 1890s. Lieutenant Palmer and his party

View from the summit over Hotnarko River

walked this route much earlier in August 1863, packing their supplies and equipment on their backs from the lower sections of the trail on the North Bentick Arm near Bella Coola to the Fraser River. His commission was to search out a better route to the goldfields and it probably was just another survey to him, but looking back on it from my perspective it seems like a gigantic effort. When I read his journal, his matter-of-fact presentation belied the difficulties he must have encountered during his journey through the dense coastal rainforest, a steep and rocky climb up the river to the valley, and then another rugged trek up and over the cliffs. At that point he does allow himself some emotion as he describes the "dizzying path" climbing the last 90 metres in elevation to summit the Precipice itself. From there it was a slog across the plateau, traversing bogs and swamps to the point that "never did we make camp with dry feet."

When I walked from our house along the short section of the old trail on the ridge, I visited with Lt. Palmer, reaching back in time and usually making a comment or two. This was not so odd as it may seem. When I viewed the old fir trees, the fire-blackened stumps, the wind-torn tops and the leaning, moss-covered trunks supporting contorted branches clawing at the sky, I knew that the lieutenant had seen the same trees and had walked under and beside them the same as I did. These were the same old firs, already two or three hundred years old when he saw them, the same trail, the same view of the Coastal Mountains and the Precipice Valley. Nothing had changed in any substantial way. How short a span of 150 years is! In a flicker in time I could be connected to the lieutenant by the firs, the bed of the trail, the sense that time is porous, full of tunnels and passages for the mind and the spirit to wander into.

So, every time I reached the little level spot partway along the trail where it bent around the spine of the ridge, I took a moment, visualized the man, imagined what he was wearing, and who was walking with him. What were their clothes like? Ragged, ill-fitting or well-fitted? How tall were they? Were they walking slowly or striding with purpose? What expression was on their faces. Was the lieutenant in the front? The middle? Following? Did he wear a pistol? I ran my hands over the bark of an old, fire-blackened snag, right beside the trail. It was a natural thing to do, for anyone who passed by. Did he do the same? Was I touching the same bark, maybe getting the same charcoal on my hands as he did? I tried to visualize the scene, to be in that time in this place, to see and smell and hear what he did as he explored this unknown, spectacular and rugged trail for the first time.

"Good afternoon, Lieutenant!"

I always wondered if I should have given a salute.

The Dancing Firs

Some days, the great gyre of the Northern Pacific spawned pressure differentials that crashed into the mountains with global energy. I've seen whirlwinds stir trees like a milkshake, leaving hundreds of them twisted and torn from the ground in a creaking, cracking roar lasting endless minutes. One memorable night shortly after we moved up to the house from the cabin, we could hear the gusts coming for several seconds before they hit; our solid house trembled and the feeling of sheer force was palpable. Ancient firs clutched the bank beside the house: gnarled veterans several hundred years old, roots exposed here and there, crooked branches jutting from deeply furrowed, leaning trunks. That particular storm was something they had lived through before, probably many times, but for us it was a new experience, demonstrating both the power of the winds and the tenacious power of these elders as they took on youthful energies as the night flowed away. The firs were dancing: not their usual stately, swaying motion, but crazy sinuous, writhing hip hop club dancing, snapping their twigs and hurling their cones into the wind in a night-long orgy of energy. When I went outside to get into the action, the clouds were ripping by so fast that the moon was in staccato mode, giving a flash-dance performance.

But the firs! Whipping from side to side, their branch ends were part of the maelstrom: needle-cloaked fingers snapping time to the primal beat of the elements. Dark brown cones were hurled sideways, bouncing off the walls and windows, cracking and banging into the night. Small branches were tumbling through the air, rising higher and higher until they finally disappeared into the darkness beyond.

We watched and listened until the storm blew itself out in the small dark hours before dawn, slowly losing our concerns about the stability of our home as we immersed ourselves in the emotions aroused by this wild dance. The next morning was still and calm, benign in its denial of the violent escapade of the night before.

Elder Fir Tree

Adaptation

A different weather lesson came one late August. The so-called summer that year had been the coldest, wettest, cloudiest in living memory. The tomatoes and squash plants huddled in our greenhouses, waiting for the bit of sun that would allow their fruits to ripen. Guide outfitters had cancelled trips, resorts had lost bookings, roads had flooded, loggers had "mudded out," ranchers' hay fields throughout the West Chilcotin were underwater, and the mosquitoes were having an orgy of endless feasting.

In an odd way, there was a value in this different weather. It forced us to adapt, to use new strategies to get along. Haying had to wait until the ground was frozen hard enough to support the equipment. Ranchers had to consider "selling down" their herds, to have fewer animals to feed over the winter. The cause of that unpleasant summer could have been variation in weather pattern or global climate change, but in one sense it didn't matter. Whatever the reason, the effects were real and immediate.

Hotnarko River making a new channel

The West Chilcotin is large enough that weather usually shifts across its length and breadth, with sun in one place and rain in another, but that year the whole region was subject to torrential rains and unseemly cold days. In

August, the snow of the winter before was still down the mountains to the tree line, twice as much as usual. I wondered how the delicate flowers could survive this perpetual snow, but then I reflected that this was not the first time this had happened in the area's long history. Resilience is in the genes of the plants and animals who live in the Precipice. Over the millennia, all manner of strategies had evolved to cope with a huge range of conditions. This was one of the real values of the ancient land that surrounded us in the Precipice. It was a proving ground for testing existing and emerging adaptations in a time of increased and accelerating climate change. The following year, the snow would melt back into more usual patterns and the buried flowers would bloom again, likely in new configurations.

Adaptation is like that. Abrupt changes are the usual result—a different size or colour, or an ability to thrive in soils that were not nourishing before. Sometimes the changes are more subtle and harder to riddle out.

I spent years puzzling out the mystery of pine trees. More properly called Pinus contorta, lodgepole pine (not the jackpine, Pinus banksiana, which grows east of the Rockies), lodgepoles are superbly adaptable. From dwarf, wind-formed sprigs a few centimetres tall, huddling behind granite outcrops above timberline, to full-sized trees at sea level, these trees have long, straight trunks ideal for building, hence the name "lodgepole." They are also good firewood when dry because of their high pitch content. In fact, some people from the Bella Coola valley come up to the plateau to get dry, beetle-killed pine for their winter firewood.

I noticed one particular pine growing beside the ridge trail one day as I was rambling along. At first glance, there was nothing unusual in the way it was growing. It was about two metres tall, probably 10 years old, eking out a living on the parched clay ridge. With its southern exposure, it got lots of light, and the spring snow melt gave it a nice drink before the hot, dry summer set in. All of this was normal for young pines living on the hogback above our home, but this particular young tree had an unusual feature to distinguish it from its neighbours. All the other pines in the area had long, straight leaders, or candles, pointing upward, guiding each tree as it reached for the sky. But not this one.

The exact mechanism that governs the growth of these leaders is only partially understood. There are theories about cells sensing gravity, assumptions about biology, sunlight, nutrient transfer and genetic codes, all in well-articulated scientific descriptions. However, none really explains the way in which a tree knows how to send one central shoot straight up and cause all the others to go sideways to form branches. There is more going on than cell biology—more than the interplay of physics and photons.

A case in point was this young pine growing straight and tall on the ridge. It had lost its central leader. Maybe ice, maybe a squirrel, maybe a careless hand had broken the candle off, leaving the fledgling pine directionless. But life is adaptable, finding ways around seemingly impossible problems.

This is where the mystery deepens. Usually in each year's growth there is a whorl of three or four buds that start to grow out horizontally at the base of the leader as a pine begins to form branches. As the leader grows vertically through the year, the lateral shoots spread sideways, cantilevering into space. With no leader on this pine, one of the normally sideways thrusting buds took a 90-degree turn and started to grow vertically. The buds on the rest of the whorl grew as usual, spreading parallel to the ground, while the former branch bud firmly established itself as the replacement spire, pulling the tree upwards to the heavens.

How had this happened? How had the tree decided to direct one branch to grow upward while the others went on with business as usual? Was there some kind of conference? Did the nascent branches draw straws? Was it a privilege or a punishment to take on the role of leader?

There is a theory in biology called morphic resonance. It postulates the existence of an energy field that living organisms follow to become whatever being they are. That is why salamanders can grow new tails, or why one cell can become a few trillion diversified ones to make up a human body. The morphic field is an energy template guiding the life process, the same way software tells the hardware in your computer what to do. This matter-energy interaction is orders of magnitude more subtle and sophisticated than the most powerful supercomputers imaginable. It is also a total mystery, except for this: the youngster on the ridge was following a pattern that had been successful for millions of years, an energy force unseen and unknown, yet fully manifest in the structure emerging as a healthy pine.

Can this be called thinking? Is it conscious? Where are the boundaries demarcating free will, energy fields and so called hardwired, unchanging outcomes? In my view, this young tree took deliberate action to conform to the life model and physical structure of pinedom. After all, it was doing what we were doing at Firhome, making our own fate.

Weather Patterns

The West Chilcotin is a place of legend and spirits, and old timers who were often larger than life. John Edwards was one of those, son of the famous Ralph Edwards of Lonesome Lake. I first met him when I was a backcountry ranger in South Tweedsmuir Park. John was a garrulous fellow, always with a twinkle in his eye and a story on his lips. He ran a canoe rental and guiding outfit on the Turner Lake chain for many years and was famous for his sticky buns, cinnamon rolls he made from scratch. I'll never forget the image of him kneading the dough on his cabin table one hot July afternoon, the sweat dripping off his face into the dough. "Just adds flavour!" he quipped, his mischievous grin erupting through a neatly trimmed grey beard.

I was reminded of John one spring that really seemed later than normal. The redwings hadn't arrived, there was still 45 centimetres of snow in our big meadow, and the river was barely open in the middle. Not only that, the pussy willows up on the ridge hadn't popped their fluffy gray heads out until two weeks before, the raised vegetable beds were still humps under the white snow and black scatterings of ash that Rosemary spread to hasten the melt, and the woodshed was alarmingly depleted for the end of March.

Is this normal? I wondered. This question arose whenever the weather was doing something we didn't like, as in "Is it normal to rain this much in January?" or "It never gets this cold in July!" and, my favourite, "It sure wasn't like this when I was a kid."

Maybe that spring felt late and cold simply because all springs feel late and cold when you are waiting for that first shirtsleeve day bursting with heat and vigour. Or maybe that really was a slow one. During the term of our 27-year-long encampment in the Precipice, Rosemary's diligently kept phenological journal came in handy when the someone said, "It wasn't this cold/hot, wet, snowy/windy this time last year. This isn't normal!" Out came the diary and the discussion, on these points at least, was settled—at least most of the time. I was known, however, to accuse her of entering false data!

But back to John. When I was a backcountry ranger in Tweedsmuir Park, I was constantly asked this same universal question. I used to fumble around a bit and mumble something platitudinous, like "Yep, it sure is hot for late August," or whatever, hoping to give the tourist the satisfaction of experiencing something out of the ordinary, thus adding some spice to their adventure.

The best answer I ever heard to the question was given by John. He'd heard the question more often than I had. One particularly memorable July day, John and I had scrambled out onto his dock with the howling west wind driving a grey, slicing rain horizontally through the air, big sleety drops slamming into our faces like rubber bullets. We helped four half-swamped, soaked and dispirited canoeists tie up to the log deck, freezing in lightweight summer jackets, their red lifejackets stained dark where the water spilled off their hats.

In the cabin later, with the heater glowing, their clothes steaming, wet hair clinging to their illuminated faces, mugs of strong tea balanced on their denim knees, one of the adventurers asked: "Is this normal for July?"

"Whatever it's doing is normal," said John simply. End of story. Just like this spring, things are simply normal.

Yes, weather is unpredictable, sometimes producing hot, sunny days followed by cold, dark ones, with tender green shoots climbing out of icy puddles along the lakeshore, with sleet, hail and wet snow blown by gusty winds. followed by periods of ethereal calm so quiet your breathing sounds like a roaring train. These and so many more clashes of opposites make up just another normal spring, yet there were times, when I looked out over the Talchako Ranges to the west of Firhome, that a sense of the magnitude of time and space they represented would wash over me. These crustal beings have experienced life on Earth for a very, very long time. The rock they are made of was created 60 million years ago, when the continental plate was much farther south. They have a presence, a story to tell, a function to perform as part of the Earth organism, changing as they followed a rhythm millions of years old. Created elsewhere, they now resided in north temperate latitudes, home of the seasons.

In Hindu tradition, there are four seasons to a person's life. The first is youth, when elements of being are formed that will meld together into a fully developed individual. Then comes the phase of building a home, gathering food and shelter for family, raising children and fully participating in society. In the third quarter of life comes a withdrawal from the material world, a time of "going into the forest," where emotional connections to life, death and the spirit of self are explored, faced and come to terms with. Finally, there is old age, where we become leaders, showing our acceptance of the great whorls of energy flows that we are ready to pass through. It is this acceptance that endings create beginnings, moving through cycles, that is to be passed on by elders.

So it is with mountains. Youth is but a distant, millions-year-old memory for them. Since the time the mountains were pushed up, glaciers had carved their valleys and they had nourished countless generations of all manner of living creatures, from tiny shrews to majestic caribou, yet each year, as the Earth spun through space and time, the mountains would begin the winter process as if for the first time.

It would start with a new mantle of snow slowly settling across the heads and shoulders of the peaks and ridges sprawling across their massive frame. This isn't the dirty, black, mottled snow of the city, nor even the dust-laden snow of a country field, but the pure, blue-white snow of the high country. Every year, we watched it coming for weeks, inexorable, implacable, slowly creeping down the mountainsides, finally to come to rest on our doorstep. The Talchakos had become a Hindu priest dispensing wisdom and truth: Everything is a cycle; what ends is a beginning.

Climate Engine

We lived very frugally indeed in the Precipice, so occasionally were able to make trips "away". After we returned from one such trip, a diving holiday in Bonaire in January 2006, I had a further understanding of adaptability. Our B&B in that Lesser Antilles island, 80 kilometres from Venezuela, had an upper deck with expansive views over the ocean. I vividly remember the all-night thunder-and-lightning storms, massive in scale and unrelenting in their energies.

Later that year I found myself reflecting on our Bonaire experience. Even though the day was dark and grey, the green of the dying willow leaves still glowed in the dim light. The whitish-green junipers had silver drops of water glistening on their lacy hands, and little puffs of wind pushed the last golden leaves from the cottonwoods, spiraling them down to the ground in long, graceful loops. The remnants of a six-inch snowfall still clung in patches to the edges of the meadows, creating a mottled mosaic of rusty brown and sugary whites. Then heavy globs of gray rain started falling in sheets. A few brave sparrows were weaving and dodging their way over to the spruce thickets, to wait out the cold deluge. As it gathered strength, the storm began to sound more and more like a train passing overhead. The clickety clack of the rain on the roof had taken on the tempo of a fast freight moving downgrade. It was late fall in the West Chilcotin, a time when all things stand in wait.

Incoming Storm

That day they were waiting in the rain. The seeds were gone, drifted away on the wind or dropped onto the ground below. The squirrels had cached their cones, and the whiskey jacks were back, cooing and whistling in their own soft way.

Where had those rains come from? For several months, the skies had been clear and blue. The ground had crackled underfoot and the fire hazard had been high. Small lakes and ponds had dried up, wells had gone dry, springs no longer yielded water, and then, literally overnight, snow and heavy rain were soaking the valley.

THE POWER OF DREAMS

In a flash, I understood. It's well known that rains ride the jet stream, which directs the storm track across the eastern Pacific, but the real key to the changing moisture patterns in the Precipice lies several thousand kilometres south, in the Equatorial Belt. The tropics are the boiler room that drives global weather cycles, running the planetary climate engine at full speed. As the sun crosses the equator, it heats up the oceans, which in turn heat the air above them. Ocean warming and hot rising air provide the energy necessary to create the cold storms which affect us here far to the north. We are deeply interconnected.

A few years later, the powerful weather machine of the Coast Mountains showed us yet another anomaly. In October, the leaves had not yet left our giant cottonwoods. In fact, they had barely started to turn gold and were continuing their rustling conversations late into the season. Usually, they would have fallen long before, spreading a golden blanket over the forest floor.

Overnight, the weather dumped ten centimetres of snow onto them. The trees looked so out of place that day, debutantes in gold wearing lacy green gowns, stranded on a bare dance floor, their feet covered in snow. I'd seen these northern black cottonwoods on the meadow's edge in many forms, including at the end of a hot, sunny day in June, when we watched millions of cotton flakes explode into the air with a majesty and grace unmatched by their frosty winter cousins. Big, fluffy and delicate, they floated through the sky: parachutes of life drifting in the warm evening currents.

These giants in our valley top out at over 55 metres, with deeply furrowed bark several centimetres thick. Bears love them. Their sweetly perfumed buds (from which Rosemary makes a healing salve) are a favourite treat for cubs and moms alike. It is entertaining to spend a warm June afternoon watching a black bear cub slowly creeping out on a limb several metres above the ground, intent on licking the buds off the branch tips. Sometimes this pleasant treat can end in near-disaster as the limb bends or cracks and the squealing youngster crashes to the ground. They always bounce back, though, seemingly unharmed but hopefully wiser.

Our home cottonwoods were directly below Firhome. They stood tall and straight, their crowns almost level with the bench where Firhome sits. From our living room high above the valley floor, we looked just over their heads. In spring, those brown, sticky buds would exude the most fragrant aroma, telling us spring had really arrived. After pollination, those seeds turn into soft balls of cotton that fill the air with snow.

Cottonwood snow in July

THE POWER OF DREAMS

Lining the steam banks, these riparian soldiers love nothing better than having their roots in water. But this habit can lead to the cottonwood's dark side, as they may not be as stable. Known as the "widowmaker," the cottonwood can topple or drop its limbs unexpectedly, like huge clubs crashing from the sky. More than one rancher or horse has been killed by this random event. Lee and his daughter were walking through our cottonwoods one year and had just reached the river when a large cottonwood crashed down just behind them, a close call indeed.

Oblivious to the danger, our horses spent day after day during bug season huddled under the great trees, nose to tail, hoping to lessen the torment of mosquitoes, blackflies, horseflies, and chiggers. The little puffs of brown dust they kicked up as they stamp their feet and swished their tails were a sure sign that early summer was here. When backlit by the rays of a slanting sun, this sparkling dust, mixed with the cotton snowflakes, would be swept uphill in a late afternoon gust, flowing over the contours and defining the form of the hillside. In the fall these trees turned a glorious shade of burnished gold, throwing colour into the valley around them. It was on my first visit to Precipice as I walked through this cathedral-like grove that I heard an inner voice telling me this was home.

Just one tree species, just one little event, just one tiny precious image, fleeting yet recurring for eons, watching snow swirling in June and again in October, brings us the variety and the sheer force of life in our forests. Weather binds humans to an immense power. On a broken winter day, hard-driven crystals of sleet bite into the face with white-hot stings. Clumps of snow disintegrate into a fine spray, coating all things below with a fine dust of searing cold. The connection with primal cold, absolute zero non-motion breaks free in the heat of frozen snow, a reminder that all is relative, that water is forever present. It's a giver of life, a freezer of cells, a creator of snow, life, glaciers, and thoughts swirling through the mists of the mind, followed by a fine plankton shower drifting downward to the deeps of the forest floor.

The Day the Sun Walked Around the Mountain

Rosemary and I each had special times of the year: seeing the first humming-bird of the season, the day the first plantings were set out in the garden under fleecy protection, or the day the river became completely frozen and silence rolled across the valley. There were a great many events that marked the ebb and flow of life in Firhome.

For me, the interplay of the moon, sun and mountains had its own significance. We may not have had Stonehenge, but we had an inner ring of 2200-metre-high mountains, backed by an outer ring that soared to over 3300 metres. The astronomical observations these megaliths allowed us were far more accurate and enduring than any man-made structure could ever be.

In March 2013, for the 27th time, I watched the sun walk around the mountain, marking for me the holiest of holy days in the Precipice. By this action the sun proclaimed that the culmination of perspective, mountains and the shifting whorls of time would continue to fulfil the timeless promise of renewal. Many events in the Precipice bore witness to this process: the emerging roar of the Hotnarko River as the ice melted, the first blades of tender green grass emerging in the meadow, the horses losing interest in the baled hay because they could find tastier feed along the meadow edge, the medley of early morning birdsong reverberating up and down the valley. All these were markers that spring had arrived.

But beyond that, for me there was one very sacred event that accurately defined the start of spring, when these miracles started to unfold. We all know of the relationship between the tilt of the earth's axis and the egg-shaped orbit carved by our Mother as she races through space. Gaia is forever trying to escape, but she is tethered by the massive gravity of the sun in an elliptical embrace so strong that the boundless freedom of the universe is off-limits for the next few billion years.

It is precisely because these chains of gravity bind the Earth to the sun that life here is possible, but that is only part of the story. Axial rotation, combined with orbital revolution, creates more than the seasons; it also produces a marvellous dance in the sky. It is not just the moon that has a lot of apparent motion, scuttling back and forth on its monthly travels. Our sun travels much further, moving at a stately pace, taking its royal time to circumnavigate the southern edge of the heavens. Moving a few minutes of arc each day, the golden ball proceeds north until June 21, when it starts to fall back to the south, to nearly disappear from our horizon six months later.

As I looked out each evening to watch the sunset, I'd note this daily increment as the sun moved up and down the horizon. The outrigger range of the Coast Mountains due west of us, which reached up a little over 2100 metres, were still high enough to make the sun disappear behind them for a couple of hours each day as it dropped lower and lower in the sky on its southern journey. It was a time of short days, as the seeming doom and gloom of winter choked the sky, stealing the life-giving photons and stashing them in great underground caverns.

Slowly, slowly, the sun began to resist the forces dragging it to the nether regions and there was a halt in the southern slide; then, one day, I'd notice the process reversing itself. The sunsets would start to appear farther north, barely perceptible at first, but there. By the time another month and a half had gone by, it was often cloudy at sunset. Often I didn't notice where things were, but then one day the sun would set north of the mountain peak. It had walked around the mountain, a guarantee that spring was surely on its glorious way.

This was my ritual day in the Precipice. Wiccans have their solstice rituals. There are Maypole dances and northern light festivals, but for me the day the sun walked around the mountain proved the order of the universe was unfolding as it should.

Coastal Invasion

Precipice Valley runs east to west, which means that sometimes the coastal weather uses it as an alleyway to sneak in behind the mountains. It would come with rain—heavy, gray rain, coastal rain, falling-through-the-milk-fog rain, splattering on the dull lime-yellow of dead willow leaves and bouncing high in the puddles. Rain, thick and heavy, beating on the metal roof with a vengeance, rain, rain, rain. Even the afternoon light was subdued, grayed with fine droplets, casting the landscape into a monochrome where edges disappeared and things melted into one another.

This is not a vignette from some sodden West Coast cove, where the tide runs free and the foaming green rollers collide with misty headlands, booming far into the night. This scene takes place on the rain-shadow side of the Coast Mountains, on the end of the Chilcotin Plateau, a place officially described as arid and classified as a high, dry, cold climate—a montane desert. It is supposed to receive about 52 centimetres of rainfall a year, primarily coming as snow. One fall we got some of that snow early, about 10 centimetres, but then came the rain, rain, and more rain, the handiwork of that year's El Niño, spreading its influence far inland.

Precipice Valley is located on a hinge line. Sometimes a massive Interior high would push far to the west, invading the coast, providing day after day of clear blue sky. At other times, the pushy ocean sent its wet armies into the Interior, giving a taste of rainforest living. Some of the Douglas fir trees in Precipice are a result of such interactions. They are a species of coastal Douglas fir that has much more frost tolerance than their coastal kin because of interbreeding with the local interior Douglas fir. The Ministry of Forests has collected cones from several of these Precipice variants to use in its tree nurseries, hoping to breed a tree that is larger than the Interior Douglas fir, yet still frost-tolerant.

This coastal invasion happened a lot in our final years in the Precipice, as the ocean had warmed enough to cause the primal energy pattern in the system to shift, reaching further inland beyond the Precipice and up onto the plateau. So there we sat, with a few little snow patches bravely holding guard as the deluge continued, their fate sealed in the warmth of the ocean's latest inland foray, slowly dissolving into the puddles around them, reminding me of how this land had once been the bottom of the ocean. It seemed determined to go back.

But then the rains would disappear and we would have the hot, dry months. The summer of 2010 was especially difficult. For week upon week the weather throughout the Chilcotin had been dry and hot, in the fiery dance of summer. Forest fires raged, the sky was blackened with smoke and ash, and it seemed as if the very gates of hell were loosed upon the land.

Then, in a seeming blink of the Earth's eye, in the first days of autumn, came the deluge. The belly of the skies split open, creating a waterfall that drowned the lands below. It was the very opposite of unstoppable fire. We were in the domain of primal water: raging rivers climbing over their banks, storming across the land, carving the parched earth into new forms, blasting bridges, roads and homes into oblivion, driving the fires of conflagration back into the earth.

That is the way of primal energy. It exists on a scale far more complex, far deeper, far subtler than we can really grasp. In the flick of a cosmic moment, some of the land is renewed as fires transform forest, and then rivers assert their ancient sculpturing powers, elements of atavism completing each other.

And just when you think you've seen it all, this comes along: coloured snow. Just before sunset one late afternoon in November, I went for a short hike up the ridge to witness the transition from day to night, always my favourite time to visit my perch on the lookout I'd named Satori bench, after a favourite place up in the mountains. I watched the clouds as they tumbled across the Coast Mountains, over the Precipice and onto the plateau. The infinite variety of the sights produced by the elements always fascinated me, but that day set new limits on what the universe can do.

When I first arrived there the sun was beginning to sink into a large bank of very black cloud suspended from one angular mountain peak to another. The contrast between the sun's brilliant yellow ball and the cloud bridge's absolute black was sharp as a razor.

As the sun slowly sank toward the horizon, the thickness of the cloud hid it from view. But just at the moment the shining disc was completely behind the cloud, the mist filling the space under the black band began to pulse with gold, yellow and brilliant white flashes. The pulses moved in quick waves, bouncing off the mountainsides and the bottom of the vee below, shimmering in intensity and duration as they reflected back to the blackness. It was like an alien jellyfish suspended in space, throbbing with life.

Then the bottom of the sun started to fall below the sharp black line on the underside of the bridge, sending rays down and out, like a child's cartoon drawing. I felt the faint warmth as a ray hit my face and I had to avert my eyes as the ancient beacon became too bright to look at.

It was then that time slipped sideways. As my eyes wandered to the sheet of snow at my feet, I realized it had started to glitter—not the sparkling when frost crystals on snow flash like diamonds when the sun or, even more beautifully, the moon strikes them on a frigid clear night, but in scintillating colour. Some twinkled green, others snapped on and off in deep red, and still others winked in yellow and orange. I was seeing the vibrations of life's core. The pulsing jellyfish was reaching out to me and the snow around me, entering my consciousness as part of the energy ocean we live in. Surrounded by snow so alive that it danced with colour, I experienced a crack in time when clouds, mist, sun and snow became one in performance art so sublime, so ethereal, that I was transported to the heart of the cosmos.

As I slowly descended the ridge in the gathering dusk, my senses were still suspended in a bridge from there to here, my slow steps marking a fresh trail to the way home.

Caribou Tradition

Over time, I learned the secret of adapting to snow by watching the wind. When we planned Firhome we arranged its location to have a good southern exposure, and nestled deep enough into the land that the winter winds blew *over* the roof, not directly at it. Our closest neighbours in this wild place, the bears, wolves, moose, deer, coyotes and whiskey jacks, had their niches as well, under the protective skirts of a spruce thicket or in crevasses in massive basalt rock pile, or perhaps the broad arms of old-growth firs, which acted as roofs to keep the snow at bay.

Winter refuge is the secret to living in the wilderness. Animals gravitate to specific winter ranges to find protection, relative warmth, forage and comfort. These ranges are found in the nooks and crannies of the Precipice Valley. They are not needed every year, but in times of heavy snow or deep cold, these special places hidden in little pieces of wetland or clumped on a dry, south-facing slope can mean the difference between surviving or being starved by deep snow or killed by extreme temperatures.

This is the wisdom of the wild: learn the secret places, learn to use what the ecosystem and the climate provide, learn to hole up when you need to, and learn to yield and use the world around you, instead of forcing it. It can't be forced.

The West Chilcotin had two major caribou herds, one living in the Rainbow Mountains to the north, where their habitat ranges across the extinct volcanoes of the Rainbow, Ilgatchuz and Itcha Ranges, and a smaller one that ranged from Hotnarko Mountain south to Trumpeter Mountain beyond Charlotte Lake. Together, they form the largest Woodland caribou herd in southern B.C. Remnants of the last ice age, these caribou were stranded here on the tops of these mountains as the ice sheets retreated, leaving them alone on these volcanic islands in a sea of advancing forest. In mid- to late winter they would come down into the timber, and we occasionally saw their tracks along the Tote Road.

I had a lot to do with caribou over the years. Caribou and raven are my totem creatures, and special to me. As part of the conservation work that came out of our Precipice experience, I negotiated the creation of the 100,000-hectare Itcha Ilgatchuz Park and an associated no-logging zone for their added protection. Caribou calve in the same place for generations, choosing spots where predators can be seen coming, usually below huge boulders or rock outcrops, where shelter and water are also provided.

The importance of shelter and memory were brought home to me one spring when I was out hiking high on the far side of Hotnarko Mountain and had a once-in-a lifetime experience. As I settled in a sheltered hollow for a lunch break I saw below me an old, very pregnant female who was not having an easy time of it, labouring through deep patches of drifted snow. As she broke into the open above timberline the landmark rock outcropping came into view. Sloshing through cold rivulets, her large, cloven hooves crushed butter-yellow and white marsh marigolds, leaving brown-black pools filling with liquid mud in her wake. Finally, exhausted, she settled down in the shelter of a small depression, downslope from a huge boulder left on the mountain's skin by long vanished glaciers. Judging from her appearance, it had probably been a difficult pregnancy. It was here, in this place used by countless generations that preceded her, that the miracle of birth took place.

While Woodland caribou are very closely related to their Barrenland cousins, they do not migrate more than a few kilometres from their spring and summer ranges in the high alpine to the winter range of old-growth forest below timberline, several hundred metres lower in elevation. As one of the few species totally dependent on old-growth pine forest, their winter food consists largely of ground-based lichens, which they reach by digging holes through the snow—a process called cratering. Their large hooves and long legs allow them to move through the trees, often staying on top of the snow between feeding sites, where they graze lichens, as well as mushrooms and other tasty bits.

The lichen the caribou depend upon require the specialized habitat that depends on a mixture of sun and shade provided under the canopy of old growth pine. Cratering is a calorie-intensive business, so the caribou need to balance energy expended with food intake by finding a well-stocked larder. That winter had been difficult. An early deep snowfall, followed by unusually heavy January rains, created a thick ice layer over the belly-deep snow. In such conditions wolves could roam freely, making it easier for them to take down their prey. At the same time, these conditions also made it much more difficult for the caribou to reach the ground lichens, so they responded by eating tree-hanging lichen, as well as moving to windswept alpine areas containing other less nutritious foods.

It was this kind of winter that the mother who struggled to the sacred birthplace had endured. I guessed she was nearing the end of her life, perhaps around twelve years of age. She was stiff in her joints and her fat reserves had disappeared, but she was still keenly alert to the scents carried on the winds, ready to defend against wolf, bear, wolverine, or any other predator of these high slopes.

In this timeless way, woodland caribou fuse the disparate elements of old-growth pine forest, specialized lichens, rock havens and unique anatomy into a specialized survival strategy, which has evolved over the last 10,000 years on the foundations of old patterns. That gives me hope.

TRAIL TALES

After Breaking Trail

Switch-Over Day

Every year, when it was 27 degrees in early August, it was difficult to believe that a mere three months later it might well be -15 and snowing heavily. There were a few rare years that this day never came, but most years it came in early or mid-November. Other years, it came around Christmas or New Year's. You never knew. No matter when it happened, though, this day was a mixed blessing. It set the course for the winter. We called it Switch-Over day—the day when the snow got so deep on our road that a few more centimetres would mean vehicles could no longer drive in or out. Every year, we had to guess whether or not a storm would get us snowed in, whether it would pass through and give us a few more days or weeks of grace, or if this was the day our mode of travel changed for good until spring arrived, the snow melted, the mud dried up and the road was drivable again. Another hour would always tell.

I used to call it "Nasty November," for I never knew what unpleasant surprises the month had in store. Our usual pattern was, out with the truck, followed by the snowmobile, and back in with the snowmobile, leaving the 4x4 at the trailhead. From then on, we would be on snowmobiles until sometime in late April or even early May. Those years the valley would be completely free of snow but the road still not driveable, and we'd have to leave the snowmachines up on the Tote Road. And then when the snow finally left, we'd be on ATVs until the road surface was dry and hard enough to take a truck without leaving ruts. Some years, we would be switched from early November to early June, as much as seven months, but the usual period was five or six months. On just three occasions in our 27 winters we were able to drive in and out all year, but this was rare, and we then still had a month of no-go in the spring, when the road was wet.

One year our Switch-Over Day was not until December. It had been a busy few months, preparing our world for winter. Seven months of groceries purchased in late October in a three-day-long whirlwind shopping trip were safely home and stored. Final checks were made outside to make sure we had collected anything that otherwise would be lost under snow for the next half year.

On the evening of the 15th it started to snow—wet, almost rain, in big, heavy flakes. By mid-morning the next day we had a third of a metre on the ground and we realized that this might be the time for us to get the vehicles out of the valley before they got snowed in for the winter. But then by noon we had clear sky, so we figured: no rush.

Then about one o'clock it really started to come down—nearly three centimetres in half an hour. We decided to get out while we still could. By then we had neighbours, so we checked and they agreed. I chained up our vehicle, a dependable old Yukon, Lee followed in his one-ton flat deck (front tires chained up) and our new neighbour Fred, who had no chains yet, brought up the rear in his pickup. I had no trouble clawing through the snow, but we did have to cut several snow-weighted trees out of the way.

All in all, the trip out to the logging road, 18 km, only took about two and a half hours. We got back home in Lee's truck, which would be left in the valley for the winter, just as darkness fell. It continued to snow all night. By the next morning, we had a new winter blanket 75 centimetres thick.

Now the real fun began. With 45 to 50 centimetres of new snow over the deep vehicle tracks, the conditions for snow machining were less than ideal. Our road was one narrow lane wide, usually with only a third of a metre on each side of the vehicle, particularly in the first six to eight kilometres out of the valley. Lee's duals on his flat deck had taken the full width, leaving no place for the Skidoos to travel but in his tracks.

The trouble is that the Skidoo stance is a little wider than the space between the tire pathway. This meant that you had one ski in the rut and the other on the high middle ground. With half a metre of new, greasy snow on the tire track and 75 centimetres in the middle, the imbalance made the machine want to either snake along or slide off into the boonies. To keep things under control you had to "cowboy" it—kneel on the seat with one leg and stand on the running board with the other, using your weight to leverage the snowmachine and steer it where you want. You hoped. It was very similar to water skiing, using your balance and body mass to maneuver on a single ski. I sometimes marvelled that people do this for fun, as a sport! For us, it was a necessity.

Our trip was made even more difficult that winter, because after that heavy snowfall dozens of trees were down. This snow was the heaviest and wettest I have ever seen. When you looked into it was blue, like the innards of a crevasse.

I had the best Skidoo for breaking trail and so was in the lead machine, meaning I came to the fallen jumbles first. When the guys behind me caught up, we'd get to work, wading through thigh-deep snow, using chainsaws to cut a path through the fall-down. Wet, messy work. If you don't get drenched by falling snow, you get soaked with sweat. You have to break all the rules: no falling pants, no helmet, no safety at all, except being extra careful. You'd hold the saw with one hand, cutting over your head or cutting into the deep snow at your feet, not knowing for sure where your bar tip was. You did your best to judge where the dead pine would whip to when it snapped near the end of your cut, where the dead alder would fall when you cut its base, guessing where the 30-foot willow would land as the snow came off and the mass came cracking down. Cutting blowdown is the riskiest work, especially under these conditions. But with experience, a slow steady pace and concentration, the job gets done and switch-over is completed.

Bringing Home the Tree

The annual Christmas tree hunt was an important ritual for us. Sometimes we prowled around the valley to find a spruce or pine, but the best was subalpine fir. After the loggers had been working near the Tote Road, we found lots of candidates in the regrowth covering the clearcuts.

You'd think that being surrounded by millions of trees would make picking a Christmas tree an easy task, even a four-metre-tall one to reach up into our cathedral ceiling. Like most of us, though, we liked our tree to be "just right." It had to have thick, even branches, no bare spots and a long, straight leader to hold the star we had made for our very first tree in the valley. Overall, it had to have a bushy appearance, with a straight trunk and spreading lower branches for hanging the large glass balls that kept the cats fascinated. Every year they sat there, motionless, their eyes flashing back and forth, tracking the slight movements of the shiny red balls or the twisting silver icicles. Suddenly one of them would leap into the tree, attacking one of these strange creatures, only to fall into the arms of needle-encrusted branches — and our acute disfavour.

Every year when Christmas was getting close, I took a sharp axe, hooked up the sled to the snowmachine, collected Rosemary, and we headed off into the bush. Eventually, we discovered that the best trees grew about 14 kilometres out, on a well-watered, easily accessible, north-facing slope at an elevation of 365 metres. The subalpine firs there had the shape and branch structure we admired. I always took care to cut from a clump where the thinning of the tree would actually help the remaining ones grow faster because they would be getting more light and less competition.

One such tree day was clear and crisp, with the mountains sparkling on the horizon, framed by a sapphire-blue sky. We went as far as we could with the snowmachine, then left it behind and followed an old moose track across the clearcut to the bank, each stride making a sighing sound as the snow fell back into the trench we left behind us as we plowed along.

Trusty axe in hand (axes always start; they don't need to be choked and cranked) we waded through the knee-deep snow, discussing the merits of various trees at length, searching for the perfect one. Of course, by now the yellow flagging tape marking the tree we had carefully selected a month or so earlier had completely disappeared into the snow, and we had to start a new search.

Our perfect Christmas tree

Then came the tricky part. From past experience, Rosemary knew to stand well back, because even though I dislodged as much snow as I could before I began, that first swing of the axe always brought down more snow from the upper branches. I remember one year I tried using a swede saw, but that just prolonged the snow fall, plus it got jammed up in the sap-filled wood.

Once the tree was down, we positioned it on the snow with the butt facing us and the limbs pointing away so they would not catch as we pulled the tree back to the road. Then we trudged back through our footsteps to the Skidoo, dragging the tree behind, carefully sliding it into the skimmer so we didn't break any branches, and gently tied it in place using bungee cords and a lightweight rope.

Every year, as I drove carefully home along the track through the timber, I thought of how lucky I was. There, on that mountainside, we had no traffic, we do not have to stand in a rainy, paved lot paying $60 for a tree, we were not surrounded by honking horns and snarly crowds. On this wilderness adventure, there was only Rosemary and me, my axe and snowmachine, out there in the middle of everywhere, heading home to a celebratory hot rum and a warm house.

Coming and Going

The winter trips I made in those early years of my environmental work were legend. I'd go on Skidoo out to Jim Glenn's cabin at Little Goose Lake and there transfer to our bush vehicle, churn through their long unploughed driveway to the highway and then on to Anahim Lake, where I'd switch to a more highway-safe vehicle and continue on to Williams Lake, Prince George, Vanderhoof, Kamloops, 100 Mile, Clinton, Horsefly, Quesnel, and all the little community halls along the way.

The first thing I did on the mornings when I had to start one of these trips was to check the outside temperature. If it was warmer than -37, then I was good to go. The time it took to suit up for these trips always reminded me of getting into the wetsuits we used to wear for scuba diving. For winter snowmachine travel, first the long johns. On cold mornings, say - 20 or lower, I'd put on the full wool Stanfield's, the ones with the trapdoor. They were an itchy, red wool-cotton blend but were really warm, with their white buttons that winked at me as I tucked them into their slots. Next came the pants I needed to wear to the meetings: not formal, but something better than my work jeans. On top of that went wool pants, complete with suspenders. Over my torso I usually wore a warm flannel shirt, then a wool sweater. That was it for the under layers. After breakfast, lots of bread, maybe some eggs, cheese, peanut butter and strong tea, it was time to stand in front of the door and put the rest of the gear on.

Skidoo trail after a snowfall

Before I did that, though, I'd usually make a quick trip to the machine to get it started. At these temperatures, the starter usually wouldn't break the engine loose, so I had to give it a few pulls by hand and then the starter would kick in—if the battery still had enough juice. If it didn't, then "quick start" fluid and more Armstrong did the trick.

After the motor warmed up somewhat, I winched the back of the machine up onto a block to clear the track off the ground. That way, I wouldn't burn the drive belt as I got the track moving, loosening it from the frozen pulleys. Once the track was spinning freely, I'd let the machine down and drive it over to the house at the end of the path to the front door.

By that time I was pretty well chilled, so it was time for the last cup of tea by the heater.

Then on went the quilted, down-filled pants, followed by extra big felt packs, with heavy wool liners. Once the pants were zipped up, I added a goose-down parka, scarf, wool toque and a ski mask, the eye holes covered with ski goggles. Finally, big leather mitts, lined with wool gloves. By this time I'd be starting to heat up, so I had to get outside. This is like diving, too, before dry suits. Once you are suited up, you start to sweat inside the rubber wetsuit and you want to get into the water quickly.

The next task was to hook up the skimmer to the Skidoo. This dog-sled look-alike had been packed the night before with the mail, empty coolers, and essentials like an axe, emergency gloves and extra toque. In the early days, we had no radio and often the phone was out, so no one outside the Precipice knew when I was leaving or when to expect me to show up, and Rosemary couldn't contact anyone to say I was overdue, so we each really were on our own.

I used to like leaving about 8 a.m. on those November, December and January mornings, so that by the time I reached the top of the rimrock and hit a place we called High Point for a little stretch, I could see the sun rising over Kappan Mountain. It was a treat to see that great ball of fire climbing over the mountain and into the sky, and I sometimes took the time to watch.

The trail to Jim's usually took two hours each way, if the trail was broken and fairly smooth. If there had been snow since the previous trip, then I put on extra large rain pants over all the rest of the gear before I left home. Getting wet from spraying snow as I broke trail was the last thing I wanted to do. Being wet in those temperatures is deadly.

Sometimes the trip took as much as four hours, if there was trail to break and there were trees down that had to be cut out of the way. To do this, I had to strip off the toque, ski mask and parka—maybe even the sweater if the tree was a big one. Using a double bite axe, I would chop the tree into two or three pieces and move it out of the way. The real trick was to move slowly, not work up a sweat, always focusing on staying dry. No snow in the mitts, no snow on the sweater, keep boots and overalls dry. Dry, dry, dry, was the key. At 25 or 30 below, once you get wet there is a real problem very quickly. In a metre and a half of powder snow you can't get a fire going, so you have to keep moving.

I can still remember all the twists and turns in that trail. There was a lot of beauty and a lot of fascination in the way the snow would settle, or how the ice would form on the swamps or the knife-sharp colors in the morning sky, the black-blue almost too penetrating to look at. At a place everyone called Big Meadow, there was often a flock of ptarmigan in their brilliant white winter camouflage plumage scurrying along the snow. I used to look forward to seeing them: a patch of life, like me, moving across the landscape.

There was one morning that I left home at a reasonable -25. I was a little cool, but once you are up and running, balancing the sled and taking the corners, you eventually warm up. If you set the pace right you can balance activity, warmth and cold. Then the ride becomes quite enjoyable, a fluid movement. The machine, operator, the trail and the forest around you become all of a piece in a symphony of trail-running. The engine tells you how the temperature fluctuates.

As it gets colder, the mixture is leaned out, because the air is heavier per unit volume passing down the venturi. This makes the exhaust get a deeper, throatier roar, like a lion announcing his dominance. You get quite used to the sound, moving up and down with the throttle, the load, the grade and the temperature. On one trip, just when I saw the ptarmigan, the engine suddenly began to roar as if that lion had a thorn in its paw. I slowed, wondering if I had burned a piston (running too lean will do that), but no, it was that in a matter of a few metres the temperature had fallen through the floor. It wasn't unusual to run into a pool of cold air at that spot. The air flows down off the Little Rainbows and settles in to the meadow system, lying in wait, its frosty eyes sparkling with the light of distant stars, waiting to flash-freeze the unwary.

I don't know how cold it was, but it had to be well below -40. In a situation like this, there is nothing to do but go for it. No way to stop or warm up. Either the pistons would hold or they wouldn't. In another few kilometres, the roar became much less, and by the time I got to Jim's the temperature was a balmy -34.

That was the travel routine: leave the Precipice on snowmachine, arrive at Jim's, have a coffee, a short chat, and transfer all the load from the skimmer to the back of the Nissan; fire it up, drive to Anahim Lake, and unload into the van parked at the school; get *it* started, which was occasionally a trial because the kids sometimes pulled the plug out of the block heater (another delay of a couple of hours as the engine warmed a little so it would start.) It's not that it had a bad battery, but the van ran on propane and got very cranky in cold weather.

Sometimes this warmup time didn't matter, though, because the person who ploughed the parking lot would pile snow up against the van so high that I had to dig it out before I could move it anyway. I kept an axe and a shovel in the van for that reason. The axe was to chop the frozen snow that had turned to ice and the shovel to clear it away once the ice chips were in a pile.

I often wonder whether, if I had told people at the meetings what I went through to get there, they would even have believed it. For a three-hour meeting in Williams Lake I had to leave the day before, go through the

THE POWER OF DREAMS

snowmachine/Nissan/van transfers, drive four hours to town on icy roads, spend the night, have the meeting the next day, then reverse the procedure, driving back to Jim's, where I would spend the night. The next morning I'd repack the skimmer, especially the perishables like veggies and eggs, into the coolers to keep them from freezing, put them well-wrapped into the skimmer, suit up and head for home. If the phone had been out, which was frequent in those early years, I had no idea what was happening back in the Precipice. Sometimes my meetings kept me out for as much as a week, so there was always a nagging worry in the back of my mind: *Is Rosemary okay?* Were there any emergencies she hadn't been able to handle? We had only the one snowmachine then, so she wouldn't have been able to leave the valley.

Looking back, yes, there were some hairy times, like when the machine started to power out near High Point and I got off to see if the track was binding and went up to my chest in new snow. I had to tramp a trail to get going again and kept the throttle pinned until I reached the top of the rimrock.

But then, to break out of the trees over the top! To have my mind smashed with the immensity, the beauty, the wholeness of this world once more, especially after a few days in Williams Lake or Victoria, was like having a mental shower. It refreshed me, renewed the energy. These are the moments I miss: those searing, deep, connecting times when the mind, the soul and the physical elements that we are immersed in become one.

At those moments, I would shut the machine off, relax in the sun and think how lucky I was.

The Broken Snowshoe

The year we moved into Firhome, 1990 was full of adventures, starting off with 53" of snow in just 36 hours. This happened in early November and was followed by another 24 inches a week later. With over five feet of new snow on the ground, it was impossible for the snow machine to break trail until it settled somewhat. It was one of those situations where you just took a deep breath, said "OK" and went about doing whatever you could.

Not that there wasn't a lot to do. Our newly built Firhome was without indoor plumbing, had plastic sheeting over the windows, only one door for the entrance, and no stairs or flooring on the ground floor. We did have lights as the solar system had been installed but the rest of the electricals were far from complete. But the wood heater blazed away, the walls were insulated and we were warm and cozy.

The snowmobile club out in Anahim heard we were more or less snowed in, and 6 of them decided it would be an adventure to "rescue" us. Unfortunately, they decided to come in the longer way, along the seasonal Tote Road. They had a very difficult time, leap-frogging one another as the lead vehicle and driver became exhausted. By the time they finally got into the valley, it was late afternoon. They decided that their original plan, to make a round trip (up the steep trail up to the top of the plateau, our usual winter route) was not in the books and went back the way they came.

We waited another few weeks more for the snow to settle a more and then took that somewhat packed-down trail all the way into Anahim Lake, since our vehicle was parked at the end of the other route, at a friend's place. Rosemary wanted to get out of the valley for a bit of a change, so she decided to go too.

At that time we only had one skidoo, my 1984 Skandic. It was a real workhorse but primitive by today's standards. No hand warmers and no suspension, limited in many ways, but it was a good trail machine, had lots of power. So on a sunny clear day in late November, Rosemary and I set off on a town trip. She was riding in the dog sled type skimmer I pulled behind, as the Skandic was not really a two seater. It was a little rough ride for her but she made the best of it, wedging herself in as much as possible. I'd already cut out the blow-downs on our usual trail, and since it had been windy we didn't know what to expect on the newer route, so I packed a chain saw and an axe. We carried snowshoes as well, "just in case".

The trip had its challenges. There had been a slight thaw after the original big snow and a bit of melt had taken place. The little streams that carried the meltwater downslope created miniature canyons a few feet deep and two or three feet wide as they gurgled downslope. The only way to get across these snow machine traps was to cut small trees and bushes from the side-hill and pile them into the trenches until there was enough fill that, if you took a run at it, you could bounce the machine across to the other side, manually pull the skimmer across, rehook and be on your way. This mode of travel got us to town although the last part, along a ploughed gravel forestry road, was especially unpleasant as we had to drive on the lumpy verge, which had a lot of gravel in it.

Once in town, after being fortified with lots of coffee, some local info, a few supplies and a lot of mail (including a few bags of mail service library books Rosemary had been awaiting eagerly) we headed back into the valley. Now we had a route with the brush bridges filling in the gorges, and a packed trail, we were in fine shape. I would judge the steepness of the approach, the width of the 'bridge' and charge across.

We were about half way along the trail when a particularly deep and wide fortified section had to be crossed. I slowed down, took a look, signaled back to Rosemary, she gave me the thumbs up and I gave the machine a lot of throttle. We jumped ahead but then I felt things get a little sluggish. Thinking I was sinking into soft snow I gave the throttle a full squeeze, full power. Still sluggish, so I looked back and was aghast to see I'd been dragging the skimmer on its side, no Rosemary in sight. I stopped, jumped off and started up the back trail around a curve to see her half buried in the deep snow, unhurt but a little shaken. I will never forget her blue toque, green jacket, and yellow snow pants all in a jumble like an elf fallen from a Christmas tree.

Finally, the laughter came and we let the tension flow away. Then we discovered that one of the snowshoes had been thrown off in the tumble; it was broken in half. A stark reminder indeed of how close she had come to a serious injury.

In the end all was well but we still have an inside joke about "Must be something slowing us up, I'm just gonna give'er".

A Canine Interlude

We both loved our animals, but Rosemary was particularly attuned to their moods. She tells this story of what happened one winter while we still lived in the Glad Cab:

I've always tried to avoid explaining animal behaviour using human motivations, but often our pets have really tested that resolve. Take, for example, this particular winter night.

Our black pup had been too young to neuter before we moved into the Precipice. Given the difficulties of getting out to the vet in Williams Lake (then seven or eight hours away) and with the nearest neighbour and dogs 40 kilometres away, we kept putting it off. As a result, Bear was nearly two years old and still unneutered when he met his first female dog.

Tuffy, a small, white ball of scruff, arrived at the Glad Cab one winter with her owner, Jim Glenn, late one cold, snowy afternoon. Jim lived out at Little Goose Lake now but had come in to check his cabin at the west end of the valley. Jim had tied Tuffy under a tarp in the skimmer he was pulling with his snowmachine, so at first she was very happy to get into the freedom of our cabin. We were pleased to see our friend Jim, and especially pleased to get the mail he'd picked up for us.

Bear was excited to have a canine friend also and danced around Tuffy, who kept trying to hide behind our legs and under the table. We decided to let them sort things out, but by the time Jim had thawed out with a hot drink it became uncomfortably obvious that while Bear was infatuated with Tuffy, it wasn't reciprocated. "Oh, she's just coming into heat," explained Jim. Tuffy had disappeared behind the couch and Bear was trying to join her, oblivious to the warning growls and yips from Tuffy. The cats, fluffy

Inskip and sleek black Mojo, perched on the loft ladder, where they could more safely watch the activity.

Minus 35 weather and a tiny log cabin were not a good combination for keeping the two dogs separated and still allowing us to keep our sanity, so, although we tried to persuade Jim to spend the night, he bundled himself and Tuffy up and left us to Skidoo the seven kilometres down the valley to his cold cabin at the west end of the valley. At more reasonable temperatures, Bear was an outdoor dog, but when it was that cold he'd nose open the door and curl up by the heater for the night. The door was harder to close than to open, and he'd stand up on his hind legs and throw his considerable weight against it, scrabbling with his claws and grunting with the effort.

On the Night of the Bitch, as it became known, Bear wasn't around for dinner. Nor had he appeared when we climbed up to the loft to bed.

We fussed, of course. Couldn't really believe he would have made the trek down the valley, following that scent that enthralled him, but worried anyway about him wandering around in that bitter cold. We finally dozed, but I had an ear out for the scrape of the door.

Finally, just at dawn, I heard that familiar sound. I sat up and waited for the corollary—the closing performance. Frigid air swirled up the ladder and across the bed. I heard a little squeak. More frigid air. Another little squeak. Too curious and cold to wait, I crept across to the opening in the floor and peered down from the side.

Our wandering canine wasn't using his usual door-closing technique. Instead, he was on all fours, just his shoulder against the door. He'd give a cautious shove, then look up at the loft ladder. Another shove, and another look. A harder shove produced a louder noise, and Bear froze. After a few moments he checked the loft again, then gave a more gentle push. He acted just like a teenager sneaking home after being out past his curfew!

Shaking from both mirth and cold, I watched the whole performance. It took him five minutes to work the door closed, without, he obviously hoped, waking his "parents." He walked quietly over to his mat by the wood heater and, with a grunt and a thump that shook the cabin, collapsed.

When we got up an hour later and stoked the heater, Bear inched around slowly until his back was to us, keeping his eyes tightly closed. Mid-morning came before he stirred again. He stood up very stiffly, drank a bowl of water, and headed for the door, all without looking my way. His door-handling abilities work only one direction, so he waited patiently for me to notice him.

"Want to go out, Bear?" I asked, trying to get him to acknowledge me.

His tail drooped, and he moved a few inches closer to the door.

"Where were you last night?" I persisted.

Now his head was drooping along with his tail.

I spent a few more minutes trying to coax him to "talk" to me, but he steadfastly refused. I gave up and opened the door, and he slunk outside.

I watched from the window. He stood with his leg lifted against a large snowdrift for an inordinate amount of time, then looked around him uncertainly. He took a few steps toward the Skidoo trail, then hesitated and looked back at the cabin. He took a few more steps and I hurried to the door.

"You weren't planning on visiting Tuffy, were you?" I asked repressively. Bear looked at me, then looked longingly at the trail down the valley.

"No!" I said firmly. Bear gave me his "Aw, gee whiz, Ma" look.

I shook my head. Bear gave one last hopeful look south and then, with a canine equivalent of a shrug, turned and slouched back to the cabin.

It was several days before Bear would meet our eyes, and he looked sheepish for another week. We learned later that Jim only knew Bear had been there because he saw the tracks in the snow the next morning. The frustrated dog had spent the night quietly circling the cabin. All that guilt when nothing happened!

That was the start of a firm, although (thanks to a spring visit to the vet) forever unconsummated friendship between the two dogs. Bear always looked slightly uneasy when we travelled down to that cabin, whether or not Tuffy was there, and we are still speculating about the reason. It *must* have been because he stayed away all night. We'd be anthropomorphizing if we said it was because he felt guilty about his suddenly awakened biological urges.

Wouldn't we?

Our Vehicles

We needed snowmachines for the winter. But we needed other specialized vehicles for the other three seasons, as well. The vehicles we moved in with were old but good: a 1984 Nissan King Cab 4x4, and a 1969 GMC one-ton wood truck. The one-ton was a straight six. It had been used by a sprinkler company and had new rings and valves. It had power galore. I added sides of 1-inch plywood and painted it grey. That box held two full cords of dry pine, weighing approximately 4,200 pounds, and would go up our steep driveway in second gear. We called it Big Red 'cause, well, it was big and it was red. (Our ATV was just as cleverly named "Li'l Red") As far as I know, it is still running like a top. I really loved that truck: four on the floor, meaning a four-gear shift on the floor plus reverse, fun to drive but 45 to 50 mph top speed, and 10 miles to the gallon. Every five years, I had to take the gas tank out and drain it. It was a metal tank, sitting behind the front seat. Eventually, condensation would clog the filter with water. The first time it happened took a while to figure it out.

The first year we were in Precipice, living at the Glad Cab, I had filled Big Red with firewood from beetle-killed pine trees down the valley and was preparing to back up to the cabin to unload it. Slowly, carefully, I started to back up, when simultaneously I heard Rosemary yelling and a scraping, crunchy noise.

Loaded in Precipice Valley

You guessed it. I'd forgotten where we'd parked our Nissan and had backed into it, scraping along one side and crunching the right front fender. Think about it. The only two vehicles in thousands of square miles, and I had an accident, backing one into the other. Go figure. We never did get that crunch fixed. We just banged it out and drove it that way.

We purchased the Nissan new when we were still in Alexis Creek, in preparation for moving into the Precipice. I also bought a used chain saw, an old green McCullough, dull as road apples. The guy really saw

THE POWER OF DREAMS

me coming. Anyway, I was going to do my logger thing and try falling. I had read a falling and bucking manual and it didn't look that hard. So up behind the town, I found an open meadow and drove across to a nice-looking dead pine.

I parked the new Nissan, climbed out and took the saw over to the tree. No falling pants, no helmet—that stuff was for sissies, right? I made a good undercut just as the manual said, complete with pictures. Then the back cut. Hey this wasn't too hard! The tree started to sway and then I realized that, instead of falling into the brush, it was heading for the Nissan. All I could do was stare, paralyzed with shock, as the tree gathered momentum and with a *thwack!* the top five feet punched the roof of our beautiful new truck. It put quite a dent in it and broke the back window.

More than a little sheepish, I drove home. The way our driveway was, anyone who drove by could see, too. I took quite a ribbing over the next few weeks. "Oh, out falling, were you?" Snicker, snicker. After that I always parked a long way from where I was working.

My next truck lesson came one Saturday in early spring. I was playing hooky from the store and exploring west of Alexis Creek to Cholequoit Lake. At the east end of the lake, a track led off from the gravel road toward the water. I started along it, put the Nissan into 4-wheel-drive, and confidently headed into the meadows.

Suddenly the steering went funny. I couldn't move the wheel at all! Then I felt a slight tipping feeling, so I stepped on the gas and opened the door—just in time to see my tires turning furiously as they sank into the mud.

It was not mud, really, it was more like fine clay suspended in water. Locals call it loonshit, and that describes it accurately.

So there I was, in the middle of this huge meadow, the Nissan sunk to the floorboards, wondering what to do. In a sense, it was my lucky day: a rancher I knew just happened to come along in his tractor, delivering salt blocks to his cattle. He ran a cable out to me and pulled the Nissan to safety. The lesson? For the unwary, all 4-wheel-drive does is to get you further out into the swamp before you get stuck. It can actually makes your situation worse if you're not paying attention to conditions.

We also had an old van in which we'd made enough changes that we called it a camper van. We had bought it from an herb company and it smelled delightfully of the various herbs they transported in it. When we moved to the Precipice we added the 1969 Ford truck, for hauling large materials like window glass and to use as a wood truck. Then, in 1992, we added a 1979 Suburban to the fleet, replacing the Nissan for town trips. In 2000 we retired the old guy and purchased a 1997 Yukon 4x4, a truly outstanding truck for our purposes; chained up, I could plow through 18 inches of snow with it. It was very comfortable to drive, a great road car, and had lots of room inside for transporting our huge mounds of groceries twice a year.

In 2004 we purchased a 1989 Suburban from a couple named Jasmine and Steven, who fled the country after a brief and ill-fated attempt to adapt to the isolation of Precipice Valley. It had a six-inch lift kit, lots of power, and looked rather prehistoric, so we called it The Beast.

The idea was to use it for driving in and out of the Precipice, possibly even all winter long in some years, but at least to delay the switch-over. The only thing it lacked for the winter trials was new boots. The tires it came with were wide, 12.5 x 35, good for climbing rock bluffs and swimming in the mud, but bad news in winter conditions. Wide tires tend to float over the snow, leading to loss of steering control and traction. The solution was to buy narrower tires, with dedicated snow tread.

Right. Well, for starters, the rim size on the old tires was smaller than the rim size needed for getting the new tires to fit. Well, okay, no big deal, just order new rims. I set the purchase up in advance with our garage in Williams Lake, so that on our town trip in late October I would pick up the new tires and rims, take them into the Precipice, put them on the Beast and away we would go.

It didn't quite happen that way. When I went to pick up the new gear, the mechanic said he thought the hole in the middle of the rim looked a little small to fit over the front 4x4 hubs. But when he called the supplier to check, the supplier assured him that the rims would fit, so I loaded them into the Yukon and headed west—and drove right into a blizzard. It took three hours to go the 100 kilometres from Redstone (halfway from Williams Lake) to Nimpo Lake. Over fifteen centimetres of snow fell that morning, adding to the 20 centimetres already on the ground at the high part of the Tote Road. There was no way I could drive the Yukon in through that. Its clearance was less than 35 centimetres. Besides, taking it into the valley would be risky. If we made it, and got even a little more snow overnight, it would be stuck in the valley for the winter and that would be a serious problem indeed.

Time for Plan B. Lee was still in the valley, and had killed a heifer and needed to get it out to the butcher, so he chained up his one-ton and chewed a path out to Anahim Lake. When I arrived in Anahim I loaded the new tires into the back of Lee's truck, along with groceries, Christmas presents and other flotsam and jetsam, and in we came, leaving the Yukon at the end of the logging road. The back of the truck was a high, open box, so, as you can imagine, as we came in it became heaped with snow knocked from the overhanging trees as we shoved our way beneath them. To get the tires and the groceries out of the truck, I had to take a shovel and dig them out of the waist-deep chunk of snow in the truck box. I didn't do *too* much damage to the vegetable cooler when the shovel hit it. Everything else came out okay.

Bright and early, about nine o'clock, I started up the Suburban, ran it over to Lee's, got his truck started, moved it out of the barn, and drove our big 4x4 in under shelter. I assembled the jack, wheel wrench, cheater bar and a couple of boards to rest the jack on, and away we went. This was the same place that Lee had slaughtered a heifer two days before. When I crawled under the front of the Beast to position the jack, the ground was quite uneven, so I got a bar to level it out. Ah. Out came a pearly white, corrugated windpipe with a chunk of bloody red meat still attached. Not something you usually have to move before you jack up your car, but Lee had been ranching cows here for only a few years, so I didn't really think about it. Chilko really liked the treat. With Mort's dog, Diaz, helping, Chilko proudly dragged this special treasure away for a feast.

Now, all I had to do was to jack up the front end, remove the big old radials, and then the pleasure I'd been waiting for, the moment that had taken two weeks of planning, 680 kilometres of driving, blizzard, a tough mountain road trip, and many hundred dollars, had arrived. But it wasn't to be. You guessed it—the rims didn't fit. The inner hole was too small.

Even though I'm sure the mechanic in Williams Lake could have heard me without any technology, I went into Lee's and phoned him. I wanted to hear his explanation. "Can't be. No way!" said the mechanic.

"Believe it," I said. Or something similarly polite.

The mechanic said he had a solution. Take a cutting torch and make the hole in the rims bigger. "Done it lots of times, no problems," he assured me.

Yeah. Hmm, I thought. What would this do to the integrity of the rims? I was going to be using them under full load, chained up, clawing though deep snow, uphill. Probably the most stress you could put on a rig, and he is suggesting I cut the inner rim support off and make a bigger hole.

I checked with a couple of people out here who have been bush-rigging things since God made the Coast Mountains and they said, yeah, it could be done. *They* had done it. "Sometimes it works fine and sometimes the rims crack after prolonged use," they said.

Another call to Williams Lake. "No problem," the mechanic said. "If the rims crack, I'll replace them."

Sometimes you take a deep breath and go for it. Heck, life out here doesn't come with a guarantee, anyway. With Lee helping, we cut the hole in one rim. It took about an hour of slow, careful work. The hole has to be dead centre and not too big, but even so it came quite close to the lug nut holes, making me think of those cracks again. Finally, I slid the rim over the locking hub, and voila! It fit. Until, that is, I tightened up the lug nuts. Rims come in many designs and this one was not offset enough to allow for the steering arm to clear its inner lip. What that meant was that, even after cutting a bigger hole, the rim still did not fit.

After another "polite" conversation with the mechanic in Williams Lake, new rims were ordered. The following week, the proper rims arrived in Williams Lake and were sent out on BeeLine courier to Anahim Lake. All I had to do was to get the old set of new tires and rims out by snowmachine to Anahim Lake and take them to Buster's shop in Nimpo Lake to have the tires taken off the wrong rims and put on the right ones. The original deal was that a complete new set of tires and rims would come out, but the mechanic didn't see it that way and just sent new rims. Rims without valve stems, I found out, so I had to call him back and have him send out valve stems on the next BeeLine trip.

The next morning, I loaded 140 kilograms of tire and rim into the skimmer and pulled it behind the snowmachine for 90 minutes, climbing 550 metres up the mountain over several long steep grades, to the junction where the Yukon was parked, then loaded them into the Yukon and drove in to Nimpo Lake, got the things changed over, made my way back, parked the Yukon, loaded my freight back into the skimmer, and headed home again. That took another day. The return trip was not too bad, except for the high-centered load of four tires pushing downhill on the long grades, overturning the skimmer so that I had to retie the load on three occasions.

In the end, the new, narrow tires fared no better than the big old fat ones. Imagine balancing on a railroad track. That is what the old tire track was like: a long, narrow, steel rail. It was impossible to stop the tires from slipping sideways off this narrow rail, throwing me sideways toward one ditch or the other. Naming this vehicle Beast had been more apt than we realized.

So I had learned another Precipice lesson. Don't fight it; take winter as it comes, when it comes. If the conditions were too much for our hardy Yukon, it was time to switch over for the winter.

A Trip to the Dentist

Travelling anywhere from the Precipice was never the same twice. Each trip had its own character, set of experiences, challenges and rewards. Very occasionally, everything went just right. Rosemary recalls this mid-March excursion to the dentist in Bella Coola:

We awoke at 6 and peered anxiously at the sky—clear, thank heavens. The clouds the night before, with the promise of warm weather, had been a worry, as our ailing snowmachine wouldn't be happy running in above-zero temperatures, but in the morning it was -30 and the snowmachine would be fine. We hurriedly dressed in our warm clothing and ate, with the cats tearing around the house and fighting, knowing our changed routine was bad news for them. Chilko came in for breakfast, looked gloomily at us, and climbed up on the couch with a big sigh. He knew that at this time of year he would have to stay home. Weighing 48 kilos, he wouldn't fit on the Skidoo with both of us.

Dave went out to start up the Skidoo and to hook up the skimmer, check that the axe, shovel, and chainsaw were all in place, and tie down a cooler we'd already packed the night before with outgoing mail and bags of library books (we had a wonderful free mail library service), and which we needed for bringing back the treat of fresh vegetables. Meanwhile, I'd be doing a final checklist: heater stoked up, trail mix and water packed, a few necessities in case we didn't make it home today, dog-run in place, his water bucket filled, cat dishes full. Bedroom door closed to foil the cats from leaving unwelcome gifts on the bedroom carpet—carnivorous offerings to gods who might otherwise keep us away too long.

We dressed in our usual snowmachine clothes, this time covering it all with rain gear, because the three centimetres of fresh snow on the track would blow up, cover us and melt with our body heat. We had extra gloves in case ours got soaked, the radio phone in case of an emergency, driver's licence for the police, money for the shopping list. Finally we were good to go.

I called Chilko to the door. He slouched out onto the front porch and climbed up on his bed, submitting resignedly to the lead connecting him to the run. The cats sat in the hall window and glared, and finally, we got onto the Skidoo to make a quick trip to Bella Coola, to the much-needed dentist.

Since a logging road had been built a decade ago, we no longer had to take the long trip around the back way, needing to change vehicles twice. Now it was an easy run when the conditions are right, out to the ploughed logging road (a negotiation we made with Highways, after the logging road was decommissioned), which in good conditions could be under an hour. The trail hadn't started to break down yet, and aside from a few impressive moguls it was much smoother than traveling our summer road. We reached our vehicle and it started—another relief.

Then the process of unpacking the skimmer began. It was covered in a heavy canvas tarpaulin and lashed down with soft flexible rock climbers' rope. Even when wet and frozen, this rope stays flexible and easy to work with, unlike the tarp, which freezes stiff and peels off the load like a giant turtle shell.

Nothing had shifted in Dave's well-packed load, in spite of the bumpy skimmer ride. All was dry and organized. It is really quite a skill—akin to horse packing—to properly put together and tie down a skimmer load. Over the years, Dave had learned the hard way through trial and error. There is nothing so disconcerting as arriving at the trailhead only to see the tarp flapping and half of your load gone.

Then we scraped the snow and frost off the Yukon's windshield, prised open the stiff, ice-encrusted doors, got the engine started, unloaded the contents of the skimmer into the back of the truck, pulled the snowmachine into the bush off the trail, covered it with the skimmer tarp, turned the skimmer over, and put the snowmachine key in a safe place (usually the console of the truck). Dave had learned not to put it in his pocket, after the time it fell out at the post office as he pulled out some money to buy a coffee. That day, when he arrived back at the snowmachine, getting ready to head for home late in the day, the key was missing. After a frantic search, he finally decided that it must be in "town," so hc drove back to Anahim Lake and retraced his steps. Thankfully, some good soul had found the key and had given it to the postmistress.

On this day, the truck had been sitting for several weeks, so it was frozen through and through. With the heater running full blast, we peeled off the layers of heavy clothing and put on unlined boots. After all, it was March and we were headed down to a coastal climate. What a pleasure to wear lighter clothing!

 It was too early for mail, but we stopped at Mort's to drop off a few things he had requested—a food bowl for Charlie the Pot-Bellied Goat and a plant hanging bracket. Then it was the drive to Bella Coola, down the Big Hill, known for its 12 to 18 percent grades, single lanes, boulder-strewn road beds and 610-metre drop-offs, followed by a lovely drive through the Bella Coola Valley. The contrast to Precipice was striking. Here, nearly 500 metres lower and 25 degrees warmer, there was green grass, apple trees in glorious pink blossoms, yellow daffodils and white-blossomed cherry trees, all in stark contrast to the white-grey world of still-frozen ground and snow-covered meadows of Precipice. We finally arrived in Bella Coola at the west end of the valley, reaching the dentist just five hours after we started our trip.

Seeing the dentist turned out to be a quick, easy-solution visit, and we celebrated by Going Out for Lunch at the Cedar Inn. Wow! Food we didn't have to prepare ourselves. The owners were Korean, and they had a complete menu of Korean delicacies. We gorged ourselves on exotic soups and other spicy dishes. Bella Coola is small but has a lot of amenities, so we stopped at the hardware store to pick up welding rod (for Klaus), the Co-Op for flour and quinoa (for Chris), and finally the Mercantile (for Mort and us) for flashlight batteries, an axe handle and the much-longed for fresh vegetables and fruit.

THE POWER OF DREAMS

The sun was shining, which was a rarity here in this wet, narrow valley, and the views of the mountains were wonderful. We enjoyed our drive back up the Hill, left the goods purchased for other people at Mort's, had a quick cuppa, and then drove back to the Skidoo to reverse the whole process.

We got home at seven o'clock, just 13 hours after we started. Not bad! One of our faster trips, and no problems. And we had fresh greens to supplement the buckwheat, peppercress and sunflower greens I'd been growing, and the 6 or 8 kinds of sprouts that we were getting very tired of after five months. (Note that "fresh" is a relative term, given how far they travelled to get to Bella Coola.)

Houdini Chilko had magically unhooked his lead and rushed joyously down the driveway to meet us. The cats were relieved that our absence was so short, and there was only one dead creature in the hallway.

Given all the things that could have gone wrong and didn't, it was a good trip to the dentist.

The Energy Gods

Routine is a very important aspect of living in the bush. In a way, it's like a pilot's preflight checklist: The more often you do something, the smoother the procedure becomes. Yet there is always that intangible component, the feeling in the gut that things are not quite right or good to go. The longer we lived in Precipice, the more we experienced this sense of timing for things we needed to do. The first spring run on the ATV in 2009 was a good example of this process in action.

Breakup was underway. As usual, the valley bottom was clear of snow and the grass in the meadows was sprouting. We were expecting the first bears any day, fresh out of hibernation and looking for a green snack. The geese were in the ponds, the trails were dry, and there was a fringe of ice left along the river banks in the shady spots. I had been thinking about attempting a town trip for several days. Part of the calculation was guessing how much snow had melted up on the mountain, as it was north-facing and 450 metres higher than Firhome. The other permutations were almost endless. *How cold has it been at night lately? Was it a bounce, or was it freezing for several hours? How warm did it get during the day? How much did those two days of rain last week melt the snow pack? Did it snow up there when it was raining down here? Did the culverts stay open or are they frozen solid, with the runoff washing out the road? How many trees came down during those last windstorms?* Lots of questions. Lots to assess.

Loading ATV for early spring trip out of the valley

I climbed up the ridge behind Firhome and took a look to the southwest. The hilltops I used as a "tell" still had snow, but there were a few bare spots. That usually meant that travel, while a bit messy, was possible. None of this was new. According to my calculations, I could have gone out any time in the previous few days, but there was always some little thing I felt

I still needed to do: recheck the chain saw, fix the muffler on the ATV, take another look from the ridge. It was nothing specific; I just didn't feel ready.

I began to think about Indigenous peoples, with a myriad of rituals, routines, observances and chants to placate the spirits, to ensure safe travel or good hunting. I've always been skeptical of such beliefs, because I know that humans cannot control weather, the movement of game, the strength of the wind, or the energy that forms the universe around us, but then it struck me. It *is* about energy, but not the energy of the wind, the rivers or the forest; it is about *our* internal force fields. The rituals, the observances, the actions, prayers, chants and all the cultural instruction are not about the power of the spirits. They are about personal human energy. It is *us* feeling ready, feeling confident, feeling the flow that makes us quiet, calm, capable, and maybe even invincible.

We all operate that way. When we feel "up" we are hell on wheels. When we feel down, everything crashes. It's like a hockey team that wins one night and loses another, depending as much on confidence and mindset as on physical skill and capacity. Sure, you need the latter, but it is the former that really makes the difference. So it is with spring. Once I have done all I feel I can do, once I have honoured the rites of observation and maintenance, once I really feel ready, then it is time to go. I am mentally ready for the challenges I might face.

Sure, the trip had its moments. Yes, there was more snow than I had anticipated, the moose had made a real mess of the trail through the clear cuts, which made for a very rough ride, and on the way back the deep snow was getting soft and I had to chew, slip and slide a fair amount, but there was nothing really problematic.

Being in the right frame of mind and attitude made all the difference. When the ATV fell through a snow bridge into a deep puddle, I sploshed knee-deep through the slush, pushing on the handlebars, revving the engine with my right thumb, spinning the wheels and, slowly, inch by inch, climbing out. When a fallen beetle-killed pine had to be cut into pieces so

I could pass, I had to find solid footing in the slippery snowbank on the side of the trail so I could use the chain saw safely. In the shady sections where the snow was still deep, I had to stand on the running boards and rock the ATV from side to side so the tires could get traction, first on one side, then the other, "cowboying the machine"; using my weight to shift the centre of gravity around.

All these things were part of the process I felt ready for. They did not hinder or stop me but simply happened in their own way. The quiet energy that arises when we let our spirit prepare for life's journey make all the difference. *We* are the energy gods.

Life at Thirty Something

Winter cold snaps were common in Precipice Valley, but their timing was unpredictable. One year, we had -45 in early December. Another year, we had -30 in early March. We never knew when a deep freeze would come. All we knew was that we would "get it" sometime each year.

When it gets a little on the chilly side, as it did one memorable January (at –32), it is a convention among West Chilcotin residents to describe temperatures as "thirty something" or, in this case, just plain old "32." It's understood that the meaning is -32, but no one needs to point that out. After all, the frost is thick on the windows, the dog really doesn't want to go outside, and the tractor needs a tiger torch blasting it for three hours before it will start so you can feed the livestock. No one would mistake a reference to 32 as anything but cold. And then there are those who really don't like the "new" cen-tee-grade numbers. They refer to temperature in what they call "real" language: good old Fahrenheit. So 32 becomes 25. You get the idea. Of course, all this is moot at 40, because -40 is -40 no matter what scale you use.

But then, you really don't need a thermometer to tell you how cold it is outside. When you take a deep breath through your nose and your nostrils feel like they'll freeze together, that's about zero. When the snow squeaks underfoot like a mouse being chased by a cat, then it is probably somewhere around -15. When it's a little colder, around -20, your throat begins to feel like too-hot coffee is being swallowed. At -25, the sounds around you are amplified in a dry, crackling kind of way. Your parka rustles and your coveralls mumble to themselves as they bend at the knees. You can feel the electric shocks to the wrists where little puffs of air sneak in when you move your arms. You begin to feel like an astronaut, cocooned in your suit, stiffly moving through frozen space.

Dressed in this attire, you attempt to start the snowmachine because, like it or not, you need to make a run to town for mail that you hope has some much-needed part. You hit the start button on the handlebars and all you hear is a sharp click. The motor is so stiff, the starter won't turn it over. Being careful not to break it, you pull the starting cord steadily, forcing the motor to turn over slowly. There is technique here. If pulled too hard, the cord will break, and that, believe me, is a true problem at those temperatures. Steady hard pull. No jerks. Slowly the engine turns over once, then twice. Now you hit the start button and, while not very quickly, the engine does turn over and catch.

If the engine won't start, and the battery just can't turn things over and you can't use the starter cord to get things moving, then you know it is -40 and your day is done. No travel at those temperatures. The torsion bars, the track, the bearings: these parts were not designed to operate in this kind of environment. They tend to seize, break, or at the very least, damage the machined surfaces.

In the middle of the night, the crack of a high-powered rifle splits the silence. Another tree has shattered, its sap expanding as it freezes, putting so much pressure on the trunk that the tree literally explodes. It can sound like a firing range out there, especially if there is a strong outflow wind that causes the brittle trees to sway, thereby causing many more to snap. You can hear the wave of sound coming down the valley, like some giant bowling lane, the pins being tossed and scattered on the valley floor. This is -40 on anyone's scale.

The horses need to be fed every day, though, no matter the temperature or weather. They are tough Chilcotin horses that have never bothered with a barn shelter. In the extreme cold they huddle against the meadow's edge, grabbing some sun if there is any, standing shoulder to shoulder with vacant blank eyes, lids half closed, in stasis, waiting. Once they hear you coming, they nicker, whinny, and walk slowly to the waiting hay, their breath hanging in foggy clouds around their heads.

If you have to sit on the tractor with your parka hood fully extended, its long snout six inches from your face, if any wrong movement at all lets the air in and your nose catches fire, this is -45. I once chopped wood at- 50. At that temperature the weirdness really sets in. Because the cold air is so dry, it doesn't feel cold at all—at first. I stood on the back porch in my underwear and a T-shirt, feeling warm as toast as I split a round. But then it hit me and I knew: there were only seconds to get back inside before flash freezing took place.

It is said, though I have never tried it, that if you have the courage (?) to relieve yourself at -55, your stream will freeze into ice crystals before it hits the snow. One has to ask, though, what happens to the apparatus while this procedure is taking place. But perhaps this is a country legend.

Seymour's Last Ride

The first map of the Precipice Valley dates back to 1863. In the 150 years since then, people passing through have left behind many strange stories about their adventures. But often when we drove the Tote Road it was the story of Seymour that we remembered.

Seymour came to the Precipice from North Carolina with his son and daughter-in-law, Steven and Jasmine, who intended to start a new life here. "Moving to the bush to get away from Bush," is how they put it. With them and enough possessions to last a century came 15 dogs, three cats, and two guinea pigs. And Seymour.

Seymour wasn't a well man. Some years previous, when he was in his seventies, he'd had a serious medical problem and his life was saved with a little shunt in his brain. The doctors told him it would need to be replaced in six to eight years, so after six years he approached his doctor—only to be told he was too old. Their prognosis? The shunt would fail soon and he'd die.

Rather than leave the elderly widower on his own, Steven and Jasmine brought him with them to the Precipice. His various other ailments—kidney, liver, you name it—were faithfully treated by the couple with various herbs, extracts, homeopathic remedies and a vegan diet—the latter much to the disgust of Seymour. (The dogs also disliked being vegan, but not as vocally.) After one visit with him, we had seen him looking longingly at the dogs' bones—yes, they fed their vegan dogs cow bones—Dave and I started visiting more often in order to sneak the odd chicken leg or bits of cheese to him. He was very grateful and declared that the quality of his life had improved. I suspect that Steven, less rigid than his wife and thinking, as we did, that Seymour shouldn't be expected to change lifelong habits at his age, knew what we were doing but he said nothing.

Seymour made it through the first winter, but eventually it became clear that he was not doing well. By the next fall, this New Age couple made the radical (for them) decision to take him down to Bella Coola to see a doctor before they were snowed in for the winter. A comfortable bed was made of piles of down comforters in the back of their old, roomy Suburban, and a very frail Seymour tucked into it.

Jasmine and Steven couldn't both go because of their menagerie, so it fell to Jasmine to transport him. She drove as carefully as possible, but since Seymour wasn't saying much, she couldn't tell if he was comfortable. She later said she'd never found the 40-kilometre Tote Road to be so long and nerve-wracking. When she checked on Seymour after finally reaching Anahim, he opened his eyes briefly, no doubt in relief at being less thrown around.

She kept going west, still with two hours to go to get to the Bella Coola hospital. She checked on Seymour again part way down the Hill (always capitalized because of the fearsome 18 percent grade and 2000-foot drops) and all was well, but her third check, at the bottom of the Hill, wasn't so good. She couldn't rouse him at all.

In fact, she couldn't find a pulse. Seymour had died.

At this point, Jasmine had two choices. Go home with Seymour and bury him, and hope that no questions were ever raised, or continue into Bella Coola to get a death certificate. So, making the safer choice, she kept her cool and continued on to the hospital, still 65 kilometres away along the valley bottom.

Thanks to some ingenuous fudging on her part and that of an understanding doctor, it was decided that Seymour actually died in the hospital parking lot, thereby avoiding the huge complications that she otherwise would have encountered with the RCMP if the death had occurred on the highway. The hospital staff were a bit bemused by all this and probably are still talking about it, especially the subsequent events.

Steven and Jasmine had already decided they wanted to bury Seymour on their own property in the Precipice. Now, normally, the process for getting permission for this takes months—up to six, Jasmine was told. But obviously those rules are for we common folk; the government office in Bella Coola had never before dealt with the likes of this flamboyant and persuasive woman from North Carolina. Incredibly, the permissions were stamped and processed in a few hours, and Seymour rode home again in his comfortable bed in the back of the old Suburban, somewhat less aware of the trip than when he went out.

This was on a Friday. The next morning, we were invited to attend a wake that evening, after Steven had figured out how to put the yet-unused bucket on his new backhoe and dig the grave. Much, much later, we were told that the wake wouldn't be until Sunday because Steven couldn't figure out how to get the bucket on, and they had decided to dig the grave by hand. Since they didn't believe in using a coffin—just a shroud, so Seymour would become "one with nature" more quickly—the hole needed to be deep enough that their pack of dogs and any wildlife couldn't reach Seymour. And soft enough for digging by two determined people. Offers of help were refused; they thought they should do this last act for Seymour themselves.

We later learned that the summit discussions about "where" continued rather heatedly, well into the night and through the next morning, but eventually the deed was done and Seymour was placed in his last resting spot, right where a rail fence had a sharp bend. We and our neighbour Lee took our ATVs west, five kilometres down the valley, to their place to say our goodbyes, making liberal toasts to this man whom we had known for such a short time but had thoroughly enjoyed.

But the story doesn't end just yet. The couple from North Carolina didn't survive the next winter, psychologically, and once again the property was sold. The new owners, Lee (who owned the property in the middle of the valley) and a friend named Fred, removed the old rail fence that was a few hundred meters from the cabin. Now, this was unfortunate, because Jasmine and Steven had never gotten around to marking the grave and the only reference points we had were along the fence itself. After much discussion, a site was selected and the new owners decided to place a grave marker there.

Dave and I strongly suggested that there be no deep ploughing anywhere in that area. Just in case.

ATV Adventure

It was that time of the spring when the snow in the valley was gone but the road was full of frost boils, snow patches at higher elevations, and soft spots caused by high water tables, so I chose the ATV for my trip. I had a meeting at Tatla Lake, east along Highway 20, scheduled for 8 a.m. Working backwards, I calculated I had to leave home at 5 a.m., allowing an hour (at least) to get to the vehicle, another half hour to Anahim Lake and then roughly one and a half to reach the library at Tatla Lake. This schedule meant I could travel at a moderate pace. If all went well, I would have 15 to 20 minutes to spare.

When I got up at 4, it was raining heavily. Decision time. I figured it wasn't -20 with blowing snow, so even though I might get a little wet, sitting on the ATV for an hour wouldn't be a problem. Fortified with a couple of mugs of hot tea, slices of homemade bread slathered with peanut butter and honey, and hugs from Rosemary, I ventured out into the morning gloom, cheerily dressed in yellow rain pants, light green felt packs, dark green rain jacket, black gauntlet mitts and a huge brown leather cowboy hat with a patch of rattlesnake skin sewn onto the front. I was ready.

At first all went well, with the windshield deflecting most of the rain, although the back eddy caused some to swirl toward my face. The brim of the big hat, when tilted just so, caught most of that, leaving a little bit to hit my cheeks and splatter over my glasses. But I could still see through the dark well enough to stay on the road and steered a steady course into the gathering storm.

After about 15 minutes and a gain in elevation of about 90 metres, the rain changed abruptly to snow, slushy and wet, mixed with little hailstones. There was no doubt about it: late winter had returned.

ATVs don't usually have windshield wipers. Nor do my glasses. For a little while I could see enough through the gray-white mist to steer, but eventually I had to take off my blurred glasses. No matter: my vision was good enough to keep things on the road, even though the edges were a little fuzzy. The real problem was that the windshield had started to collect snow, to the point that it became an opaque white screen, blocking my view entirely. Leaning over to the side so I could see didn't work. The full force of the snow hit me squarely in the face. Things came to a near halt for a while.

Eventually, I devised a strategy: I used my right hand on the right handlebar, allowing me (rather awkwardly) to both steer and work the throttle with the same hand. I was then able to use my left hand as a wiper to clear the snow from the top of the windshield, giving me a small window to see through. I didn't see the humour at the time, but it would have been a strange sight to see me crabbing along, half-crouched over the seat with my arm swinging back and forth like some demented dog wagging his tail.

Finally, I was up into the clearcuts, nearing the end of the journey and feeling rather smug as I chugged along, with soothing thoughts of a warm car followed by a hot coffee in town. Then the ATV died. It sounded like a balloon whose neck had been let go, sputtering noisily for a second before the silence descended. I tried the starter a couple of times, but I could tell this was not going to work. There was no life at all.

So there I was, at 6:15 in the morning, 15 kilometres from home, sitting on a dead ATV with a tree-bending wind blowing hard and seven centimetres of new snow covering 15 centimetres of old snow on the road, and more coming down.

So I started walking out to the vehicle. Not too far, really, on a good day. But at this time in the early morning, carrying a wide cooler containing my clothes and kit plus outgoing mail, breaking through the crust with each step, trudging into a blizzard, the snow and sleet stinging my face as it was driven horizontally into my line of travel, I began to wonder what I was doing here.

Step by step, and without my glasses, I focused on the swirling surface before me. As the cooler became heavier and heavier in my arms I had to be careful not to trip or lose my balance when I broke through the crust. The last thing I needed was to stumble and fall, breaking who knows what, so it took all my attention to carefully place my feet and forge ahead. At times the blizzard blew its sharp snow crystals into my face so hard I couldn't see at all. When that happened, I just stopped, stood there, my head bowed to the gale like one of our horses, waiting for the wind to slacken a little before I could take another step.

I finally reached the car, wet and chilled but overall fine. The sweetest sound you will ever hear at a time like that is not the soft cooing of a voluptuous lover or the emotional notes of a soaring aria. No, the greatest sound in the whole world comes when the grinding of a starter is followed by an explosion of noise as a vehicle's engine jumps to life.

The rest of the trip was uneventful; the meeting went well and I had a good visit with friends. It is part of the karma when you live in the back country that machines will always break down when you need them the most. I suppose this is part of the soul experience I chose in this manifestation. It took the better part of a day, but in the end I was able to temporarily fix the problem with the ATV and made it home, where I could do a proper repair job before the next trip.

One Lucky Dog

One time in late May, when we could finally drive our truck, we were very low on groceries, so Rosemary decided to take a much-needed break, combining shopping with a visit to family and friends. She had been in the valley since the end of December and was ready for a change.

The plan was simple. We would use the Beast for the rough stretch, then transfer her load of goods—including four large totes of bedding plants (a gift for her niece in Pinantan Lake)—at the end of the road. I would leave the Beast there and follow her to town with Lee's car, which had been waiting with ours to be brought into the valley. Perfect. After tying Chilko to a run between two fir trees, we did the last-minute stuff and headed for the end of the Tote Road. The trip was uneventful. We had only to clear out a couple of small trees and negotiate a series of mud holes where the road was still under water.

Once the load was transferred to our town machine and Rosemary was ready to leave, I jumped in Lee's truck and followed. I had to go to Anahim, because Lee was expecting machine parts in the mail, along with insurance papers, so I needed to hang around and pick up the mail when it was ready, usually about 2 p.m.

Instead of going directly to Anahim Lake, though, we took a short cut to Nimpo Lake using an alternate logging road, which led to a convoluted passage through the West Chilcotin Mill to Highway 20 and then east to the coffee shop in Nimpo Lake. This was not the usual route. In fact, we rarely used it, but we did that day.

We had a great cup of coffee in the Nimpo bakery, along with a cinnamon bun or two, then I said goodbye to Rosemary as she headed east along Highway 20 to Williams Lake. I went back west to Anahim Lake along the highway. I still needed to fill in a few hours before the mail would be ready, so I dropped in to see a couple of friends. By the time I had chatted the morning away, it was not quite noon and I still had a wait ahead of me.

What to do with myself? I decided to go to old Mort's place and hang out. As it turned out, two of his friends from Vancouver also had stopped by to say hello. They were looking for something to do, too, so they suggested we all go to Nimpo for lunch. Since I had already been there once that day, I nearly said, "No thanks," but then I figured, "What else am I going to do?" So Mort and I piled into Lee's car, while the others used theirs, and off to Nimpo we went.

The drive to Anahim Lake from Nimpo Lake is not too long, about 16 kilometres. Near the entrance to Nimpo Lake, you cross a bridge where the Dean River flows under the highway on its way to the coast. As I came around the corner, I saw a big cream-coloured dog loping along in that broken chassis gait they have when moving across country.

"No," I cried. "It can't be!" But sure enough, as we passed by and slowed down, it was Chilko, in full cross-country mode.

Chilko on the run

I stopped, opened the door and called his name. For the first couple of seconds he just crouched, not sure of the strange vehicle, but then recognition came and he gave a deep-throated bark and bounded forward. Such energy and passion! He jumped into the back seat, crushing the freshly laid eggs I had bought from friends in Anahim. No matter, he was with us and safe.

When we got to the coffee shop, it really began to sink in. This dog had slipped his lock—I later found out I had not secured the catch properly—run nearly 50 kilometres in a few hours, and had ended up on the highway, where I had found him.

The distance is not the issue. Lots of dogs can go 50 kilometres. What got me shaking, and what I think is the really huge part of this story, is that Chilko followed our scent along logging roads, through the busy mill complex, then figured out to turn east along the highway to follow the vehicle that Rosemary was driving.

This was not a nice morning. It was raining heavily and the roads were muddy, yet he followed our track through unfamiliar territory, knew when to turn right, turn left, over muddy, mucky logging roads, across cattle guards, across several other vehicle tracks heading every which way, and was still able to decide which way to turn when he reached the wet highway. One mistake, and he would not have followed the correct route. I will never again be so supercilious as to think that we humans, brains or otherwise, have a lock on the abilities needed to be on this planet as intelligent life forms.

But then, beyond skill, there is luck. If I had decided not to go back to Nimpo for a second time, if I had not gone back to my friend's for a second cup of coffee, if I had dawdled for a few more minutes, if, if, if. If I had not come along when I did, if 10 or 15 more minutes had elapsed, then Chilko would have passed the coffee shop in Nimpo Lake and headed east along Highway 20, inevitably losing the scent of Rosemary and the Yukon in Williams Lake. We might never have known what happened to him. I would have gone back to the Precipice and he would simply have been missing. Eventually we would have thought about him drowning in the river and being eaten by grizzly bears or cougars, but I would never have thought of him being able to follow us by scent alone.

Yes, he had a tag, and yes, he may have eventually been reported. Maybe. But he was not traffic-wise, and there were many, many, things that could happen to a Precipice dog unfamiliar with cars and trucks on 300 kilometres of lonely highway. The point is that the miracle arising from the incalculable series of events that led me to see him on the highway in those few moments of possibility will be forever lodged in my memory. Mysterious beyond any scientific rationale, the connections that led to his rescue are the very stuff of life. Chilko was indeed a very, very lucky dog.

INTERFACE

Fire cloud above Precipice Valley

In Case of Fire

One consequence of living in the wilderness is the most obvious of all. You are living in an interface zone, an edge you take with you at all times. Sometimes you live on one side of it, sometimes on another. Sometimes they conflict. There are moments of danger and decision that reveal your character. You find out who you are.

Interface with wildfire is always a present danger in the West Chilcotin. Over the years, many fires came close, but none ever invaded our home. The big old firs around us had burn marks as high as eight metres up their furrowed trunks, though—evidence that Precipice was not always so lucky.

In August 2010, we received an evacuation order—the second one in the past six years— telling to us go to Williams Lake as fast as possible because of an out-of-control forest fire heading our way from the west. We had only a few hours to evaluate more than 24 years of building, gathering and accumulating the things we needed, or at least thought we needed, to live in remote Precipice Valley.

The breeding ground for the fires of the West Chilcotin is a corridor running from the north tip of Lonesome Lake up to Anahim Peak, in the area known as The Gap, where the Dean River punches through the Anahim Volcanic Belt on its path through the Coast Mountains to north Bentinck Arm. It is there that coastal air masses smash into Interior patterns, often creating high winds and vicious lightning storms in early to mid-summer. Sparking and cracking late into the night, these outbursts of primal force hurl spear after spear of white-hot energy at the forest, exploding trees into balls of flame.

Because these storms are often without any rainfall, or at best very little, their conditions allow the incendiaries tossed from the sky to create circles of fire. These nodes of heat and smoke grow quickly. In the space of 24 hours there can be a roaring fire chugging across the landscape, virtually unstoppable.

This is what happened near Firhome that mid-August. In fact, one particular electrical display created at least half a dozen fires. Growing quickly, some of these burns joined forces to become monsters covering several thousand hectares within a few days, while others, like the one called the Heckman Pass Fire in Tweedsmuir Park, grew in just a few hours into unmanageable fires too big and fast-moving to contain.

We awoke that morning to find Precipice Valley full of smoke. We had difficulty breathing, we were very concerned, and we needed information. I called the local air services, the highways manager, and a couple of ranchers out west on Highway 20, and was able to triangulate the location and size of the fire. With relief, we decided that for the moment it did not pose any threat to our tiny community.

The next day we received a recorded message telling us that we had three hours to leave the valley and head all the way into Williams Lake. It was followed by a very strongly worded email ordering us to do the same thing. This was in contrast to the information I had put together and the risk assessment I was undertaking regarding our safety. Later that day, the warning was repeated, presenting us with a vision of a wall of fire shrieking through the Precipice.

We were faced with a decision: to follow the official order, based on a policy to make sure that if anything went wrong government would be blameless, or rely on our in-depth local knowledge and assessment.

Part of the decision was based on a choice of route. There are three ways in and out of Precipice. The Tote Road climbs out of the valley on the south side. The old telegraph road, then our phone line, climbs up the steep hillside to the top of the Precipice in the north, and winds across the plateau east towards Anahim Lake. It is just barely drivable by ATV. The old pack route, the Sugar Camp trail, can be followed either northeast along the Hotnarko until it eventually climbs up to the plateau and out to Anahim Lake, or westerly along the hillside above the Hotnarko, before dropping down into the Atnarko Valley. Only one route, though, would allow us to take any possessions beyond necessary records, a few clothes, and our animals. If we wanted to drive in a full-sized vehicle, it had to be the Tote Road.

We decided to pack and get ready, while continuing to monitor the situation, and to be prepared to leave quickly if the fire became immediately threatening. I was in frequent contact with the local air service office, which gave me an hour-by-hour status of the fire's behaviour. They were flying firefighting crews to fires and making reconnaissance missions, so they knew exactly what was going on. I knew the owner well; he had flown me and my crews in and out of the mountains for several summers when I was a backcountry ranger for B.C. Parks. As well, I had flown a lot when I was the community liaison person during the fires of 2004. These flights gave me a good knowledge of the lay of the land and how serious the threat was, so I was confident I could make an appropriate decision.

In the end we decided that if we could use the Tote Road we would take the cats and dog, computer hard drives (now is that a sign of the 21st century or what?), some clothes, valuables, a few pieces of artwork, journals, necessary medications, documents, and other personal items. It wasn't much, but it would fill two vehicles. How, though, do you pack up a quarter of a century of work building a home, creating gardens, gaining intimate knowledge of the valley with its secret places, the ebb and flow of life here across the years? Not possible.

It was quite a mental jolt to go through the process, realizing that our home, a labour of love and determination for all those years, would be on its own. The capriciousness of the fire gods would determine its fate. We had no insurance, because the rates had climbed so high after the last spate of wildfires that we couldn't afford them, so if the house and buildings burned, that would be it.

In 1986, while we were still living in the cabin, a fire did come to less than a kilometre away from us. Crews were flown in, sprinklers were set up at our building site, and helicopters were used to keep close check on the fire's progress. The fire was stopped and things went well. Similarly, in 2004, a year of many wildfires in the Chilcotin, sprinklers were set up at remote tourism lodges, again in the face of unstoppable fires, and buildings and infrastructure were saved. But this year, 2010, we were told that these types of actions were no longer available, that the government no longer had the resources to protect remote homes like ours. No remedies other than evacuation were available. It was sobering. We could no longer turn to government for help. We were on our own.

We never did leave. Once again, we dodged the bullet. But with increasing fire activity, decreasing government resources and plain luck, we knew there would be another moment of decision. Rosemary carefully filed away our lists of "must take" items and "take if room" items, hoping they would never again be called upon.

Fire is part of life in the Precipice, part of the eternal connection between the bowels of the sun and the fire that warms us at the cave mouth. The lesson of fire is clear: We try to cope, but we can never control or dominate. We can simply lighten our load, be quick on our feet, and hope for the best.

Sacrament of the Hearth

While I often pondered the issues of wilderness, the human mind, and the interactions between them on an abstract level, there were many times I engaged in a more practical analysis of the situation. One morning, I stopped while tending my solar panels and scanned the frozen white vastness around me. What was life like here before chainsaws? Before snowmachines? Before satellite communications? Before propane and gasoline? One hundred years ago, none of these things existed here, yet there were people living up on the plateau in the West Chilcotin. Their technology was horses, small cabins, snowshoes for winter travel and cutting firewood with axe and crosscut saw. They ate potatoes and maybe some carrots, beans, flour, cured meats, dried fruits and berries, along with whatever they could shoot, trap or snare, and occasionally if lucky, flavoured with salt, pepper, and sugar.

And further back? To pre-European days? Life must have been even more spare. There were no rifles, just bow and arrow, spears, deadfall traps, or pits dug along the trails. Using the ancient Grease Trails to the coast, people here traded furs for coastal Oolichan fish oil used for lights and cooking and for fish to supplement a predominately meat diet. Dried fruits, berries and roots made up the rest of the fare. Instead of small cabins built by trappers, which were small (often 2.5x3 metres with maybe 1.8 metre headroom in the middle, housing one or two people), winter dwellings for the first peoples in this inhospitable land consisted of the more spacious Quigli Hut, half-buried in the ground and covered over with poles and dirt, with moss lining the inside for insulation, and crammed with whole families.

Like the trapper's cabin, these constructions were smoky, either too hot or too cold, and provided the minimum shelter for survival. Imagine a -30 December day, with two metres of snow on the ground, and you're out there gathering branches and small logs to keep a fire going. Skinning, cleaning and cooking meat over such a fire couldn't have been an easy task. The old trapper's cabins had a fireplace in the middle, with a smoke hole in the roof like the Quigli Hut. We've spent a few days during the winter in one of these old cabins, far in the bush, but even though I had a chainsaw for the firewood it was not a fun trip. We breathed smoke and spent the night tending the fire and fighting away furry creatures that were also seeking the warmth during the night. So, when I hear of nostalgia for the "good old days," for the movement to go back to the life our ancestors had, white or native, when I hear these sentiments, well, I truly wonder: If the speakers ever had to experience the physical reality for a few winters, would they still feel the same? I very much doubt it.

But then, all the luxury we experienced in the Precipice Valley was floating on a sea of oil, which will either shrink considerably or dry up. Either way, it will force change. The change will not, however, include going back to yesteryear. Those skills are mostly lost. They can, perhaps, be reclaimed, but the insurmountable hurdle remains, and it is psychological: Can anyone truly envision going back to the era before oil, or more drastically, to the stone age? So there is the question. What will life be like in the bush after oil?

For the moment, though, we had wood. There is a saying that heating with wood "warms you twice—once when you get it and once when you burn it." The first time, you get warmed by handling the wood. On those cool autumn days when you make a foray into the bush, fall, yard (haul to the truck), buck (cut into pieces) and load onto the truck a couple of cords of firewood, you break a sweat for sure. The second, more rewarding time comes when you are sitting in front of the heater on a snappy cold winter day, basking in the orange red glow of a hot fire. Practicality aside, wood also offers mystery, a spiritual dimension in which one experiences a much different warmth hidden in the secrets of fire and creation.

Each morning slowly, carefully, I would pull each night's ashes to the front of the firebox. I could feel the grainy ash on the bottom layer, the remains of once-strong trees that lined the ridge where they had grown. For nearly 150 years, those trees survived the gusts of November storms, the fires of blazing August, the twists and turns of sun, moon and cloud, until they finally succumbed to pine beetles. In requiem, I felled these seedlings of the early 19th century, now beetle-killed and dead, bucked them into short logs and hauled them to my woodshed, where they waited patiently, row on row, their newly exposed growth rings telling a 150-year-long story of drought, cold, wet summers, insect attacks, and the triumph of survival in this harsh climate. In their final winter, these snippets of a heroic tale became the next offering in the cycle of ashes to ashes and dust to dust, so it was with attention and humility that I raked the morning embers to the front of the firebox.

Perhaps wood will be our last technological fuel, just as it was the first. After all, our wood heater in the Precipice was a modern marvel, constructed of steel, cast iron, fire brick and draft controls, each part of a well-thought-out design. The glass in the door was a product of the space age. Over 370 C on one surface and a mere -3 on the other, the material did not shatter, crack or buckle. I once saw a demonstration in which a piece of this glass was heated red hot by a welding torch on one corner, then that corner was plunged into ice cold water. Nothing happened but a bit of steam. The glass was unharmed, a true wonder of our age. This was the stuff in my cast iron heater door that allowed the magic of oxygen mating with molecules of carbon to be seen close up. This was the core of life. This energy release, whether from the bowels of stars or the corpses of pine trees, made the reality we lived in possible. And, most miraculous of all, I could sit in the comfort of a cushioned easy chair, sipping a warming drink, absorbed in a galactic display of warmth, experiencing a moment simultaneously unique and ubiquitous, thanks to some very new technology put to work for very old ends.

Eventually, this necessity evolved into sacrament. The smooth flow of the granules into the opening leading to the lower chamber as I cleaned the fire box in the morning had a feel like coarse sand flowing down a steep-sided desert dune. Then the red sparks in the grey ash started to blink on, little stars gaining life as the new wave of oxygen blew across their tiny faces. Faint whiffs of smoke filled my nostrils, evoking memories of youthful hand-holding around campfires, faces full of hope and expectancy, bathed in the yellow glow of crackling flames.

It was odd, in a way, that the very oxygen we needed to live and breathe was the same oxygen needed by these little chunks of charcoal to heat up and ignite a new fire to heat us and our home.

The details were important. Old fir burned differently than middle-aged pine or young spruce. Each had its place. Fir burned hot. In fact, so hot that it would be possible to use fir bark in a forge to shape horseshoes. It didn't work well as heater wood, though, especially in cold weather. Fir needs a constant flow of fast-moving air, and even then it leaves big coals that eventually clog the firebox.

Spruce and especially cedar, on the other hand, are flashy showgirls, burning fast and furiously, sparking and tap dancing in the firebox, releasing all their heat in one go. They are good for quick morning heat—they get things goin' —but they burn themselves out quickly.

Lodgepole pine is the best. It is full of pitch, so it burns hot. The old trees, the 150- to 200-hundred-year-old ancients, have tight, hard growth rings. Dry, they burn slowly, evenly, almost like coal. These are the logs for knife-edged cold winter nights.

These thoughts moved around in my head as I stirred the coals to nurture the little suns with fresh wood—first with the brash spruce, then, once fully started, splits of the old pine. Soon the transmutation of sunlight to living being to static wood back to light and heat was complete.

That morning ceremony of tending the hearth consisted of emotions and movements that recognized the spiritual nature of fire, by reaffirming the infinity of creation borne in the cycle of time and energy. Living in concrete boxes heated by unseen forces controlled by thermostats and driving around in steel cages warmed by gas engines, on the other hand, is a sure way to lose touch with this ancient reality. We will someday need it again.

The Silent Butler

We loved living in the bush, but we liked our comforts, too. We eventually had a hot tub that I built in the tiny guest bathroom, an en suite bathroom, a fully equipped kitchen—complete with microwave and dishwasher—and a lot of old oak furniture. One of my favourites was the oak buffet in the front hall. Our "Silent Butler" always had a story to tell, no matter what the season. We all have some variation of it, we country dwellers: the table, chest, or shelves that stand just inside the entrance door, the humble servants that receive your hats and gloves, your bits and pieces, and patiently store them until you need them again. Part of the transition to get from the outside to the inside, these clever components of household functionality are many in design, myriad in shape, individual in appearance, yet universal in function. Ours was a buffet style and did as much or more than any Victorian butler could. It held our essentials until we needed them again, and it did so without complaint, without requiring anything more than perhaps some oiling every decade or so and the shelter of the hallway where it was located.

Built in a different age, when craftsmen used their hands to create useful sculptures, our hallway butler performed its tasks without needing to be paid for or fawned over. It even moved with us when we left the Precipice. How could we leave such a servant behind?

Our butler measures 130 centimetres wide and 60 centimetres deep, has two narrow drawers across the top that act as eyebrows, a chest-wide drawer, and two doors beneath. Unfortunately, we do not know its history, beyond the fact that there are pages from an old newspaper dated March 1923 used to cushion the mirror in its frame. So, for more than 85 years, this time capsule from a different age has been performing its tasks silently, without complaint. That aside, much can be said of that solid sentinel that guarded the entrance to Firhome.

Take the drawers. They contained seasons of mystery, from hand warmers to bear bangers for scaring the bears away without hurting them. Then there were the compartments below, which held ripening tomatoes in the fall, squashes in the winter, and miscellany — such as wood-burning kits, odd pieces of leather, a softball, and tennis balls for the dog to chase in the spring. It told the story of those whom it served, which meant that it also sported a propane torch, an 8 mm wrench, a medium-sized slot screwdriver and a pair of water pump pliers (water pump pliers? Google it): mute evidence of the time in January 2012 when, out of the blue, the water line froze up. I won't dissect that story here; suffice to say that it was a big problem.

I had planned to put the tools back into the workshop the next day, but, well, the next day arrived and my attention was captured by a cougar that had arrived on the scene. Late the previous night, when going out to the shop to get some supplies from the storage area, it was sprawled on the nice dry platform outside, and, while not actually attacking, was so unafraid that it had to be scared off, its yellow eyes glowing and long tail switching.

That is why there was a 12-gauge shotgun above the chest, with #3 aught buckshot shells in the ammo case, beside the water pump pliers and the torch. These items sat beside the usual tumult of gloves, goggles, toques, dog leashes, collars and earplugs. That particular night I went back to the house and fetched Rosemary to hold a flashlight and ventured forth again with the shotgun. I had no intention of shooting the beautiful creature, which looked like a giant sealpoint Siamese cat, but cougars are quite unpredictable, so discretion was the keyword. As it turned out, it was gone when we returned to its comfortable and sheltered bed.

Of course, our butler also held a multimeter to diagnose problems, such as the dead battery in the snowmachine the morning before or the state of charge in the solar batteries, to see if the factory meter was really telling the truth about how little sun we had had and how much power we were using.

The meter sat atop the shop manual for the snowmachine. I'd had to replace the clutch assembly on the Skidoo a few days before because of, well, a long story of torque, snow conditions and slope. Too much RPM wears out a motor; not enough and you can't go anywhere. A balance has to be struck between elevation and condition. The manual is a guide, but there is a lot of art in the application. So the torque wrench that held the manual in place on the sideboard had a lot to say about creep, power curves and other not-so-fascinating issues.

And so it went. Stories that sturdy silent friend could tell as it waits patiently beside our entrance door, uncomplainingly receiving the tools of our everyday lives, a silent midden in real time.

Sharing with Bears

The meadow below our living room at Firhome was a favourite spring hangout for both black and grizzly bears. When they first come out of hibernation, these animals eat only vegetation for a few weeks until their digestive systems start working again. Precipice Valley was at a lower elevation than the hibernation dens at the base of the rimrock, so our meadows were the first place that had fresh green grass. It was always a thrill to see a huge grizzly sow lying down among the dandelions, using her large claws to pick out the perfect blade of grass, nodding her head the same way cows do as she munched away. Every spring we were treated to this show. It is a true privilege to see a sow with two or three tiny cubs slowly moving across the meadow as they dined on the fresh shoots, mamma standing on her hind legs every once in a while to sniff the wind and check for danger.

A friend who visited one spring and wandered around our little valley counting bears logged 18 different grizzlies and 16 blacks! Most of them left by summer, moving down into the Bella Coola Valley for fish and berries in the Atnarko River, but we still had to be careful when moving about in the valley well into mid-summer, making sure never to get between a sow and her cubs. A few always stayed for a few months before moving to the alpine for fresh greens and marmots until mid-August. We never had a problem when we had a dog with us. Although even Chilko was much smaller than a bear, the bears were nervous and kept their distance.

We found out what a difference a dog makes during the year after Hobo died and before we got Chilko. One day, Rosemary was by herself and walking home towards Firhome along the flat section from the Glad Cab when she spotted a grizzly sow and two yearling cubs on the other side of the rail fence. The sow decided that Rosemary was too close to her kids and charged.

The fence wouldn't have stopped the bear or even slowed her down, but when her cubs followed, she turned back to send them further away. With no defence, Rosemary just kept walking, heart pounding, avoiding looking directly at the bear. The sow bluff-charged twice more. It was with huge relief that Rosemary finally reached the end of the straight driveway between the meadows and turned uphill to continue to Firhome. I suspect that the sow was relieved, too.

Black bear in cottonwood by driveway

One sow came every spring for several years, sometimes with one or two cubs and one memorable year, with four. We called her Ginger, because of her reddish-brown coat. We were speaking about bears one year with Chris Czajkowski, an eco-tourism/writer friend who lived on Whitton Lake, 80 kilometres deeper into the mountains. When we described Ginger bear and her distinctive marking, she said "Oh, that's *my* Ginger bear." There was some very rough country between us, so that bear really did get around!

We usually did not fear the bears, although we were very careful to keep an eye out and give them plenty of room. On occasion, something would alarm a sow and she would send her cub or cubs up a tree, usually a big cottonwood. They looked deceptively cuddly, sitting there in the crotch or on a big branch. Our driveway up to the house had a corner that was about 40 feet up the slope from the valley bottom, so that the middle of the big cottonwoods were at eye level. It was very special and a bit scary to see one of these bears sitting 20 metres away and looking directly at you.

Bears are very territorial. You rarely saw more than one bear in the meadow at a time, and the grizzlies were boss. If you were watching a black bear grazing and it suddenly took off, you knew a grizzly was around. Sure enough, a few minutes later the griz would appear. If it was a sow, she would vacate when a grizzly boar arrived. There was a definite pecking order. But that particular meadow had a few dips and rises, and looking down from our living room we were fascinated one spring to see a black bear grazing peacefully in a hollow, unaware of its enemy the grizzly just a hundred metres away. We watched for a long time, but they never did see or smell each other.

Black bears do the same as the grizzlies, kneeling down on their forearms to graze, but although not as large, they are more dangerous. The big males especially will actually stalk humans. On one occasion, as I walked over to the workshop, I saw one of these big boars entering the roofed area in front of it. When I shouted and waved my arms, the bear turned and started up the slope behind the shop. Then he did a remarkable thing. He sat down on the slope, just as you or I would do, for two or three minutes, legs splayed and big stomach sticking out, looking as if he was contemplating his navel. Then he made up his mind, walked along the slope parallel to the shop and started to come down behind it. He was flanking me. It made me pretty nervous. I grabbed a can of bear spray I had handy on the workshop bench, and when the bear started to come around the corner of the building I rushed at him and caught him in the face with the spray. The bear woofed and ran up slope as fast as he could. You never can trust a black bear.

A Herd of Grizzlies

Other points of interface are less dangerous but require no less adaptation and no less laying down of memories that will sustain us in times to come. This particular adventure took place along the Atnarko River, not far from Stuie in the Bella Coola Valley.

Grizzly leading cubs on Hwy 20

THE POWER OF DREAMS

"There's one," Stefan said, pointing to the base of a cedar tree.

"Yeah, and it's wet too!" I said. What Stefan had been pointing at was a "rub" tree, one which grizzly bears use to mark their territories. The bark was smooth, sloughed away by the bear's back as it marked this corner post, a ritual these bears observe on a regular basis. Judging by the wetness on the base of the tree, it had been performed by a bear who had just come out of the water.

We were exploring an old homestead on a misty Saturday morning in September. Our friend Stefan, a bear biologist, was always interested in bear behaviour, so he went back to the truck to get his camera, leaving Rosemary, Stefan's wife Eva, a fish biologist, and me nervously scanning the nearby terrain. And, sure enough, while Stefan was gone, a large, brown shape climbed over the lip of the river bank and headed straight toward us.

The bear was a young adult male. He looked like he was used to people and was coming to check things out. Not willing to take any chances, we backed away slowly, keeping our pace steady and continuing to watch him without making eye contact.

At that point, Stefan returned. The young boar stopped, looked all four of us over and veered off up slope into the cedar forest. He was in prime condition and we could see the spiky brown fur rolling over his muscles as he sauntered into the trees. He was typical of young males, who often have unusual colouring; his panda face was mottled with orange and gray. There are many variations of colour on grizzlies, even some with orange and white patches on their necks and torsos. By the time they are three, this colouring disappears and they usually take on the uniform dark orange-brown. Grizzlies are long- lived, averaging about 20 to 25 years, with females usually outliving males. Old males (called boars) will turn to a silvery colour on their necks and shoulders. Then they are known as "silverbacks."

We continued to back away slowly, keeping an eye on the route the bear had taken. He circled around and eventually headed away from us, downstream. His choice may have been based on our increased numbers.

Stefan told us that bears can count and that they usually don't approach groups of four or more people.

But little did we know the best was yet to come. After spending the night in Stuie, at the east end of the Bella Coola Valley, we headed home back east along Highway 20, which parallels the Bella Coola River as it flows through Tweedsmuir Park. Salmon fishing was in full swing that weekend, so traffic on the usually deserted highway was busy, with fishermen going to and fro. We were cruising along, in no hurry, when we crested a small hill. Rosemary saw some movement at the side of the road on the uphill side, so I slowed down and pulled over. We made out the shape of a grizzly on the left side up a low bank, standing behind a big old furrowed fir tree, steadily watching us. It was difficult to see, as the dark brown coat blended well with the fire scars on the fir bark and the forest shadows surrounding it.

To give the bear some room and to see what it would do, I backed down the road, leaving lots of space between the bear and our Yukon.

Then another bear, slightly smaller than the first, appeared. So we figured we were seeing a sow with a yearling cub, probably trying to cross the road so they could get to the river and the waiting meal of spawning salmon.

Then we saw another bear. Then another. Three young grizzly bears, all with the same near-black colours, all nearly as big as mom. These bears would have been born the previous winter, so they were probably 15 months old, quite a pawful for a female grizzly to handle. Especially when trying to cross the highway.

We could tell that momma was definitely upset. She was snuffling, pawing the ground, pacing back and forth and arching her neck, trying to see up and down the roadway, and trying to pick a safe time to cross. The cubs took turns standing up on their hind legs, obviously just as impatient. Each time the sow started to come down the gravel cut bank to cross the road, another vehicle would roar into view, chasing her and her cubs back into the forest. All the time, they were getting more and more jittery.

Finally, we saw her make up her mind. After one particularly scary vehicle, with a large Thule roof rack on top that whistled and must have looked really weird to her, disappeared down the road, she lunged down the bank to the road, the cubs running behind her.

I've never seen such a sight. Sixteen grizzly paws kicking up dust, gravel rolling noisily downslope, all hitting the highway helter-skelter. It was like a herd of horses, except this was a herd of grizzly bears. Strung out in single file, the silhouette they made as they were skylined on the hump of the black pavement, framed by the white sidelines, was a scene we'll never forget.

Momma and her three grown children trotted along the pavement for a few metres, then turned off onto the shoulder towards the river, where they melted into the forest, leaving no trace. Driving ahead to see where they had gone, we discovered a well-worn trail, probably used by generations of grizzlies to move across this valley from the upper slopes to fishing spots in the river.

We drove off, lost in the wonder of the experience but also thinking of those fly fishermen we had seen standing on the gravel bars, the forest at their backs. If they knew what was headed their way . . .

Grizzly Encounter

The last thing on my mind was a grizzly bear. After a long, hot day I was walking back to camp, a thick cloud of black flies hovering above my orange hard hat, my khaki B.C. Parks shirt damp with sweat and a red chainsaw heavy on my shoulder. My mind was focused on the cool waters of Octopus lake where I could take a refreshing dip on a cool sandy beach before tending to the horses.

As park rangers working for the B.C government, my partner and I were charged with finding and brushing out the ancient trade routes which led from the Chilcotin plateau to the Bella Coola valley. In use for thousands of years before European settlement, these trails were major trade routes linking the first nations of the B.C interior and the coastal peoples of the Bella Coola valley and beyond. In fact, obsidian tools shaped from deposits found in the west Chilcotin have been found as far south as California and as far north as Alaska; proof of just how far these trading routes extended.

California also was the last thing on my mind as I approached the trail junction a couple of miles from camp, where I saw the sign post tilted at a crazy angle, nearly flat on the grass. "Well, he's done it again ", I thought as I approached the supine 4 x 4 post, the trail sign split in half and twisted sideways, pointing aimlessley at the sky.

When we began the summer's work, one of the first things Jim and I did was to erect a signpost which would guide hikers to the lake beyond, a mile or so to the west of the main trail which led across the flats and eventually dropped down several thousand feet to the Bella Coola valley. Known as the Burnt Bridge trail, this route was followed by Alexander McKenzie on his historic trek of 1793 when he reached tidewater at Bella Coola. He was the first European to cross America north of Mexico, making a continental traverse fully eleven years sooner and a thousand miles longer than the Lewis and Clark expidition of 1804-5.

It was exhilarating to stand on that spot, letting the imagination fill in the details of what McKenzie's party looked like, how they were dressed, what equipment they carried, the First Nations guides sure footed and quite knowledgeable, leading the way down familiar trails that were used for millenia for trade and occasional raiding for coastal plunder.

No fur traders today, no Indian guides, just a signpost pushed over pointing aimlessly to the ground. The evidence was clear: tooth punctures, red blond hair, claw scratches; the post had been knocked over again by a big old grizzly as he ambled along this convenient travel, surveying his domain. We never did figure out whether he used the sign as a scratching post, or whether he took offence at its upright position. Maybe it looked like a challenger to his domain.

This was the third time in as many weeks that the post had been shoved over. Definitely not a random occurence, this attack on the sign was deliberate and done with energy and thoroughly. I did not stop to fix the problem then but I made a mental note that we needed to come back later and try again. Maybe the old griz would take the hint, but I doubted it.

The June days were long, 16 hours of daylight ensuring time for trail work farther from camp each day. We often used a packhorse for the fuel and the saws, but it was tricky business. The mixed gas had a way of leaking from the spouts of the small containers, the saws were not at all balanced, and even though we tried to secure the plastic blade guards, they always seemed to slip, exposing sharp saw teeth and spitting chain oil onto the pack saddle rigging. Horse blankets, pads, tarps, ropes and a sawbuck saddle were the tools used to secure the loads, using a rope arrangement know as a "Diamond". In the end, after a long day of brushing trail, it was just as easy to throw the empty saw over your shoulder and head for camp. The horses agreed.

So here I was, lost in reverie, when I came around a sharp bend in the trail and there he was--a full blown silvertip easily over three feet tall at the shoulder, sauntering along, head down, walking straight towards me. I immediately stopped, put my head down, avoided eye contact. Taking a deep breath, I stood very still. The bear also stopped, sniffed and snorted, almost like a sneeze.

He had a slight musky smell, not unpleasant, more like a combination of wet dog and horse with an overiding scent of grass. Sounds strange, I know, but that is what he smelled like, almost like fresh hay. But then, at this time of year, that is what their diet consists of, grasses mostly along with some fruits and berries. The bears migrate down the the valley bottoms in late August where they feed on salmon, but until then they are primarily herbivores. From our home in the Precipice we watched those early bears, and there is no sight like a full grown grizzlly, slouched down on his forepaws, nibbling on fresh grass daintely picking out the tender shoots, a fine early summer salad. Such a huge animal and such delicate eating habits.

Well, now what? I dare not turn around, that would invite chase for inquisitiveness if nothing else. Running would be even worse, that would be an invitation to follow, possibly attack and maul. A full grown grizzly can outrun a good saddle horse for the first 50 yards, so there was no way I was going to make a run for it. I could not step back to far or too quickly as I might fall over backwards, and that would for sure be a bad thing. So with my eyes cast down, my head sloped off to one side, I carefully backed up a couple of inches. I tried to exude calm, diffucult to do with my heart racing and the hairs on the back of my neck standing up.

Then the bear did the most amazing thing. He stood up on his hind legs, walked off the trail a few feet to a large flat boulder. And sat down. Just like you or I would sit on a park bench. He sat with his arms on his thighs, started chewing his cud and snorted. He looked for all the world like a gentle grandpa sitting in his favourite rocking chair. All he needed was a pipe. As he looked away I took my cue and slowly sidled sideways until I was around the corner, then I slowly and very carefully retreated up the trail, sneaking looks back over my shoulder as I picked my way back along the way I had come.

Jim had been finishing up a bit of brush cutting, using the last of his gas, so he was a few minutes behind me. "What's up?" my partner said as he came into view. "Just a griz up ahead," I said, "let's give him a few minutes to clear out." So we had a little chat and then not wanting to startle him, noisily walked back down the trail and around the corner. The bear was no longer is sight, nowhere to be seen. I guess he was looking for a way out the same as I was; bears are not naturally aggressive unless threatened. This bear was just like me: out for a stroll and not looking for trouble.

We kept a sharp eye out all the way back to camp, but we had no issues and saw no bears.

THE POWER OF DREAMS

The next day I went back and dug a new hole, erected the sign and marveled at the experiences I was privilege to on my job here. And sure enough, a few days later, when I passd this way again, the signpost was down, the sign split and the turf torn by scratches. "That's it!" I thought. Bowing to the inevitable, I simply made a small rock cairn put the sign on top of it and called it a draw. That bear left the pile of rocks alone and we could still read the sign--a win win for all.

Horsing Around

Not all our neighbours and friends were human. It is one of the facts of the wilderness. You rely on species other than your own, and they learn to work with you in return. It is part of the interface.

For most of our time in the Precipice we had horses and fed them, along with Lee's herd, in the winter. In the first two years, we used a pitchfork to feed loose hay from a stack: 14 horses once a day. It could have been the Middle Ages. Rosemary tells of the time in early winter when I was away and she was feeding:

There were strong winds that day, and with Dave away I had a struggle to climb to the top of the high haystack carrying a pitchfork, very aware of the horses waiting eagerly below. Annie, the herd boss, trotted back and forth, shouldering the others away so she would have first dibs at the hay. At the top I braced myself against the wind and tossed the first forkful of hay down to them—but the wind was so strong the hay blew right back up! This happened again and again. I didn't know whether to get frustrated or laugh hysterically at the shocked horses as their dinner was snatched from them. As romantic as it was to feed from an old-time stack, I wasn't entirely sorry when Lee switched to square bales.

Once we learned to ride and pack horses, we took many pack trips into the mountains. I was fortunate that when I worked as a backcountry ranger for B.C. Parks in the early '90s, I patrolled the Rainbow Mountains on horseback for several years. It was the experience of a lifetime.

Class is in session

But before that, when we were still in Alexis Creek, we had met a cowboy who managed Spain Lake Ranch, about a 45-minute drive north of the town. He was an excellent rider and knew everything there was to know about horses. In preparation for moving west, I arranged for him to find a saddle horse for Rosemary: a surprise for her birthday. He brought a young horse up from the Fraser Valley. It was a beautiful blood bay stud colt coming on two years old, tall and confident, with a crooked white blaze running down his face.

He and Rosemary were instant friends. "What is his name?" Rosemary asked.

Simple question, but we didn't get a direct answer; we got a story. It seems that when a new foal is weaned and taken out into the world, it is a custom (so we were told) to ask the first person who sees the animal to give it a name. In this case, it happened to be a young boy. When asked the question, "What will we call this horse?" his reply was "Who knows?" So, that became his name: Who Knows. Every time someone asked his name, we were reminded of Abott and Costello and their "Who's on first?" comedy routine.

THE POWER OF DREAMS

Who Knows

He was a big horse, a Morgan-Quarter horse-Arabian blend 17 and a half hands tall, with an even temperament, but untrained. Later that spring he was gelded, and when we moved we took him into Precipice, where he mingled with Lee's bunch. Rosemary loved to ride him—his height made him a very smooth ride—and I took him into the mountains when I was rangering.

We purchased our second horse in the summer of our first year in the Precipice: a six-year-old gelding called Cayuse. I learned a hard lesson about the care of horses that fall. We had gone to Williams Lake on our semi-annual shopping trip in late October. As we were tight for time and we were worried about having an early snowfall. I didn't pull Cayuse's shoes. I just turned him loose in the meadow.

When we got back, we were shocked to see Cayuse standing on three legs, not moving. When I went over to him, he tried a step but could only hop. I will never forget looking down to his right foreleg. It was swinging free in circles, a chilling sight: broken at the knee, and only held on by the skin and sinews. While we were away, there had been a heavy frost and some of the ground had frozen. He must have broken the leg when he slipped on the slick ground, all because I had thought I was too busy to pull his shoes, and ignorant as to what could happen.

I had to shoot him right then and there, 30-06 between the eyes. I am still overwhelmed with sadness when I think about it. I used the truck and dragged him upriver to the upper meadow. In a few weeks, all that was left was the skeleton. Nature doesn't waste anything.

That next spring we went together with Lee and purchased a small dappled roan called Takia, a sturdy, unflappable creature you could ride or pack. He was a bumpy ride, but you could trust him.

Then came an even smaller black and white pinto. Rosemary promptly named him Harlequin, which was quickly shortened to Quin. He arrived in the valley wearing a large chain for a halter, was scarred around the throat from some baling wire used to hold the halter on, and it was obvious he had been abused. He would not let me near him for several weeks, and he never did like men. He simply showed up in our meadow one morning, joined the herd and became one of ours. In spite of his small size, he could jump any size fence and could have left any time. But why would a horse want to leave Precipice, with its early green grass? We advertised in the Anahim and Nimpo stores but had no response.

Despite the abuse he had suffered, though, Quin was gentle and a wonderful pack horse, completely unflappable. We had him for years, but one spring when we turned him out into the big meadow on new grass he foundered. Rosemary tried to nurse him through, confining him to an open barn and walking him in the irrigation ditch several times a day to cool his painful feet. But the second year this happened, he was in such misery that in the end, after discussing the issue with a Williams Lake vet, I had to put him down as well. Another tough and painful decision, but a part of living so far from any services.

Stealing a Ride

Jim Glenn was a veteran horseman. He and his family had lived at the west end of the valley for many years but had moved out to Little Goose Lake, near Anahim, the year before we arrived. During our first winter, his horses were still in the valley and we fed for him.

The year we moved into Precipice, Jim took a job with B.C. Parks, working the high country in Tweedsmuir Park on horseback as a backcountry ranger. He must have figured that because we had horses and all the riggin' I knew horses, so early that following spring he suggested I sign on with Parks so that he could take me as his partner into the mountains for a summer job patrolling Tweedsmuir Park on horseback, locating and clearing old trails, establishing new routes, aiding hikers if needed and generally giving B.C. Parks a presence in the backcountry.

At nearly a million hectares, Tweedsmuir Park is the largest provincial park in B.C. Designated as a park in 1938, this vast wilderness area is divided by Highway 20 into Tweedsmuir North and Tweedsmuir South; two very different landscapes. The area north of Heckman Pass contains the volcanic Rainbow Mountains, while the south part contains some of the highest mountains in B.C., a rugged area accessible only on foot or by floatplane. The 600-metre-deep Atnarko trench, a world-scale rift valley, runs for a hundred miles through the region, connecting the Bella Coola valley with the Kleena Kleene valley. At the higher elevations, glaciers sit in solitude among high peaks, the last bastions of the former ice age.

Ranger Dave on Who Knows

North of Highway 20, it is horse country. The Rainbow Mountain range is the eroded remnant of an extinct volcano that last erupted 12 million years ago, forming a huge cone over 80 miles in circumference. The area is now primarily long, sloping ridges and flat plains radiating from the centre of the old eruption. The dramatic colours on the slopes are the main attraction, but because the terrain points in all directions it is easy to get lost. It's imperative to follow the hiking routes. Old trading trails also cross the centre of the Rainbows, as well as the range's western edges.

Riding in the high country and getting paid for it was a gift from heaven. What I failed to recognize and understand was the degree of horsemanship required for such backcountry riding. Starting my first tour, we needed to get the horses moved from their winter range to the trailhead in Heckman Pass, along Highway 20. That first morning, Jim took off at a trot and so did I, gripping the saddle horn for all I was worth. I then began to think I had made a mistake: this was no trail ride! Eventually things settled down, and we rode up the trail to the top of the Precipice, across the plateau and to the corral where the horses were already gathered.

It took us two days of slow, roadside riding to move the horses from Anahim Lake to Heckman Pass. Then we took a serious look at all the saddles, pack saddles, ropes, tarps, cinches, halters, reins, all the gear we would need for a 10-day trip. Jim began to teach me the art of building a load for the pack horses to carry from camp to camp. These were big, strong horses, weighing around 360 to 450 kg, and although still a little out of shape after the winter, seasoned backcountry animals who knew the routines.

While you could ride some of the pack horses, it was generally true that pack horses were pack horses and saddle horses were saddle horses. Tying on the load for a pack horse is a true skill that takes a long time to learn. First, you groom the back and sides of the horse with a stiff bristle brush, removing sand, needles, burrs, whatever the animal had rolled in or walked through the previous night. Next, you drape a saddle blanket over the horse, a little forward on the back, closer to the shoulders than the tail. On top of this, you set the pack saddle or sawbuck, which looked like a miniature sawhorse for bucking firewood. Then you tightened the cinches. This was only the initial cinch. The horses would often suck in air to expand their girth, trying to fool the packer into thinking the cinch was tight. You soon got wise to it, though. Finally, ropes were laid across the saddle, ready to receive the pack boxes. This was the trickiest part. The boxes had to be as equal in weight as possible. Some packers used scales; others (like Jim) placed them side by side, hefting first one then the other, move a few articles from one to the other until the load felt balanced. Forty pounds for each box was the usual.

Balancing the boxes was a critical step for ensuring that the load rode evenly on the horse's back. Just a few pounds either way, and with each step the horse took the load would exert more pressure on one side than the other, eventually causing the load to roll over the slide and under the horse's belly. When that happened, all hell would break loose, or as they say, there would be a "rodeo" as the horse frantically tried to escape the packs.

Once tied to the sawbuck with a series of loops and careful slip knots, a top pack of lighter essentials such as sleeping bags and clothing would be laid in the center between the upper arms of the saddle. This in turn was lashed down and a large tarp was put over the whole load, which was then tied with a series of special knots pulled tightly to secure the whole assemblage. Because the shape of the crossing ropes in the centre of the load formed a diamond, the whole process was called "throwing the diamond."

It took me the whole first summer to learn how to load a horse the correct way. A good packer could do it in half the time and still have the load stay centred for a day's ride of about 30 kilometres. Sadly, the men and women who possess these skills are a vanishing breed.

Dave and packed horse

Saddling the riding horses was simpler, but it, too, demanded a special skill set. We would alternate riding days for these horses to keep them fresh. Those movies of galloping across the desert all day are good for the screen, but in the real world we usually rode at a leisurely walk, making the whole process easier on both the rider and the horse. When you are on a 10-day-long ride in the wilderness, keeping your horse in good condition is the most important thing there is.

We filled the pack boxes with food and basic cooking gear and set off at a slow walk. This degree of slowness wasn't necessarily our decision. It is a universal trait with horses that when they are heading out on the trail they tend to go slowly, having to be nudged along to keep on the move.

The first day, we made it to a base camp in a swamp meadow called Octopus Lake (from the air it looks like an octopus with its arms spread). Because this was mid-June, the camp was very wet and the feed was still poor. On the other end of the scale, the mosquitos were in full bloom, but with enough industrial strength DEET we coped. We also put dope on the horses, a tricky business at times, especially when it had to be applied to their undersides. They had a habit of kicking swiftly inward (wouldn't you?).

Our task in the alpine was to find and cut out the old trails where needed and to follow them as they moved across the land. Once I got a feel for it, I could ride into a swale, look across it and determine where a trail would go. It was always a thrill to cut out a bunch of small trees and find the old trail bed still there.

There were two types of trails; the older ones that had been made by human feet, and those made by horses. Human pack trails walked differently, took the grades at a different angle, and were more meandering, less direct. Horse trails were wider, more deeply incised, and tended to be more aggressive on the slopes.

According to local lore, the horse replaced human packers in the 1860s. There were times, following a horse trail, when you could see where it crossed an older, deeper trail that had been walked for centuries before pack horses arrived. On that first tour we brushed out and built rock cairns along the route from Octopus Lake to MacKenzie Pass, where Alexander Mackenzie passed through on his epic journey to Bella Coola in 1793.

Another old route called the Capoose Summer Trail was a spectacular ramble across open alpine and open meadows. The rugged Coast Mountains looked so close, I felt I could reach out and touch them. Practically speaking, each day's ride was a little longer than the one before, as we rode further from camp, identifying the trail.

When after a few days the feed for the horses was still not very good, we had a helicopter drop off a few bags of oats: a coffee can full for each horse in the morning, and, for the last four days of the tour, another one at night. This regimen gave the horses more energy, but it also made them a little "hotter" to ride.

There is an old cowboy saying that a person who does not know how to ride a horse, yet gets a good horse to ride that does what it is supposed to on its own, is "stealing a ride." I received a lesson on the meaning of this homily on going-home day, when we rose early, ready to go back to Heckman Pass and civilization.

Horses have an absolute sense of where they are on the trail. They know instantly when you head out what direction they are going. On this morning, when we turned east on the back trail, instead of heading west as we had been doing, they started to get really full of energy. On top of that, the four days of double oats rations gave them more jump.

I was riding Who Knows, and he took off down the home trail at a full gallop. Scared, I pulled hard on the reins.

"Rein him in!" Jim shouted. "Rein him in!"

"I can't!" I shouted back, holding up two broken reins. My horse had simply tossed his head and broken them.

Jim managed to get in front of us and turned my horse into a clump of whitebark pine, where we were able to cool him out. I made a new set of reins from 3/8-inch poly rope and hoped that would be strong enough to hold even him.

The next time he tried the home-run trick, I knew what to do: I turned him in a circle, keeping him in control all the while. I was no longer "stealing a ride."

One of our horses was called Salsa. She sported a short-haired, reddish-brown coat with a black mane and tail. Her ebony eyes glittered with energy. My friend and partner Jim liked his horses to have a little "life," as he put it, and Salsa certainly provided a lively ride.

The morning she got into serious trouble was one of ethereal beauty. We were camped beside Octopus Lake, which was large enough for a float plane to land and take off from. A rising sun had stained the fluffy clouds, turning them into pink candy floss strewn across deep blue heavens. Jim and I had gotten the morning fire going, and Jim went to check on the horses while I got breakfast started.

When Jim came back, he muttered something about horses that left camp not being worth keeping. He figured the time and trouble it takes to round them up cuts too much out of a day's ride.

That day, they were all accounted for except Salsa, who had slipped her drag log, a heavy log each horse was tied to which allowed them to graze but not leave camp. We were only mildly concerned, though, since she rarely wandered far from the other horses. Our camp was beside a small stream, right where it emptied out of a large, swampy area, probably an old beaver pond. As we had found out in an adventure in the Precipice with Merritt's D6, in these meadows the grass was growing on a mat of roots and mud about a metre thick, floating on a liquid goo of muck that could swallow anything you put on it. Our meadow was firm, but others were not. We had to be careful where we walked or rode in that area.

With a belly full of fried onions, eggs and sausage, complete with two cups of cowboy coffee (two handfuls of grounds boiled in a blue, chipped and dented enamel pot, strong enough to get anyone going), I moved out across the golden meadow with a battered red coffee can full of oats, shaking it and calling out for Salsa. The noise of the oats rattling around in a can is something horses can hear for miles. It was the routine, and I was sure she would appear out of the nearby timber.

No luck. However, as I moved through a narrow neck at the end of the meadow and glanced into the next opening, I saw what appeared to be the head of a horse sticking up over the top of the swamp grass. Moving closer, I saw that it was Salsa, completely submerged in mud except for her head and neck. She had fallen into an old beaver channel, wide enough for her body but too narrow for her to climb out of. It was a deadly trap.

Salsa was not a big horse, maybe 340 kilograms. Part Arab, part Quarter horse and part who knows what else, she had a long frame with a high arched neck and very narrow withers. She had been working hard. I could see where she had pawed ahead of herself, trying to climb out, but every time she had stepped forward, the bottom layer had broken into pieces and she had sunk back into the muck. She was on the edge of panicking, and the whites of her eyes were showing. Exhaustion was already setting in. I hurried back to camp and collected Jim.

The first thing we tried was digging a platform at a 45-degree angle to the old beaver trench. This was not fun. The black, frigid water was chest deep as we shovelled and dug and sank and dug some more.

Finally, we thought there was enough room for Salsa to clamber up and out. Jim went back to camp and saddled up his other saddle horse, Nick, then tied a long rope from his saddle horn to the halter shank dangling below Salsa's chin. When he lunged forward, I slapped Salsa on the hind quarter with another piece of rope as hard as I could.

She almost made it, jumping forward, with her front hooves digging into the platform, but it started to crumble and she did not have enough energy left to push out with her hind legs. We didn't know how long she had been in the water, but she now had reached the point that horses reach sometimes—she simply gave up. Her head lolled sideways, her breathing slowed and nothing we did would make her move at all. She just lay there, waiting for the end.

We almost gave up, too. Then Jim had an idea. He remembered an old-timer telling him about the power of a Spanish windlass, how it could be used to winch trucks out of a bog hole. Well, we figured, if it could pull a truck out of the mud, why not a horse waiting to die?

The roar of our chainsaw split the still morning air as we cut two sturdy poles, one about 2 metres long and 15 centimetres in diameter and the other about 1.5 metres long and a little slimmer, both green and supple. We sharpened the larger diameter pole on one end and drove it into the ground halfway, using a big rock as a pile driver.

Taking Jim's lariat, we lashed the other pole crosswise, forming what looked like a capital T. I took two 50-foot pack ropes, twisted them together and looped one end under Salsa's belly, behind her front legs. It certainly was refreshing to drop into black, cold, stinking swamp water to put a rope under a horse's belly as lay there, depressed nearly to death.

We wound the other end of the rope around the upright post below the cross bar and then started to push on the outer ends of the handle. The leverage was amazing. As the post slowly turned you could see the rope getting tighter and tighter, starting to lift Salsa partly sideways. She must have felt a lot of pain as the rope dug into her sides, and we hoped that would spur her into action.

We were pushing as hard as we could, putting tremendous pressure on the post, the rope and Salsa. Something had to give. And finally it did. Salsa's head shot up, she grunted, and with a piercing squeal she exploded from the trench, mud, grass, rope and all. We quickly dried her with saddle blankets and tied her to a picket in the warm morning sun.

Half an hour later she was eating, good as new, the old glitter back in her eyes. The lariat we had used to tie the handle on with was so tightly twisted that we had to cut it off. Jim was quite upset, wondering if the horse was worth a good lariat, well broken-in. In the end he concluded it was. Salsa lived many more years, always giving spirited rides into the mountains, beaver meadows and all.

Lost—or Misplaced?

We had been living in Precipice Valley for just a year when an old school friend who had relocated to Florida came for a visit. I'd arranged a ride for her from Williams Lake to Anahim Lake, where I picked her up for the trip into the Precipice Valley.

By the time we got on the road, it was dark. I'd seldom driven the Tote Road at night—in fact, I'd rarely driven it on my own, so I wasn't as familiar with the turns and twists as Dave was. The road seemed much longer at night, but we had a beautiful full moon that led us west. Frances and I were chatting, getting caught up with the past decade of events since we'd last seen each other, and I wasn't really paying a lot of attention to the drive. After all, there were no side roads, no other traffic.

Suddenly, the moon was behind us. *Behind!* How could that be? I frantically tried to remember if I could possibly have taken a side track, even though I was sure there weren't any. I stopped the Nissan and got out. Frances nervously asked me if we were lost, and I of course tried to pretend I wasn't worried. I walked back up the road towards the beautiful full moon—and realized that I had just negotiated a sharp switchback in the road without realizing where I was. Breathing a sigh of relief, I got back into the truck and continued along the now-darker road, until it gradually turned towards the valley and the moon reappeared where it should have been.

Frances had travelled a lot in some remote areas in Guatemala, where she had started an organization called Adopt-A-Village. But the next morning she explained to us that wherever she went, if there was a road there were people. She had never experienced anything like the wild land we called our home.

A few days later, she said she'd love to go for a ride. She liked the idea of riding up to Hotnarko Mountain, which she could see from the valley bottom. So, I saddled up Who Knows and Takia, and we set off. We had an ATV trail running from the valley up to Precipice Lake, and then a short diversion through the woods to a large open area called Johnny's Meadow.

A few decades ago a rancher from the Bella Coola Valley, Floyd Mecham, had a line cabin up on the Tote Road just above Precipice Valley and moved his cattle up to Precipice each year. He decided to cut a trail up the side of Hotnarko Mountain so he could access some natural meadows up there, for use as more summer range for his cattle. This trail started "somewhere" at the end of the large meadow near the lake. Feeling possessive about his trail, having paid a worker to help him to lay it out, Floyd hid the beginning of it. I had been up there a few times, but earlier in the year, when the bushes weren't so heavily covered in leaves.

After walking the horses back and forth across the end of the meadow a few times without finding the trailhead, much to the disgust of the Canada geese trying to feed there, I found an old deer trail and decided to use that, hoping it would lead to the the trail we wanted. I regretted not taking our dog, who would have set us right!

But the deer trail soon vanished, and we found ourselves bushwacking. My big bay horse was very tall. The horse Frances was on, a little Appaloosa, wasn't. I was concentrating on our route and hadn't realized that the fallen trees and brush that my horse simply stepped over with his long legs were a real obstacle for the little guy that Frances was riding. It wasn't until she called out to me, sounding partly scared and partly annoyed, saying that Takia was hung up on some brush, that I paid attention to what was happening behind me.

Frances looked very hot and disheveled. Her tight blonde curls were full of fir and pine needles and even a few twigs, and there was a rip in her shirt sleeve. I'd been in the Precipice for just a short time and already I'd forgotten that not everyone was as relaxed about riding off-trail as Dave and I were.

We got Takia untangled and drank some water. Then, for the second time in a few days, Frances asked me if we were lost. I looked up at Hotnarko Mountain on one side, and over to Kappan Mountain on the other side of Precipice Valley.

"No," I replied, trying to sound confident. "We aren't lost—just a little misplaced." I knew that if I kept those two landmarks to my left and right sides, we eventually would intersect the "proper" trail.

And that is what happened. We both sighed with relief when we turned up that trail and saw the mountain in front of us. The rest of the ride up to nearly the top of the 2100-metre mountain was easy, once we negotiated a wide rockfall on the side of the mountain, and the 360-degree views were spectacular.

We headed back down the mountain, the horses finally deciding they knew the way after all, and found Johnny's meadow with no problem. As we rode through, the huge flock of Canada geese flew up in a mass, honking at us as they circled.

Forty-five minutes later, we arrived back home. We unsaddled the horses at the Glad Cab, turning them out to feed before we walked up the hill to Firhome. Dave greeted us with a big grin on his face, saying he knew we were on our way and had dinner nearly ready.

"But how did you know how long we'd be?" I asked.

"I happened to be outside and saw the geese take off up north from where I knew Johnny's meadow was, so I knew you had disturbed them."

Frances marvelled at all this. "I can't imagine living somewhere with so few people around that Dave knew it was us, not someone else."

Frances enjoyed her visit with us, but she never let me get away with anything as I showed her around . . . for some reason she kept asking me if we were lost!

Life Cairns

Being paid to work in the outdoors, camping in the wilds of Tweedsmuir Park, lounging in the lush colours of multicoloured flower meadows, embraced by some of the most idyllic surroundings to be found anywhere as we cleared established trails of winter blow-down and chased spring up into the alpine, was an adventure, but the real adventure started when Parks asked us to go into the more remote parts of South Tweedsmuir, well beyond the trailheads.

Our first base camp was on Turner Lake on the Turner Lake Chain, a popular three- or four-day canoe loop in the high valley between Glacier Mountain and Mt. Ada. Our supply was from the Nimpo Lake float plane base, and our trips were 10 days on, four days off. Our task was the same that we were given in the Rainbows, but on foot: locate old trails, build cairns and pioneer new routes across the terrain. These trails couldn't be marked by signposts as they were almost all above timberline. I especially liked building cairns. There is something quite satisfying about lifting the rocks, picking the right rock for the right place, making them balance, knowing that they were markers for those to come.

Dave building a cairn in Tweedsmuir Park south

Turner Lake feeds Hunlen Falls. At around 280 metres, it is one of the most impressive in Canada. Jim and I were the first crew in to scope out this area and our mission was to give B.C. Parks an assessment of the state of the trails and any work that needed to be done.

Tweedsmuir Air had flown in a canoe, along with our other supplies, so one of the first things we did was to explore Turner Lake. As we entered the stream that left the east end of the lake, we quickly came to the footbridge to the falls. A red sign attached to the railing warned of extreme danger and commanded: "Passage beyond this point is prohibited." Of course, we assumed that as authorized personnel we were exempt from the prohibition, so we blithely paddled under the bridge and headed downstream. It was a very quiet day, with only a breath of wind. Everything was calm and peaceful.

As we approached a tight bend in the stream, we decided to tie the canoe to a low branch of a large spruce and go ashore. As I stepped around the base of the tree I froze. Not 10 feet away, the lip of the falls disappeared into a mist as the creek tumbled into oblivion. Jim stopped beside me and we just stood there in silence, the realization sinking in that, had we not stopped when we did, we would have gone over the brink to sure death. I still shudder when I think of how close we came that day. It was a sobering lesson.

A few days later, we went farther west on Turner Lake to do some more exploring. On the end of a point that juts out into the lake, we saw what looked like clothes flapping in the breeze: an odd and rather eerie sight. We landed and cautiously approached the fluttering clothes to discover that, indeed, this was a clothesline strung full of clothing: shirts, jeans, socks, a full line indeed. One end was attached to a large pine tree and the other to a sturdy cabin, complete with a porch. As luck would have it, as we climbed up onto the porch we heard a shout from across the water near the end of the lake, so we sat down and waited. Fifteen minutes later, a spry man with a full white beard and a stout walking stick strode from the pine forest to greet us.

He was John Edwards, son of Ralph Edwards, known as The Crusoe of Lonesome Lake. Once we got acquainted, he told us that he left his laundry out on the line when he was away, figuring that people would assume someone was home so they would not come near. John had unusual logic for sure.

The following year, I flew higher above Turner Lake with a small crew, to land on Ptarmigan. Once again we found and reestablished old routes, developed new hiking experiences, mapped them (no GPS in those days), wrote trail descriptions, and built cairns along the best routes for others to follow.

Hunlen Falls and Turner Lake

It was both a challenge and a thrill. First, I'd get out the map, examine the contour lines, elevation, aspect, size, distances and proximity for possible peaks to hike, then work out the logistics for food for the several days my crew and I would spend away from base camp.

THE POWER OF DREAMS

One such area was a small lake located at timberline on the slopes of Caribou Mountain—a modest 2200-metre peak guarding a series of broad alpine valleys. Called Ptarmigan after the birds who spent the summer around its shores, this lake was large enough to fly a Beaver aircraft in and out. The rule—not so useful in metric—is 5000 feet of lake at 5000 feet elevation. There are a few alpine lakes that meet these criteria, and luckily Ptarmigan was one of them. I had spent a couple of weeks the previous summer camped on its eastern shore, scoping out possibilities for new routes leading from base camp, along the northern shore, then up and over a steep ridge to a large, flat-bottomed valley with many lakes, glaciers, waterfalls and streams. Set against the serene beauty of the Coast Mountains as a backdrop, this was the kind of perfect alpine wonderland we wanted to open up for hikers.

To establish one of the routes, we needed to explore a path to reach a col (a pass) suspended between two fractured peaks. So, up we went. Scramble here, back down and retry another line over there, getting a feel for a good route over the scree, between boulders the size of transport trucks, across snow patches, along the edge of the vertical cliffs dropping into the small lake far below.

In all, it took several days of exploring to locate good ways to reach the valley we'd chosen and finding the best angles for walking the slopes in a relatively safe, easy manner. Routes could not be too steep, nor too long. They had to miss the boggy parts, cross snow patches safely, and, most importantly, they had to find those special viewpoints for rest stops that make it all worthwhile.

Once the way had been chosen, we'd build cairns to mark the path for those who would follow. My style was to make just enough, so that when you reach one of the cairns, another one will come into sight, gently leading up and across the bare mountain. If you build too many cairns, the feeling of wildness, aloneness, is damaged. If you don't build enough, the way can be lost.

In the end, we provided three access possibilities into the new valley. Once there, the hikers were on their own, with no more cairns to follow. It was now their turn to explore new routes and to continue the process. They would experience the particular pleasure that comes when you find your way through new country, picking your own line of travel, learning to read the landscape.

Wild Spring Rains, Hard Drives and Reality

By the late '90s, developing technologies had allowed Rosemary and me to become more easily involved with environmental issues. When I was working on an environmental campaign I would often spend days in my office in Firhome, on the phone and the computer. It was like any other office job. I rearranged landscapes on maps, rejigged budgets, devised strategies for cabinet decisions, worked on community plans and wrote business plans. The work sometimes became so intense that I simply never got outside.

It was after a few days of one of these deluges of indoor activity that I fled out of the house into a rainstorm one day and let it wash over me. Wild spring rains sharpened the air, filling it with ozone, a glossy mist and the bite of zest borne on tiny droplets, stinging the nose and cheeks as they float by. It was at times like these, as I stood in the rain on the ridge, watching the roar of the swollen river explode over the valley, that I was fully aware of the distance too often put between me and the physical world in which I lived. I remember writer Gary Snyder saying that even in the dirtiest, most desolate inner-city landscape there will be weeds growing in the cracks and grass on the margins. "There is wildness everywhere," he said. So there is. We just have to see it.

Walking in a city, with nothing but traffic noise made by the scrape of machinery, the squeak of tires, the roar of exhaling buses, complete with the hissing of air brakes and the rat-a- tat of jackhammers keeping time, seems to require an iPod to drown out the din. With earbuds jammed into our ears to block out the surroundings, we go obliviously from place to place. In offices, where bulletproof glass blocks out the helter-skelter noise of the street, computers take over. The mind now becomes the prisoner of hard drives. Little spinning disks set our confines. Ergonomic hardware determines our pathways. Tiny pieces of electronic gadgetry become the vehicle for human imaginations. Whether we're on the Net as some avatar in a virtual-reality environment or simply working through the rote tasks of a standard application, the electronic world becomes the world of existence. It fools us. We are able to change realities within it, even change worlds at the click of a mouse or the stroke of a key, all severed from planet Earth.

That's not our life, though. We are first and foremost beings in a physical body, evolved and attuned to be present in an earthly reality.

That is why, even in the Precipice, it was so important to find a wild place outside of our cosseting nest and stand in a spring rain. My full suite of senses was aroused by the primal contact with wind and spray, ears and eyes fully engaged with the rest of the body, emotions and energy connected, rising, and touching the core of being. Wild spring rains exposed the electronic reality for the sham it really was—a third-rate, dangerous impostor—and held me in the cycle of life, in which birth follows death, validating the timeless truth of being and the reality that none of us can control the vast forces in which we are enmeshed. Standing in the spring rain allowed me to build maps up from the ground of being.

COMMUNITY

Music night in Firhome

The Neighbourhood

For the first few years in Precipice, winters were solitary affairs. Our nearest neighbours, Lee and Pat Taylor, had a small horse ranch a couple of kilometres away. They had been homeschooling their two girls but decided the kids had reached an age where they needed to be more integrated with their peers, so they moved to Vancouver the year we moved in. Aside from occasional visits during Christmas, Lee came in the late spring and usually left in November. We had winters to ourselves, with the nearest neighbours over 50 kilometres away. Rosemary talks about the changes in our community:

At first, we'd been happy to feed Lee's horses through the winter, because ours herded with them in the meadows, but with Dave away so much, it left very little time for building Firhome when he was back in the valley. I could manage the feeding in a pinch when Dave was gone, but I didn't have the ongoing strength to do it regularly.

Lee started bringing in caretakers. Mort was the first, arriving the fall of his 65th year with a broken leg. He wasn't particularly good with machinery—the word "inept" was invented for him—and the broken leg kept him from getting firewood, so that first winter with Mort Dave spent a great deal of repair time with him as well as filling his woodshed.

Mort left after two years to be closer to town. A series of caretakers followed. The first long-term ones were Patti and David (Jorgie) Jorgenson, with their three young children. They had been boat logging for years and were very accustomed to being self-sufficient, so when Jorgie went out on a sustainable logging contract, Patti did just fine on her own.

It was nice for me to have another woman in the Valley, and Patti and I did have many adventures together. I recall one "dark and stormy night" in January when both our Davids were away from the valley. Of course, as often happened at that time of year, the ancient phone line was down somewhere. Hobo alerted me to a visitor—I hadn't heard because of the blizzard. I hurried downstairs to the front door and there on the front porch were Patti and the children, Aileen, Maria and Ty.

"May we come in?" Patti said in a very small voice. She'd gotten her snowmachine running—no small accomplishment in such cold weather—and loaded everyone on it for the 15-minute trip through the snow up to Firhome.

After I chided her for not just walking in, we got settled with hot chocolate and she told me the story. Their chimney had blown over and was lying on the steep roof! The old cabin had a double roof and the insulation was dry sawdust, so Patti was understandably nervous about fire and didn't dare run their wood heater. The outside temperature was around -35. Staying in the unheated cabin overnight wasn't an option. But they couldn't leave it unheated very long, either, or all their perishables would freeze. That meant that moving up with me wasn't a long-term answer.

The next morning was clear, so we headed back to their cabin to see what we could do. The chimney had toppled off its base cleanly. That was good. Patti felt that if we could just get it back vertical, and ran ropes for support, it would hold until the weather warmed and repairs could be made. Patti monkeyed up onto the roof and slung a strap around the chimney, with a rope down to a Skidoo. By carefully backing the Skidoo, and with Patti guiding it, the brick chimney slowly straightened back on its base. Problem solved.

The men had figured out by now that the phone lines were down and each had alerted B.C. Tel. They were both told that it was too cold for a lineman to go out and check. And then when the weather warmed up it rained hard, the usual brief January thaw, and it was "too wet" for working on the line. They had a point, because the only way to travel was by snowmachine and the rain made slush over the various swamps and puddles. Patti and I had no further emergencies, though, before our backup Davids returned.

The Jorgies stayed for four years, having another baby, Ida, before they left. We grew very close to them and remain good friends.

Jorgies and Dave

After Lee gave up on the idea of raising Percherons, since there no longer was much of a market for them, he started ranching cows. We felt that they were harder on the landscape than horses, but they did provide an excuse for a very large party each year in late May or early June, when the cows had to be moved up the Precipice hill to their summer range. On Cattle Drive Weekend, people came in to help accomplish this, some with horses and some with ATVs, while others came just for the two-day party. Lots of food, lots of music, lots of good friends.

There were two lakes by the Tote Road above Precipice Valley, before our road dropped down into the valley iteself.. The smaller one, which we dubbed Lilypad Lake, was in front of a line cabin that Troy Gurr and Floyd Mecham had built. It was permitted by the government because Floyd Mecham had some summer cattle range and used to drive his cattle every year up the Sugar Camp Trail from the Bella Coola Valley. When age and ill health stopped the Mechams from using the line cabin, Troy and Lorrein Gurr from Hagensborg, also in the Bella Coola Valley, took over the cabin, cleaning out the massive pack rat and mouse damage, and making it livable again, visiting whenever they could. So we got to know them as well and had many happy times with them, from sitting around huge bonfires by the lake to snowmachine expeditions across the rimrock to frozen Hotnarko Falls.

Steven and Jasmine, the couple from North Carolina, bought the Glenn place at the west end of Precipice Valley around 2002 and moved in, with their horses, dogs, cats, and guinea pigs. They made it through a couple of winters, but the third was too much for Jasmine. In the late winter of 2005, she fled, saying she needed to go back to Carolina to deal with some real estate issues and would return. Dave took her out by Skidoo, wondering why she had so much stuff with her. That left Steven alone, and by the time he realized she wasn't coming back, he couldn't follow because their second vehicle was on the wrong side of the deep, semi-frozen river. He was in pretty bad shape psychologically and was desperate to leave, but he had all the animals to deal with. Somehow it fell to me to find homes for them—another process that couldn't be completed until after spring breakup. Eventually, I was able to place them all. During that two-month process, I got to know a lot of good people by phone and over the internet. It was very time-consuming but worthwhile, so I enjoyed doing it.

Fred Reid, an organic farmer from Abbotsford, bought the cabin and some acreage from Jasmine and Steven, while Lee bought the remaining acreage, needing the hay from the meadows for his expanding cattle herd. Fred had been in the valley a few times, as he had met Lee when they both were involved in organics. He loved the Precipice and jumped at the chance to move in.

Right about then, we were making plans to go to New Zealand for eight weeks. While we were away, our house sitter, Monika from Germany, met Fred. They fell in love, married and are still in the Precipice together. They have created a large organic farm on their wonderful bottom soil (I say, enviously). A few years later, Fred's daughter Farida met Barry, a Dutch wwoofer—and now they too are married, with two children.

What can I say? It's a magical place.

Inspiration, Chickens and Sanity

Even though we lived remotely, we learned that in sparsely settled areas like the Chilcotin (an area the size of Switzerland but with fewer than 5,000 people) folks living several hours away are still considered neighbours. One of the things that attracted us to the Chilcotin in the first place was the individuality of the residents. Conformity was not part of anyone's vocabulary! A wonderful example was the story of Johnny and the chickens.

John and Mary Lou Blackwell were a couple of those people we called neighbours, even though their winter home was a of couple hours' drive away in Anahim Lake. They owned Moose Lake Lodge, which was just "over the mountain"; in other words, north of the Rainbow Mountains. John owned a venerable floatplane which he used to supply his business, flying guests and groceries from his dock on Anahim Lake to his remote lodge, which had no road access.

John might have been old Chilcotin, but he realized that the world was changing and that the needs of his clients were changing also. So, he adapted to the desires of his more demanding clientele, putting in a garden for fresh greens and keeping chickens for fresh eggs. And therein lies another Chilcotin story.

Imagine this: over 60 squawking chickens packed into assorted boxes, cages and other containers, being stuffed into various recesses of a bush plane. The only thing not full of chickens was the pilot's seat and the floats. Well, the pilot's seat for sure. I watched this process the first time as Johnny snapped the doors closed, climbed into the cockpit, with the co-pilot's seat beside him filled with crates of beady-eyed chickens, watching every move. As he closed his door and buckled up, the chickens grew eerily silent. The plane made a long, quiet taxi to the end of the lake, followed by a shattering roar as it gathered speed on the glassy surface, foamy white water cresting in waves behind the floats.

Slowly, gracefully, the metal bird took to the air full of chickens; birds within a bird. Where else but in the Chilcotin would such a scene take place? Out there in the still-wild west, things are done in ways that make sense, ways that may not be conventional, ways that may not be the norm, but which serve the people and the environment they live in.

That is not to say that there haven't been a few ideas tried out over the years that seemed sensible at the time but were just a little odd, given the isolated location. Take the bizarre scheme of the "Chilcotin Beaver Lady." In the 1930s, she moved from Europe to a very remote corner of the Chilcotin to build a beaver ranch. She had a log cabin built and a small meadow cleared and proceeded with her mission. Before she could complete her plan, beaver felt hats fell from popularity. The cabin is still there, full of pack rats and collapsed roof logs, a silent epitaph to that wonderful little bit of insanity.

However, this plane full of chickens was not some crazy plan to create a chicken ranch out in the middle of nowhere. It was the result of some very clear-headed thinking. The lodge where the chickens summered had been thriving for several decades. Over the years, as the business had grown, so had the demand for increased variety in the menu. Today's guests are no longer content with just moose meat and spuds. Today's resort clientele are more discriminating. They want communications, satellite TV, gourmet meals and all the comforts of home. When your operation is a 45-minute flight from the nearest tiny village, with no road access, these things are not easy to provide.

But then innovation stepped in. Bernie, the chef hired by the lodge a few seasons before, had been in the country for a long time. He was trained in the European style and was known for his elaborate pastries and other succulent goodies. He was also the owner of 60 chickens and supplemented his winter income by selling eggs to the locals. When the lodge hired him to run the dining operation in the summers, naturally enough, discussions around the chickens ensued. Over the next couple of seasons, the plan evolved of creating a summer home for the chickens at the lodge.

At first, John was dubious. Fly chickens to the lodge? Then fly them back out again in the fall? But then some creative thinking started to kick in. Easily accessible organic eggs for the clients! It would no longer be necessary to scrounge for farm eggs around the Anahim area and then fly them in. The flock would ensure the lodge had fresh organic eggs daily. This would be a good selling point to the avid fisherman or hunter—and the price was right, too. The lodge owner used to dispose of the organic wastes from the kitchen with a propane burning system, and its downside was huge: flying in the propane meant using more airplane fuel, there was more CO_2 released in the air from burning fossil fuels, it didn't smell all that great and, of course, there were the costs of all that to consider. Now the chickens ate the peelings, the discarded salad and other tasty waste, and the composted chicken manure fertilized the chef's garden, which grew much of the greens needed for the kitchen. Once the chickens arrived, the garden was bigger than ever. Things had come full circle. The chickens had a summer house, the chef had fresh produce, the clients had organic eggs and salads, and the lodge owner saved time and money and left a smaller carbon footprint.

Floatplanes stuffed with crates of squawking chickens just reaffirmed our conviction that the Chilcotin was the place we needed to be—after all, a lot of people considered us a bit weird also!

Do You Have a Hammer?

Johnny and Bernie definitely can be credited with creative thinking with their fly-in chickens. But one of Lee's caretakers, an interesting character named Klaus, took problem-solving to new levels.

Klaus was very old-school. He often worked with power tools, such as angle grinders, bandsaws and table saws, without using guards or other safety devices. One cold January he was making a door frame using an industrial shaper with a 5-centimetre spindle to rout the curves and grooves needed to house the panels. He was guiding a long, awkward rail by hand, no fence, no guard, when he hit a small knot, causing the rail to jump. His hand slipped and slid along the piece into the 5000 RPM spindle.

It was after 4 p.m. on a -25 winter afternoon and already dark. I had come in from outside, taken my boots off, put my feet up on the stool, and was warming myself by the heater when the phone rang.

"Have you got a hammer and a sharp knife?" said the hurried voice on the other end of the line. "Well . . . yesssss," I replied. "Good, then I come right over and you cut my finger off." *Click*. The phone went dead and I stared at it for a long moment, letting all this sink in. Although Klaus usually was a man of few words, this conversation set a new benchmark for brevity. I put my boots and jacket back on and went outside to wait anxiously for his arrival, while Rosemary collected first-aid materials and prepared for the worst.

Within five minutes I heard the whine of his snowmachine. Up the hill and into the driveway he came, stiff-backed and glassy-eyed, with no coat, shirttail streaming behind, his full beard frosted white and hair straight back. He looked more like a ghost from Christmas past than my neighbour.

Somehow he had managed to work the throttle and steer the machine with his right hand, even though it was wrapped in a big glob of blood-soaked paper towels.

I led him to the dining room table, where Rosemary unwrapped the paper towels to reveal that what used to be a finger but now was a piece of white bone with ragged pieces of flesh hanging to the side, from the middle knuckle to the end. The nail was still attached, but at a weird angle. The whole finger was curled in the fetal position.

"Whiskey," breathed my neighbour. He slugged it back. Then, "Cut it off," he demanded.

"No way," I said.

We figured he was in shock, so Rosemary dressed the finger in gauze and bandages and called the about-to-close clinic in Anahim Lake to see if someone would wait there, while I went outside, fired up our Skidoo and got it ready for the trip. By the time I got back, Rosemary had dressed Klaus in some of my heavy snowmobile gear, complete with down coveralls and jacket, extra-large mitts to accommodate the bandage, and her warm blue toque. Klaus is many kilos and several sizes smaller than I am, so he looked for all the world like a little kid dressed up in his dad's clothes, but we didn't see the humour at the time.

The trail was rough and bumpy, but Klaus stoically hung on behind me. Forty-five dark and worried minutes later, we were at the car, parked at the end of the logging road in the turnaround where the highways crew always stopped ploughing. After a nervous few minutes while the car decided if it would start in this cold weather, we drove another half-hour to the clinic in Anahim Lake, where the nurse took one look at the blood-soaked bandages and, after hearing the description of the finger/shaper machine encounter, said, "You guys have to go to Williams Lake."

It was now after 7 p.m. The finger had been mangled over three hours before, but my neighbour still insisted he didn't need any painkillers. We stopped for a warming coffee at old Mort's place, then off to Williams Lake we went.

After four hours of icy driving on dark, deserted Highway 20, we were in Emergency, the doctor shaking his head and trying to provide options. All this took a few more hours, and we were both exhausted.

After the trip and the trauma, it was not the time to make a decision, so we went to a helpful friend's home for the night. It wasn't much of a night. We arrived after 1 a.m. and left again at 6:30 so we could be back to Emergency to catch the same doctor before his shift ended at 8 a.m. By then, my oh-so-practical neighbour had made the final decision: to have the top two thirds of his right index finger amputated. Since he is right-handed and enjoyed playing guitar, the decision was not easy, but with the spectre of numerous trips to Kamloops or Vancouver for the surgery, to see a plastic surgeon, rehab, and no guarantee that the finger would ever be really useful again, removal seemed to him to be the best solution.

It was quickly accomplished and we were back in the car by 10:30. We grabbed a drive-through lunch and then drove the endless hours to the snowmachine and another 45 minutes back into the Precipice. And finally, pain pills were accepted. Talk about a high pain tolerance!

But the day wasn't over yet. The cows needed to be fed, huge round bales of hay needed to be delivered by tractor, and ever-stubborn Klaus insisted on driving the tractor while I cut the binding twine, kept the frozen bales rolling and acted as gateman and cattle shooer. Once that was done, we went back the couple of kilometres to our place, for the good hot meal Rosemary had waiting and a debrief.

And so it went, one of those little things that can happen when you're running power tools. Traumatic anywhere, just much more complicated out there beyond help.

In any case, the next time someone phones you and opens with, "Do you have a hammer?" be prepared.

Bringing Home the Puppy

By March of that year, Klaus was getting lonely. His Great Pyrenees Diaz, a former dog of Mort's, had been with him for three years but had been killed by a buck deer the fall before. As a bachelor, he did not have any companions aside from his cows and horses, so he decided to get another dog. This was not just a sentimental decision. A good dog is an invaluable partner around a ranch, helping to guard cows and horses, keeping rats out of the grain bin, alerting you to unusual occurrences such as the cows getting into the hay barn, and, yes, lying at your feet in front of the fire on a deep cold winter night. So he borrowed our *Dogs of the World* book and started researching.

Klaus finally made his decision. He was going to get a Komondor. Choosing the new stock guardian dog was the easy part. Getting it into the Precipice was another matter altogether.

There aren't many Komondor breeders. Klaus finally found one in Whitehorse, Yukon. The breeder was expecting pups at Christmas, so he ordered one. When it reached eight weeks, the pup was old enough to be flown to Vancouver, where another dog breeder from Aldergrove, Johanna, had agreed to be the transition point between flights. The little guy would then be flown to Anahim Lake, where we would pick him up and bring him home by snowmachine.

We headed for town on a Monday morning with two Skidoos, Klaus's for backup and my larger one to carry the large dog crate. The weather was okay, but as we neared the logging road where my truck was parked, the snow and clouds started to roll in, obscuring the mountains surrounding us. The closer we got to Anahim Lake, the thicker they became, but as we rounded the airport corner the clouds lifted a little, so we were sure things would be fine for the plane to land.

There's no control tower at our Anahim airport. The administration office was so small that we could hear the pilot talking to the ground crew as she was making her final approach. Even though we had enough ceiling over the airport itself, a snow squall south of the runway obscured visibility below acceptable limits, and the pilot radioed she was going to abort the landing attempt and return to Vancouver.

So there we sat, eyeballing the lowering cloud banks, absorbing the radio chat and the import of the turboprop's thrum as it bore unseen through the slate grey murk above us, GPS-ing it back to Vancouver. So near, yet so far.

Even worse, when I called Rosemary, she told us that the sun had broken through over the Precipice. In fact, she had seen the plane go over from Bella Coola on its way to Anahim where we waited.

Oh, well. Back to the snowmobiles, the run back to the Precipice and a call to Aldergrove, asking Johanna to turn around and go back to the Vancouver South airport, her second long trip that day. Then, after considering the weather predictions and the twice-weekly winter flight schedule, we decided to wait for the next try until Friday, when the conditions were supposed to be cold and clear.

Sure enough, on Friday we awoke to -25, with a few clouds scudding across the horizon. Since we didn't have to leave until 11, I had time for an extra coffee, to let the day warm up a bit. About 10:30, as I was getting geared up, Klaus roared up on his machine and pounded on the front door. He wanted to know why I was 35 minutes late; we were supposed to meet at the bridge, down below our place. He was cold from waiting and also was worried about meeting the plane on time.

It turned out that after our last trip out, when he had lost his watch on the trail, Rosemary had given him one we had kicking around. What none of us noticed was that it was set for daylight saving time, making Klaus an hour ahead. Once we got that sorted out, we were on our way, bouncing along on the hard, mogul-filled trail to the truck at the ploughed logging road.

This time, the sky was an unbroken blue and the plane landed smoothly and quickly and taxied up to the apron, with the port engine exhaling puffs of blue smoke as it shut down. We walked over to the nine-passenger Bandera and watched as the pilot opened the hatch and nimbly scampered down the ramp, ducked under the wing and cracked the cargo door. And there, surrounded by beige, black and blue luggage of all shapes and sizes was Puppy, lying in his crate, blinking and yawning, without a care in the world. His coal-black eyes, set in a snowy white face, scanned the new landscape with cool aplomb. He looked like Frosty the Snowman without the carrot nose.

After a short walk to do his business, the puppy was loaded back into his crate, and off we went to the trailhead. There we put the crate sideways on the back of my larger Skidoo, strapped it down with ropes and bungee cords, carefully wrapping it over all with a blanket for warmth and stuffing towels on the inside so puppy wouldn't be jostled around too much. As I slowly pulled ahead, Klaus watched from behind to see the reaction from the passenger. Did he jump and howl? No way, not this dog. He simply lay down, put his nose between his feet and looked straight ahead. I guess after four plane flights and many hours in the back of a car in rush hour, he could do snowmobiles standing on his head.

Bringing home Kosmo

It was a very slow trip home on the rough trail, so puppy was eager to get out of the cage. But do you know the first thing he did? He took off into the deep snow and got stuck trying to reach a cow on the other side of the fence, nearly buried in the snow with only his head visible. No slouch, this pup! He was going to be a great one.

His new name? Kosmo. Kosmo the Komondor, owned by Klaus. Isn't that kosmic?

Jimmy and the Pot

Mort, who had originally spent two years in Precipice Valley in the late '80s, caretaking for our neighbours the Taylors, had been living outside of Anahim Lake. He wasn't expecting us that morning in 2004. Dave had told him we were heading to Williams Lake soon so I could do my spring semi-annual grocery shopping and Dave could attend a meeting, but not that we were stopping by to give him a planter (actually a plastic-lined milk crate!) full of chard, his favourite green.

Mort was living at a ranch property called Trail's End, looking after the place while the owners decided what to do with it. It was a great place for him and all his animals, but it got pretty tough for him there after a few years, especially after his creek dried up and he had to haul water (by ATV or Skidoo, depending on the season) for himself and his livestock. Mort was getting on; the year before we had thrown a large surprise 80th birthday party for him out at Nimpo Lake, attended by people from across the Chilcotin and Cariboo. Now he was 81 but still living as independently as possible.

So anyhow, as I said, Mort didn't know we'd be arriving, but we weren't worried as he was always very welcoming. His various AWDs (advance warning devices) greeted us—Cactus, the gimpy border collie; Bones, the elongated hound, Nicholas the llama, and Charlie the goat. But no Mort. We pulled up in front of his old log cabin and got out, and Mort appeared on the stoop. His usual erect stance was a bit slumped, and he wasn't wearing his trademark Stetson.

"I've got a Problem," he announced peremptorily. Not, "How are you, good to see you." Then he sort of caught himself. "Er, come in and have a cup of tea,"

"We're in a bit of a rush," said Dave. "What is the problem?" he asked a bit nervously, thinking of his scheduled meeting in town. Mort's ongoing problems had a way of being very time-consuming.

Mort came over to us, carefully locking the gate behind him. He needed a fence around his cabin to keep chickens, curious goats and llamas out of his cabin. "It's Jimmy," he announced. We automatically looked across the field to where his two huge Belgian draft horses were feeding, apparently quite happily.

"I made my usual Anahim trip yesterday, and before I went I gave them some grain. I gave Jake his in the rubber feeding bin, but I couldn't find the other one, so I put Jimmy's ration in my big old enamel pot. You know the one—with the flowers on the side?"

Mort shuffled a bit as we distributed pats among the various pushy animals. "And . . ." encouraged Dave.

"Well," continued Mort, "when I got home I didn't notice anything at first. But then I saw that Jimmy wasn't walking quite right. It was like a clump-clump-*clank*."

Evidently Jimmy had stepped in Mort's enamel pot—and it was a perfect fit. So there was Jimmy, going about his business as if this was a normal occurrence, his butterscotch coloured flanks harmonizing nicely with the yellow flowers on the pot.

"I tried hammering it off, but it didn't budge," explained Mort. "I phoned people last night on my radio phone but couldn't raise anyone to help."

"Okay, let's take a look," said Dave, and off we went. Yep, that pot was a perfect fit. Punky and Bulldog, our local farriers, couldn't have done it better.

Mort put a massive halter on Jimmy. It looked like something a window washer on a high-rise would feel safe in. I held the horse while Mort hovered anxiously. Dave tried the hammer, and Mort was right—a hammer wasn't going to do it.

Dave working on Jimmy's potted foot

"What else have you got? Tin snips? Hack saw?" asked Dave.

Mort was rummaging around in his tool kit. "How about fencing pliers?"

"*Fencing* pliers?" repeated Dave faintly. Those large pliers are great for cutting fencing wire, but awkward for anything else.

You know what those heavy-duty enamel pots are like, right? Thick rim around the top, built to withstand any abuse. But fencing pliers are what he had, so fencing pliers are what Dave used. He started snipping around, trying to rip the metal. He's pretty strong, but even *his* tough hands were starting to weaken.

"Here, lift up that foot," he instructed Jimmy. Jimmy obliged, Dave checked the pot again, but it was still tight as . . . well, really tight. Jimmy plonked his foot down and rested most of his 900 kg on it. We all looked at the pot gloomily. Dave picked up the fencing pliers and went at it again.

"I'm making some progress," Dave finally announced. Jimmy turned to look as if to say, "Hey, I'm enjoying that shoe!" I hung on to his halter, snapping pictures with my other hand. My town clothes were liberally covered with drool and horsehair, and Dave's . . . well, it was obvious he was going to show up at his meeting looking like he just came from a West Chilcotin backwoods. (Oh, right, he did!)

At last, Dave had made enough cuts that he could rip the metal. One last foot lift and off came the mangled pot. Dave held it up triumphantly. You could see the imprint of Jimmy's shod hind foot quite clearly.

We hastily offloaded the crate of chard plants and got ready to leave. Jimmy started eating grass again, probably wondering what the fuss had been about.

Mort walked us to the truck, holding the destroyed pot. As we pulled out of the driveway we heard him say plaintively, "But I *liked* that pot!"

Rescuing Fred's Snowmachine

Out in the bush, stories of friends, like stories of horses, are often about rescue. Usually, they come on the heels of a spirit of adventure supported by a feeling of technological superiority —a bad mix. Take snowmachines. Snowmachines are truly ingenious inventions. Trail sleds nowadays are lightweight, can tow up to 450 kilograms and take two or three passengers, all with ease of handling and good suspension. Fred's snowmachine was a, well, a little bit of an older model, but it was still a good machine, I assure you. He had used it all winter to yard logs for a cabin he was building, putting some very hard hours on the sled's drive train. Then it was late March.

Sometimes the snow conditions up on the plateau behind us were so perfect that they were begging to be used. It wasn't the deep powder sought by the downhill fanatic, or the drifted snow needed for igloos. It was crusty and soft *all at the same time*. For a few days it had been quite warm, even raining a bit. Then the temperature had dropped, followed by several centimetres of new snow. This gave a hard surface, with a nice cushion on top, which would support a snowmobile with ease and give a great ride.

The day was perfect, clear blue and sparkling, so Fred, Monika, and her son Philipp, visiting from Germany, decided to go up to the rimrock and then cross-country to Hotnarko Falls for a picnic.

Unfortunately, Fred's snowmachine had other ideas. As they were breaking out of the timber up on the rimrock, getting ready for a glorious run in the open, his machine stopped dead. The engine ran fine, but the track sat there as solidly as if they were encased in cement.

A short inspection revealed a broken drive shaft. Sand, from using the machine for logging in the mud, had worn the bearings so badly that they finally seized. This was a major breakdown, not something to be handled in a meter of snow, no matter how forgiving the crust. The expedition to the falls became instead a weary trudge back home on the trail, five kilometres of tough walking, leaving the machine sitting stubbornly where it had seized up.

Over the next couple of days of steady conferencing and enthusiastic sharing of wisdom, a rescue plan emerged. We would wait for a frosty morning and then take Lee's big trail machine, complete with its banana-shaped metal skimmer, and two other machines for backup, and haul the broken sled back to the shop. In other words, a well-thought-out military operation.

We got a fairly early (for us) start, over at the shop, where friend Barry was welding the tow bar on the old skimmer so it would be strong enough to pull Fred's 200 kg machine. Once that was welded and hooked up, we loaded a chain saw, a pick and a shovel, a digging bar, straps, ropes and whatever else we figured we would need to get the job done. The digging bar and the shovel were to make a path around a large boulder that had slid down and blocked the trail on the side hill. The saw was to cut out the fir tree that had collapsed across the trail further up, which would make passage with a towed snowmachine very awkward. The ropes and tie downs were to keep Fred's machine on the skimmer. Perfect.

We arrived at the scene and heaved Fred's sled over on its side, positioned the skimmer next to its track, then rolled the snowmobile over into the skimmer. So far so good. Once the sled was tied down and set on the trail bed, things would go smoothly.

On the side hill, the new path we put in worked well, too, although it *was* tough going over the mud and clay. We had to unhook the skimmer with the snowmachine on it, because although Lee's machine was meant for towing, the bit of friction caused by the aluminum skimmer bottom on the muck proved to be too much and things came to a standstill. Even then, we had to push on the handlebars, me on one side, Lee on the other, to get his sled over the bare patch.

It turned out that wasn't so bad, because after that the *real* grunt work began. We tied a sturdy rope into a big loop on the skimmer's tow bar and pulled. Nothing moved. Finally, it took the four of us, all yoked together, giving everything we had, to pull the loaded skimmer over the so-called trail we had built across the mudslide.

Finally we were down the hill and into the yard and then the tractor was put into service. We wrapped a logging chain around the snowmachine, hooked the chain to the bucket on the front end of the tractor and raised it until it swung freely in the air, all according to plan at last. Gently, trying not to jerk too much (the tractor is an old Universal, a Russian-made relic with a bad clutch), the tractor crept toward the shop. As it went, we pushed and shoved the snowmachine to keep it at the proper angle while Lee lowered the bucket to set the sled's track on the ground at the entrance to the work area. From there, it was another tug of war as we pulled the damaged sled into the repair area. *It* had a wooden floor. We could work at last.

That afternoon, after a much-needed lunch break, we took things apart. Replacing the broken shaft was a serious repair, yet doable even with the tools we had at hand. Getting the track off was a very tricky business, though, as the springs that guide it are under a lot of tension. We had to unbolt it very carefully and pay real attention as the mechanism dropped free.

Once we figured out what parts to order and how to install a new drive shaft, we phoned the order in to the dealer in Williams Lake. He called back the next day to say that the parts were on backorder and that it would take about a month to get them—par for the course around here, living as we did at the end of the end of the supply chain.

Fred switched projects and started to work on his new greenhouse, getting ready for spring. All he needed for that was a hammer and nails, things not too likely to break down. The rest of us had gone about our various winter tasks, philosophical about the enforced delay.

Rescuing Merritt's Cat

The Tote Road wasn't part of the highways system, so keeping it passable was the responsibility of Precipice residents. After much clever negotiation by our neighbour Lee, the government agreed to provide a small amount of money for "in kind" contributions, for doing basic work—like putting in culverts or repairing washouts. We were always trying to maximize the return for this amount. One of the ways to do this was to rent equipment and do the work ourselves. That is why this particular machine was in the valley. It belonged to Merritt Sager, who ran a ranch up on the plateau, outside of Anahim.

And so, one day in early spring turned into another adventure with our neighbours, this time rescuing the D6 Cat Merritt had rented to us for a very low rate in order to improve the road. Lee would operate it and Rosemary and I would pay for the fuel, and then I would pay Lee back for his part with feeding time in the winter. That way, we got the job done for about half what it would cost to go ahead and hire somebody to come in and do it. I even did the layout, the grades and elevations, and ran the ribbon. It was quite a learning curve, all before the cat blade touched the ground. For the new road, that is. Rancher Lee was so excited at the chance to run this new Cat with its power-shift clutchless drive, decelerator system and mega horsepower that he just had to put on the brush blade and go clear some more land.

The old-timers who did the original clearing for Lee's fields stopped at the banks of a previous watercourse, piled the windrows along its edge and created a barrier that limits the size of the meadow. Never shy of hard work, these men worked with horses, axes and brawn. They were very good at reading the land, knowing where the best ground was, interpreting the subtle signs and messages that indicated good pasture and good soil. Lee was about to learn why they stopped where they did on the north side of that particular meadow.

At first the clearing attempt went well. Those pesky alders, willows and cottonwoods snapped and died as they were thrown under the shiny steel plates of the 15-foot-long treads. Then the bottom dropped out. Literally. Once upon a time, industrious beavers had built a dam on that ancient stream. The pond was gone, but the mud bowl created behind the dam was still there. It was hidden by a layer of some sod and trees, but the pool of "loonshit" was still there, a deep depression filled with pudding-like black ooze—lying there, waiting, a primeval, mindless, protean creation. The perfect trap for an arrogant D6 and its human handler.

The call to me for help came late in the day. I had just time enough before dark to go over to the north side of the field, peek behind the windrow and see the hamstrung D6, sunk over the track up to the cab floor on one side, listing at 45 degrees, stuck fast in the maw behind the old beaver dam. In the dusk, the equipment-yellow paint on the superstructure contrasted sharply with the soft greens and pale whites of the new aspens.

When I got there, Lee fired up the monster and spun the tracks a few times. If there was a hood on the D6, we would have raised it, stood around, poked and prodded, then agreed, "Yeah, she sure is stuck, all right." Male wisdom of the ages. But with no hood, there was nothing to do but raid the root cellar, drink cold homemade beer, and hope that maybe the elves would come in the night and lift the Cat out onto dry ground.

A couple of late-night calls to other keepers of the male wisdom of the ages, and a plan was formed. Bright and early at 9 a.m. the next morn (well, it was a rather late night) we set off to rescue the D6: 20 tons of steel and rubber hoses full of hydraulic fluid slumped over in a stinking muck hole several metres in diameter and who knows how deep.

Overcast and muggy. Black fly heaven. Bug dope, ransacked brains, strong backs and desperation drove this operation.

The Cat had a grapple on the back, mounted on a large, curved arm. Operating much like the pincers of a lobster claw, it was usually used to pick up bunches of logs and skid them to the landing for pickup. Plan A was to get the grapple high enough out of the muck to put a log in the pincers and use this to raise the back end of the Cat so we could put logs under the track to get some footing.

Trouble was, the claw was deep in the muck and there was no way to raise it high enough. So we made a platform out of logs, shoved it under the arm behind the grapple's attachment pin, lowered the grapple arm into the muck, sank the platform, raised the arm, built another platform, lowered the arm, buried the platform, raised the arm, built another platform, lowered the arm, raised the arm, lowered the arm . . .

Eventually the platforms stopped sinking and the back of the cat started to be lifted when we lowered the arm. A third of a metre. Digging down into the muck, we created a space under the lower tread. Into this space went 15-centimetre-thick logs, and then . . . lower the arm, let the weight of the Cat sink the logs, raise the arm, new logs, lower the arm, sink the logs, raise the arm, lower the arm, raise, lower, raise, lower . . ..

After three endless hours, the grapple was exposed enough that we could put several logs in the claw and then build a platform under the claw for the logs to push against, lower, raise, lower, raise. Hot, mud-covered, stinking ooze, bug swarms, sweat running in rivers, this was a Precipice jungle. Finally a lift that exposed the whole undercarriage. A half a metre more, and we'd have enough space to build a bed to drive on.

That's when the grapple lost its balance point and collapsed sideways, throwing the Cat off the logs and back into the muck. Nothing to do but go back at it: raise, lower, raise, lower, raise lower, raise . . ..

Cutting aspens and alders to provide the blocking for the platforms, I kept thinking of the destruction we were creating. Noticing the black bear claw marks on the greenish white bark of the aspens. Thinking of the bear cubs sent up these trees for protection by their mothers. Thinking of the tender spring buds the bears climbed these trees to eat. Thinking of the death of these trees and how long it would be before they knew they were dead. Was it when the chain saw bit into the flesh of the trunk, spewing white chips onto the black soil? Was it during the next few months, as the tree dried up, slowly starving for water and nutrients? Was it when all of its body had been eaten by ants, other insects and bacteria that the tree was truly dead?

The image of the translucent green leaves falling in a slow arc, backlit by a brilliant blue sky, the first moment of death, remained in my mind. I was not pleased to participate in this, the rancher's adventure, yet there I was, helping my neighbour and myself, for I too would kill trees to build the new access we had planned. No saints there that morning.

Six hours later, finally, the job was done. Then the moment of truth. Lee hooked up the winch on his little 1950s D4 to the back of the big D6.

He quickly taught me the rudiments of the power shift decelerator system: push the levers, rev up the huge diesel engine, make eye contact, thumbs up and "give 'er."

Shudder, roar, and the monster began to move. Then, as quickly as it had gone in, the machine was out on high ground—having climbed out of that hole on the bodies of those aspens and alders.

Then came the adrenalin rush, a high-five, smugly approving our innate male wisdom. The D6 was now free to continue its career of helping the agriculturists dominate the land.

I wondered how many more beaver traps were out there. I suspected there are many more to come, many that we can't even imagine. And I'm not sure if we remembered, when we returned Merritt's pride and joy, to tell him of the mud bath we had given it.

WWOOFERS and other Volunteers

Around 2002, with Google and access to many websites thanks to our satellite system, we discovered WWOOFERS. That acronym stands for "Willing Workers on Organic Farms." Volunteers would sign up and post their particulars, while the would-be hosts did the same. The expectation was that wwoofers would travel to the place of their choosing, usually in a different country, and work half time in exchange for meals and accommodation and the cultural experience. Many also hoped to improve their English.

Reading through the offerings, we realized that the term "farm" was flexible. We would certainly qualify, with our large garden, endless handyman work, and wilderness location. Through carefully worded emails, I became adept at selecting people who would fit in to our little Precipice community. This was not an easy task, as few of the volunteers had ever been exposed to a situation where there were no stores, no junk food, no easy access, and they would be surrounded by endless wilderness full of potentially scary wild creatures. We learned that it was far better to have a couple, or two wwoofers at once, so that after we had shown them the lay of the land, they could be comfortable doing things on their own.

Dave and I are both very private people and cringed at the idea of sharing our home with strangers, especially in the morning. So we came up with the idea of housing them at the Glad Cab and providing food for breakfasts down there, then sharing lunches and dinners with them up at Firhome. The volunteers all thought it was wonderful to be living in their very own log cabin!

Wwoofers Gerben and Meijke with their catch

We taught them how to use our ATV and showed them the lakes on either side of our valley, where we kept our canoe and a couple of rowboats. They had the experience of canoeing and fishing; Dave showed them how to follow trails and fall trees, while I taught the interested ones how to bake bread, make pizza, preserve food, and grow your own food. In response, they eagerly helped us get firewood, maintain the gardens, build fences and rock walls. It was a few years before we realized how exotic our lifestyle was to these predominantly urban people. We also signed up on other similar websites such as HelpX and Workaway, and soon had more applicants than we could handle. Our two neighbours thought this was a great idea also, so that often we had four or five volunteers in the valley at the same time, from different countries around the world.

As a result, the social activities in the valley increased, and over the years we met many wonderful people. They were all ages; some just out of school, looking for life experiences before they moved on to jobs or university, and others who simply wanted a sabbatical from their demanding jobs, be it a banker, medical doctor, or accountant. Some were retired but still eager for new experiences. Once we had two fellows from Belgium who hadn't met before. One spoke only French and the other only Flemish, so they had to converse in English! They got along famously. Another time, a bridge builder from Australia came to us at the same time as a blacksmith from Scotland, both with such strong regional accents we had trouble understanding them, but they also worked together happily. We called them, privately, Mutt and Jeff, since the blacksmith was a towering six-foot-four, while the bridge builder was nearly a foot shorter.

One of our more interesting finds was a family. We were a bit dubious when we first read their application, as they had two very young children with them, but we liked what they wrote and decided to take a chance. They were from Scotland also; Tom is a solicitor (and plays a great fiddle!) and Becs, a skilled artist, worked with a wildlife foundation. They decided to give their kids, aged four and six, a world experience before they became too enmeshed in their schooling and set off for a year, travelling around the States and Canada. Later, I laughed to think that I had been worried I might end up as a babysitter, as the kids were remarkably mature and independent, a joy to have around.

That was the year of the great floods on the Atnarko River, in the Bella Coola Valley. With their usual summer fare of berries and fish no longer available, many grizzlies came back up to the Precipice, where they knew would find good feed as they had spent early spring there. The two children, Kai and Freya, were fascinated by the bears. *Too* fascinated, and Tom and Becs decided they should leave the valley until the bear population thinned out a bit. We gave them our old, somewhat-camperized van, and off they went, to drive into Tweedsmuir Park and hike up in the Rainbow Mountains. They came back after that adventure to spend another few delightful weeks with us.

We'll never forget all the enthusiastic volunteer workers who graced us with their presence over the years. As much as they may have learned from us, we learned equally from them—an international experience without leaving our home.

Pets and Vets

There were no veterinarians west of Williams Lake. We were very fortunate in having Williams Lake–based veterinarian Carolyn Walsh, who provided a much-needed service for the Chilcotin Plateau and the Bella Coola Valley via a mobile clinic organized in the back of her truck. She would set this up in various locations along Highway 20.

In years gone by, we would have to go all the way to Williams Lake. From our valley, our trip was easily five hours each way if the Tote Road and highway conditions were good, and so had to include an overnight stay in town. When we had heard through the grapevine that the new vet was passing through that week, we made several phone calls, found the person who organized the visits for her, and finally tracked her down at the community hall in Hagensborg, a little village in the Bella Coola Valley.

She had a full schedule for the rest of the week, but agreed to meet us at Mort's place in Anahim Lake that evening before she went back east to

Tatla Lake (nearly halfway to Williams Lake), where she was booked for a big animal clinic the next day. No problem. This was another routine planning issue, like getting in supplies or firewood, or making sure you have all the parts needed to keep the various machines running smoothly year-round. We discussed the logistics of coordinating both our travel times. Caroline said she would phone us in the Precipice when she left Hagensborg. Because it would take us the same length of time to drive to Anahim Lake as it would take her to drive up the Hill, if we all left Precipice at the same time, in theory all of us would arrive at our friend Mort's house in Anahim Lake approximately two hours later.

Chilko and Kosmo

We wanted to make Caroline's stopover worthwhile, as it meant she'd have a very long day, so we also took Klaus and his Kommondor Kosmo, who was 11 months old by then, so the 100-pound puppy could

THE POWER OF DREAMS

get his second rabies shot. On top of that, Mort had three dogs: a black and white female pit bull and two brown-and-white streaked miniature Shiatsu cross-somethings that were smaller than his two cats. One of the little somethings needed minor attention, as did Louise, Mort's aging marmalade cat, so Carolyn and her assistant Carey would have lots to do.

So there we were at Mort's, with Caroline using his kitchen table as an examination bench. The wood heater was glowing, cats complaining about the dogs, dogs sniffing and whining. But Caroline and her assistant managed it all with a cheerfulness and grace that calmed owners and pets alike. It was really quite a scene, with five excited dogs milling around while Louise and a smoke-grey Persian named Elvis presided, perched on the back of a big old black leather chair.

Soon, the tests were done, the samples taken, the shots administered, the ointments applied and advice given. The team packed up the mobile clinic, loaded it into a big mud-splattered 4x4, and headed off east along the highway to Tatla Lake, while we drove south into an outer space reality.

It was a socked-in West Chilcotin November night. As we entered the snow-covered, tree-lined passage that is the second stretch of the Tote Road, ice crystals did a twinkly dance in the headlights. It was an ethereal trip, gliding through the darkness in this winding tunnel, our vehicle becoming a spaceship exploring an alien ice world on the fringes of the Milky Way. We couldn't help but compare it to our lives before the Chilcotin, times when our animals had to go to the vet and we would fight heavy traffic with an unhappy cat yowling at us over the blare of car horns, or holding a sick dog that we were so anxious about. Instead, we were on the Tote Road, having this special moment that reminded us how lucky we were.

ON THE PLATE

Dave cooking a freshly caught trout

Applesauce

The original ad for our property in the Precipice promised an "orchard." This turned out to be half a dozen sticks in a partially cleared area across the river. The explanation was that the horses and moose had chewed them down and that they would recover, but even though I started protecting them from the critters, they stayed dead.

Once we got a bit organized, we bought two three-year-old apple trees and a couple of hardy plums and planted them around the cabin. This foray into orcharding went not much better than David Gladden's had. One by one, the trees died, either from a harsh winter or from being girdled by rodents.

Soon Rosemary planted two more apple trees up at the new house site and yet another two at the cabin. When we moved out of the Glad Cab up to the house on the ridge, it didn't take long for the bears to discover our absence and raid the oldest tree, the first one we planted down at the cabin. After we propped up broken branches a few times, we started to worry about the main trunk. Plus, we were really unwilling to share our apples. My solution was old-school: I surrounded the tree with an electric fence run from a regular car battery.

The black bears didn't like being stung—maybe bad memories of raiding bee combs—and learned to stay away, but the grizzlies were more stubborn. One crisp fall day, Rosemary and I discovered that three of the four wires were broken through and trailing away from the tree. I'd love to have seen that grizzly as he frantically tried to escape the persistent shocks he was receiving as he tried to untangle himself! Still, the fence had done its job—the tree lived on. Our smaller tree there had just started to have blossoms, so, success within reach, we circled it with another electric fence, because as much technology as that took, it's the little things that matter.

But the frustrations continued. Every few years, we'd lose a pollinator up top *and* the one at the cabin. We had figured out that as the crow—or the bee—flies, it was too far between the two sites for any kind of cross-pollination, but our attempts to rectify the problem never succeeded, except once. That year, both the lone cabin tree and the lone house tree were covered in beautiful blossoms, but neither had a pollinator tree. Rosemary played matchmaker by carrying branches back and forth between them and placing them in buckets of water under the trees, hoping to keep the bees and apples happy. The results were mixed. We had one tree full of apples, but most weren't suitable for storage.

Rosemary salvaged a bushel of apples from that tree, the old, long-suffering tree down at the cabin. After using the best apples, we were left with a motley, brown-spotted, misshapen bunch of fruit that looked like the worst grounders you have ever seen.

But waste not, want not. We skinned them, then sliced the pulp into sections and made applesauce. In the first applesauce years, I took one look at the big pile of little apples and my first thought was that this was too much work for so little return. It would be easiest to compost them and buy some applesauce from the store in Williams Lake and be done with it, but you couldn't buy this kind of apple sauce. For one thing, it was more than just organic. It was frozen in freezers powered by solar panels. The packaging was recycled. There was no CO_2 production in its making, transport or storage. Its only carbon footprint was that the tree which grew the apples was sequestering carbon as part of its life process.

The chore of peeling this forlorn bunch of apples soon became an enjoyable task: one of my annual rituals that made the world turn round. Simple. We just picked the tree clean, peeled and cored the apples, and made the sauce. It had that definite sweet sharp taste that can only come from fresh apples picked on a cool September afternoon, and that made all our work worthwhile.

Hunting

In our early years the shoestring we lived on was very short indeed, and to supplement our diet I hunted both deer and moose in Precipice. Aside from putting food on the table, this was a wonderful time of exploring the secret hills and valleys below the rimrock.

To the north of Firhome is a 300-metre-tall escarpment. Its top 15 meters consist of a vertical cliff of pentagonal, rusty black basalt columns. On the slopes below the cliffs is a band of old-growth Douglas fir. Many of these trees are a meter at the butt and hundreds of years old. They are magnificent, with reddish-black bark, gnarled and wrinkled with centuries of fire, wind and sun. You can slip your entire hand into the curls and folds of the ancient, six-inch-thick skin.

It also was excellent mule deer winter range. In the late fall, starting in November and running into early January, they came down from the high country and hung out in these forests. I usually spent four or five days in the trees amongst them.

The first few days, I was not strictly hunting. Even if I got a chance to shoot on the first day, I never did. Over the years I'd gotten to know the slopes fairly well, and I'd learned what was in the next dip, what ravines the deer liked to be in depending on wind, sun, snow cover, temperature, recent activity, weather patterns and so on. Basically, I hunted the ridges and either shot across to the next one or down into the ravine. I didn't like uphill shots too much. They really were tricky, especially over a hundred yards.

In those first few days, I just liked to see who was who, what groups of bucks were hanging out together, where the does were, which I wouldn't shoot in case they were pregnant, and what groups were still formed. Sometimes there were still a few big bucks in with the does, but usually the bucks were grouping up to spend the winter together, and the does the same. (While all mule deer occupy the same range, they separate like this into same-sex bunches.) Once I'd figured out where they were and what they were up to on any given year, I decided which one I wanted, selected the place, and then really got to the hunt.

On actual hunt days, the psychology changed. I can't really describe it, except to say that my level of awareness and concentration went way up the scale. I moved very slowly, perhaps a few meters an hour, sensitive to wind, noise and especially the scents. I smelled the trees, the bushes, the sun on snow, and, when I caught it, the unmistakable smell of the buck. That is when the tingles would run up the back of my neck, the emotion and adrenalin would rush in, and another being would take over—especially if I smelled him before seeing him.

I tunnelled in and became a non-thinking creature, using all my senses: hearing, smelling, tasting the scents, using the legs and the mind to do one thing: be stealthy and get close; stay on the right side of the wind, creep forward while the head was down feeding, freeze an instant before the head came up, make no noise, always have a tree or a boulder beside me or be in the fork of a clump, something that didn't outline my profile and covered my image. Slowly, slowly, slowly, maybe an hour to cover that last 45 metres to the spot I'd chosen to shoot from.

When I got there, my pulse really picked up. I carefully rested the rifle, got braced, and sighted through the scope. The absolutely elemental, primeval feeling at this point was like no other. All consciousness was concentrated on this one moment. I re-checked the wind. I looked for stray twigs and bushes that could deflect the bullet. Then, all thinking ceased. I took a deep breath, slowly let it out and . . . the next thing I knew, the animal was down, shot through the head, one quick, clean kill. I didn't really hear the shot; it was a felt thing. The actual moment of shooting, that last concentration as the trigger was squeezed, all that was lost to conscious memory and volition. That moment was eternal, housed in the being of human, in the ancient mists of time and survival.

Then I awoke. Was it as good a kill shot as I had hoped? No sign of movement. I approached, rifle ready for that second shot if necessary. It was then that I realized what I had done. The killing, the elemental nature of it all. It was then that I returned to full consciousness on this level. It was an experience that only those who go through it can describe. A connection to all that we are, have been and could be.

But also, it was often at this point in the hunt that the "oh, damn" reaction would occur. Damn, I had been so into the hunt that I hadn't realized I was *that* far up this hill and *that* far from the trail and the ATV or snowmachine. Oh well, out with the knife and here we go. On good years, it was all downhill.

I could go on and on about the drawing and quartering, the way it feels to take the snow and cleanse the heart . . . but that isn't something to dwell on. I'm not arguing for hunting as a sport, and I'm certainly not defending the beer-drinking road hunters, or the dog-using simple killers out there, but it is true that all animals must die. Seeing (and hearing), as we have, an animal hamstrung by a wild predator and gutted alive is not pretty. Finding an old, toothless moose dying in a swamp isn't, either. When I put a bullet through an animal's head after being with it in its home, it is a thing that I wish could be done for me when the time comes, with respect: fast, clean, and painless. What more is there?

So yes, we are predators. Whether we bond in the sense that we hunt together, or in the sense that the lone hunter can return from the hunt, tell his story and know that others understand, is a needless dissection of the issue. For me, hunting is a shared human experience through time and space, and that is what wilderness is for. It is us.

We hunted only the first few years of our time in the Precipice. As soon as we could afford to, we bought our meat from local ranchers up on the Chilcotin Plateau. I missed the days preceding the shoot, that amazing heightening of senses, but not the rest of it.

Catching a Rainbow

A lake above the Precipice Valley was known locally as Johnny's Lake or Precipice Lake, but Rosemary and I liked the name our friend Nancy gave it: Sweet Wind Lake, after the hot, scented winds of August that slid across its rippled surface. This small jewel was a 15-minute ATV ride from Firhome, followed by a 15-minute walk through the trees. We thought of it as our private lake on the northern edge of the estate.

Although a plane could land on it, the lake was too small for take-off. So even though 1- to 1½-kilogram rainbows were not uncommon, the lake remained a secret to even the most avid fishermen.

Dave with Rainbow, and Chilko watching for more

It had great rocks for sunning and small cliffs for swimming, the Little Rainbows for a mountain backdrop. We left our 17-foot Grumman aluminum

THE POWER OF DREAMS

canoe there year-round for accessing the other side and the swimming rocks, and, of course, for fishing.

The fishing was good. This day, on a whim, I was using a damsel fly, an insect that usually hatches in May or early June, but the trout didn't seem to notice or care that the fly was out of season. The instant my fly hit the surface, there was an explosion of water, sending my line whining away into the deeps. That image of the white fly floating gently toward the smooth black surface, so gentle, so calm, fluttering peacefully through space that was violently transformed into a seething, roiling surge of primal energy will stay in my mind a long time. As I played a fish, slowly bringing it closer to the boat, I caught a glimpse through the peaty water of its sleek body, shimmering brassily in the midday sun.

Once into the net and in the boat, the pale yellow fish became a silver dart, flashing its rainbow red and pink colours much more vividly than I had seen them in the water. I thought about many things as I took the hilt of my knife and clubbed that superbly-adapted creature to death and yet, as I felt its teeth on my fingers, their sharp points raking my palm, I thought about how this fish had been trying to eat the fly, and how it would kill a smaller fish without hesitation for a meal. No quarter would be given by this arch predator in the lake.

So, I thought, now it is your turn. The predator becomes the prey. Rainbow trout are killing machines. It is what they do.

Rosemary and Chlko were with me that day. We beached the canoe, pulled it up on the pebble shore, and after a few minutes foraging among the trees brought an armful of dry twigs and branches to the beach. Setting two flat rocks on their sides, I build a fire between them, laid an old oven rack that we kept in the trees for this purpose across the top, and once the fire had burned down to a bed of coals laid the rainbow down, wrapped in tin foil with the butter, French sorrel and lemon slices that Rosemary brought. Carefully tending the fire and keeping the coals fueled just right, I soon had a meal fit for a king! And of course, my queen.

Like the rainbow, as it swims satisfied through the weed beds after a tasty meal of minnows and the odd dragonfly nymph, I had no remorse, no feelings of guilt, just the wonderful tastes on my tongue and the boundless enjoyment of eating this fish on a spectacular afternoon, sitting on the shore of a wilderness lake.

And this pleasure recurred. During the following winter, when we had some smoked trout as a snack during a day on the trail, I would think again about that day and the big one I had caught on a damsel fly on a perfect sun-filled September day, on a lake where we were alone in the world and living deep in time.

My Perfect Birthday

We often were asked, "What do you do in there, don't you get bored?" Or, "It must be nice to have all that free time." This is probably the biggest misconception that people have about remote living. They think you have all the time in the world, that you are living a laidback life. Nothing could be further from the truth—even with the modern conveniences we had worked into our lifestyle, we were constantly busy. As this incident shows, not even your birthday is sacred.

It was February, and I was expecting the usual birthday pampering. After a leisurely breakfast, my most energetic activity would be to select a perfect book and lounge in the sun on the couch until a perfect lunch, with maybe a glass of wine, then a snooze in the sun for the afternoon. I knew Rosemary would have bought something special on our last shopping trip nearly four months before, so I was looking forward to a surprise birthday dinner followed by the most sinful chocolate cake imaginable.

That's when I made the mistake. I decided to take advantage of all the solar power coming in on this perfect sunny day, so I ambled downstairs and threw the switch that activates the water pump in our well, located at the bottom of the steep slope in front of the house. It usually took about two minutes for the water to be pushed up the 80 metres of pipe so it could fill the inside cistern which was our holding tank for the house system.

I waited two minutes, two and a half, then three, but there still was no water coming in. "Uh-oh," I thought, "This not a good thing."

I shut things down, restarted the pump and took careful note. Pump drawing full power, but still no water. Two possibilities arose in my mind, neither of which fit into my birthday plans. It might be a broken pipe on the hillside, or worse, something wrong in the well, such as a pump bearing gone, or the line and the pump disconnected, leaving the pump lying uselessly on the well bottom.

Nothing for it but to get dressed in wool pants, coveralls, felt packs and all the cover-up clothing needed for a cold morning. Turn on the pump. Slither, slide down the steep hillside over frozen ice and a metre of snow, looking for a leak. Bad news. No visible leaks. Back up the hillside. Turn off the pump.

It was at times like these that I started to wonder what I was doing here. Why didn't I live in a warm tropical climate, a place where water lines did not freeze and the ground was covered in sand and palm leaves, not a metre of snow?

As I poured a coffee, my mind's eye wandered off to Costa Rica's eternally warm climes, but no matter how hard I concentrated on tropical images, the water line was still frozen and I had to do something about that. So, I finished my coffee, slid my boots back on, and got dressed for the next operation. I had to go down to the well site and check things out.

I knew this was not going to be a one-trip fix, so I took the cover off the snowmachine, got it started and headed down the driveway, across the hayfield, through the cottonwood grove and back over to the base of the ridge directly below our house, where the well lay 30 metres from the river, cool, clear and snug in its sandy gravel home.

The system was a drain-back operation, which means that the line emptied every time the pump was shut off. That way, the water pipe could sit on top of the ground, not needing to be buried. Besides, burying a water line down a 60-degree slope full of fir trees, boulders and clay was not a viable option.

There were three splices in the ¾-inch conduit about fifteen metres from the well, where a big black bear had chewed a few holes in it five years before. These gave me a convenient test point. By disconnecting the line there, I would be able to determine if the water was at least getting that far.

The switch to operate the pump was up in the house, properly located in the breaker panel. This made it difficult to reach when standing down at the well. The solution was to take a whistle with me, like the ones hockey referees use to call penalties, part of our emergency gear for trips to the mountains. After a little digging in the summer closet, the whistle emerged, was tested in the house (much to the disgust of the cats) and back down the hill I went.

After disconnecting the line, I blew one long, hard blast on the whistle. This was the signal for Rosemary, who was waiting outside on the top of the ridge, to run into the house and throw the breaker to start the pump. Instantly, I heard the pump in the well humming, but still no water spurted from the line. Two long blasts on the whistle and the pump stopped.

Back up the hill. Time for another coffee. This time the beaches were full of sun, surf and string bikinis. This still didn't fix the pump, so I hooked the skimmer to the back of the snowmachine, loaded on a six-foot digging bar, a shovel, a pickaxe and extra mitts, and headed back to the well. The snow on top of the well was very crusty and frozen in layers. Digging into it was like carving chunks of Styrofoam. I cleared a circle the size of the well top, about one metre in diameter. November's torrential rains had left a layer of ice on top of the frozen ground. Now, laid bare by the shovel, it glistened in the noonday sun.

The digging bar was an old drive shaft from a 1940s flat-deck truck. Weighing about 14 kilograms, it was sharpened to a point on one end and flattened like a chisel on the other. I'd had it for years—old faithful. Crunch, clang, squeak, the pointed end bit into the ice. Then I began to dislodge the rocks. Even as I grumbled, I admired the thorough job I had done when I had covered the top of the well with rock and soil to keep it insulated. This well-done job was in response to the time the well had frozen because of inadequate cover and I had to heat it with a tiger torch for two days, but that is another story.

I gradually uncovered the pressure-treated plywood that covered the access hatch on the top of the well. Chilko really wanted to throw his 50 kilograms into this project to help me, so he was right in there, digging and snuffling away. Finally, I prised the cover off and looked down into the dark recesses of the cement casing. So did Chilko. I kept a close eye on him, because if he ever slipped into the narrow well, I'd never get him out before he drowned. With him frisking around, I used the pull line and raised the pump to the surface, all the while taking care to coil the ¾-inch line and not kink it. I didn't have any extra pipe. If this one got broken, that would be it for the well until spring, and we'd had enough of hauling water during the years we lived in our log cabin.

After disconnecting the pipe from the pump, I laid the wiring aside, covered the hole with the plywood and examined the pump. I found a blockage in the pipe below the elbow that entered the well casing. Frozen. This had never happened before. So nice to have a new twist on things.

On the way back up the hill, Chilko stopped dead in front of the snowmachine to investigate some intriguing scent, so in order to stop from running him over, I stopped too. Right under a big fir tree that had nothing but ice under it. It is one thing to maintain momentum while in motion, but stopped, the machine slid backwards, right over the section of pipe I was dragging up the hill for thawing in the house.

The language I addressed Chilko with was not very polite. Fortunately, the pipe wasn't damaged by the incident, and I was able to hang it over the heater to thaw the ice plug and clear the line.

All that water reminded me of the outside showers by the beach at Uvita in Costa Rica, gaily painted in greens and blues, depicting the blue whales for which the park was named. It was for visitors to wash off the salt water after a swim. This sandy expanse of the beach was over two kilometres long, flat as a billiard table, and on that day we were the only ones there.

Back to *this* reality. Dog in house. Pipe thawed. New hose clamps, screwdriver, butane torch to seal the clamps, new insulation to go on the pipe section. Finally I was ready to fix things!

Dave's perfect birthday meal

I piled onto the snowmobile and headed down the hill again, consoling myself with thoughts of Rosemary slaving over my perfect birthday dinner, in between running up and down stairs and out on the ridge to listen for the whistle so she could attend to the pump switch.

THE POWER OF DREAMS

I hooked things up, blew the whistle, and the pump hummed and the water flowed, right up to the house the way it was supposed to.

As I was filling in the hole to re-cover the well head, I looked at the sand, which made me think of beaches . . . this sand had been deposited by the Hotnarko River over many centuries as it flowed in various channels on the valley floor. Who knows? In another incarnation this very sand might have been cleaned on a tropical shore, where it sparkled in the midday sun.

By the time I went back up the driveway, put the tools and the snowmachine away, shed my outer layer of winter clothes and resumed my position on the couch, it was well into the afternoon and my favourite patch of sun had moved on. But there was still the wine, a perfect dinner and a wicked chocolate birthday cake to look forward to. Rosemary had performed magic. Cooking without running water between shivering forays to the ridge, she had created a birthday meal fit for paradise.

Of Mice, Packrats and Men

Some Octobers, if the frost arrived before the rains, autumn in the Chilcotin was spectacular. The leaves along Highway 20 would turn a brilliant yellow, backlit by the morning sun, exploding into one's eyes like mercury lights in a stage production.

Alas, all was not beauty and warm sensuality when the harbingers of the changing seasons came calling, though. When you live so close to wild nature, you are under constant siege. Mice, voles, squirrels, woodchucks, bats, and birds all see your cave as the best one around, so as winter approaches they naturally want to move in.

Of all those, it is the pack rat that is the most troublesome. Pack rats are related to the Norway rat, but they are much more handsome. With rounder faces, bushy, flat-ended tails and furry brown-gray coats, they have an endearing look, especially when they sit up onto their haunches to look you over. From the first frosty night in mid-August until winter lock-up, all cabins, homes, sheds, barns and vacant buildings are vulnerable to these squatters. Maybe it was a roof ever-so-humble, or a loft with its nic, fluffy quilts or, even better, a pantry full of great goodies: nuts, seeds, flour, raisins, dates, a cornucopia that never ends. All these would-be denizens had to do was figure out a way to get inside these great winter digs.

Mice are the sneaky ones. They can crawl through the tiniest holes and wriggle into the smallest crevices. But pack rats are not nearly so subtle. They are a straight-ahead bunch. Kick the door in if they can. Noisily bump-thumping all night long, these masters of demolition never give up. They have been known to chew through one-inch fir roofing boards, through 90-pound roll roofing, tunnel straight up through the wall to the upper plate, find a way into the roof, and then chew down into the room below.

Pack rats must have an amazing understanding of spatial dimensions. How else can you explain one now-famous (and long gone) pack rat that chewed into the gable on the west side of the house, went across the roof, up and over the rafters, into the wall on the opposite gable, tunneled down two metres and chewed through the wall until it, voilà, hit the middle of the pantry, at floor level, where all the goodies were sitting below the shelves of inedible canned goods? NASA has nothing on a Precipice pack rat.

It is unfortunate that pack rats are so good-looking, cuddly even, because they are very destructive. They have two scent glands in their hind quarters which exude a molasses-like substance that they use for marking their territories. The greasy, odiferous scent trails they leave behind are unbelievably tenacious. If they are dropped on wood, carpet, mattresses or other fibres, it is nigh impossible to remove the sharp, acrid stench. The smell is very unpleasantly distinctive. It makes your stomach curdle, and once anything has been anointed with this oil, the odour will linger for years.

Aside from this unique perfume, pack rats have an interesting habit. They are very polite, making sure that they trade for everything they take, such as spoons for eyeglasses, or hay for raisins. They are very particular about this.

One decided to relocate into the Glad Cab after we first moved up to Firhome. Because a very heavy snowfall kept us otherwise occupied, we didn't discover it for a month. In that time, the pack rat filled the double enamel sink with all manner of tasty leaves, cones and berries, in exchange for the knives and forks, cleaning supplies and even some small pieces of pottery stolen from the kitchen drawers and cupboards. She then built a nest in the loft, from fibreglass that had been used for chinking between the logs, furnishing it with all her treasures that she dragged up a steep ladder. Then she gave birth to four kittens, and that's when we discovered her. It was a situation that had to be dealt with. A very unpleasant duty indeed.

Later, in spite of our best efforts, a pack rat invaded our large, walk-in pantry in Firhome. Regardless of its politeness in matters of trading, it and its penetrating smells had to go before it destroyed months of supplies.

Trap in hand, a length of string over his shoulder, and peanut butter/raisin bait in his pocket, the Precipice's human resident sets the scene. Pack rats are very inquisitive, but fast and tricky. An ordinary rat trap will not work. There are two kinds of pack rat traps that can be built, though. Some people set the trap in a length of stove pipe. This Precipice human prefers the another way: a large and solid wooden trap. To build this trap, you make a wooden box about eight inches square and two feet long. Cover one end with chicken wire, then take a chain saw and cut a slit along both sides, about 15 inches long. Then you put something shiny, like tin foil, maybe a spoon or two, a dinner knife, whatever, in the far end, up against the chicken wire. Next, take a #3 Connibear trap (Google it), bait it with raisins and peanut butter squeezed into the toe of an old nylon stocking, tied into a bundle and attached to the bait-holding prongs of the trap. Firmly.

Then set the trap—it has a spring so strong that only a strong arm can do this—and slide it into the slots so that it just clears the bottom and the springs have room to collapse when the trigger is sprung. Put the box containing the trap in an area frequented by the packrat, with the chicken-wire end facing the light, so the shiny things are lit. Then tie the chain attached to the trap to a chair leg, table or a big piece of firewood, whatever is handy, because very occasionally the rat may be only partially caught, in which case it can drag the trap away.

The rat really, really wants to get at that shiny stuff, so it can't resist going into the tunnel after it. Then it senses the raisin/peanut butter mix and starts on the nylon-encased package to get at the mixture. The trigger trips and you have caught the pack rat. The Connibear snaps its back or neck instantly. At least, that's how it is supposed to work.

But this particular pack rat, wily and cunning, stole the bait without tripping the trigger, and began its 3 a.m. shopping spree in the pantry. Our bedroom was directly below the pantry, so we were awakened by its clomping around. Rosemary was convinced it was wearing snowshoes. We listened in vain for the snap of a sprung trap. It never came.

The next night, it was time for a different strategy. We decided to bring in a reinforcement known as the best little hunter in the West: Precipice feline Mojo, appropriately dressed in black. This was an extreme solution, since Mojo wasn't very much bigger than a large pack rat. Our larger cat, Obi Wan Kenobe, as befitting his name, felt it was beneath him to engage with lower creatures, so Mojo won by default.

So there I was, at 3 a.m. again, standing at the pantry door with cat in arms, waiting for the rat to resume activities. I heard it arrive by way of its still mysterious route. I quickly slid open the door enough to toss the cat inside, then slid the door closed. All went quiet, then after a few minutes, *scrabble! squeal!* and the rat was caught. Not dead. Caught. As we soon learned, this particular Precipice feline doesn't kill, not right away. So, wearing thick leather gloves complete with arm-protecting gauntlets, I slid open the pantry door and the game of "catch the pack rat before it can run behind the piano" was underway.

Rosemary had blocked a potential escape route, the stairs down, with a large piece of cardboard and stood guard, also rather scantily dressed for the cold house. We must have looked an odd trio: a pack rat being chased, under and over chairs, tables and couches by a black cat and a slow-moving human. Finally, the Precipice feline chased the now-winded pack rat (not to mention the gasping human) behind the piano and waited for me to do something. I managed to drag out one side of the heavy old piano, just enough for Mojo to slide in. He squeezed in and easily caught the pack rat. He slid back out and brought it over to me, like an emissary bearing a gift, full of pride over his large catch.

This time it was resident 1, pack rat 0. When the cat dropped the rat, I quickly swooped up the dazed—but still not dead—animal, took it outside and used a fire brick to crush its skull on the porch railing. Nasty, brutish and short, to quote an infamous judge: the downside of living so close to wild nature.

Did I mention this was done in the nude, in below-freezing temperatures, with the wood heater long out? And for those of you who think the rat should be live-trapped and transported to some other location—where? our neighbour's ranch?—the pack rat can and does travel literally miles to return to its chosen home.

And so it went; the changing seasons shared the world over by mice, pack rats, men and squirrels. Yes, squirrels. Squirrels were a very strong presence in the valley, especially around Firhome. One was always trying to get to the feeder, or burrowing into the roof, or scolding from the limbs of the big fir by the deck, with a shower of fir cone crumbs tumbling from his teeth. One memorable little guy even learned to walk, tightrope style, on the clothesline that supported the big bird feeder. Two legs on the top line, two on the bottom, he crabbed along, finally making the platform. After enjoying his antics for a while, we foiled him by changing to a single wire.

October was the squirrels' busiest time of year. The sun was taking a little longer to climb over the ridge, the mists falling in from the mountains were taking longer to reveal the blue sky above, and the burnt gold leaves on the aspens were beginning to flutter groundward: silent messengers, flagging the slow transition from fall to winter. A light wool vest went on over the shirt, and hard hats would once again be needed to be worn around the workshop.

The swallows were long gone. So were the hummingbirds. The grey jays were back, though, along with the nuthatches and the usual ragtag assortment of chickadees, settling in for the winter. The wood shed was full (better than money in the bank), and soon the last big wind would blow and the deep stillness of winter would set in, the river would go quiet, its voice gagged by frozen layers of ice, and the meadows would be smothered in silent layers of snow. Soon the heater would be on every day, soon the last cottonwood leaf would drop from the highest branch, and soon we would see our breath in the midmorning air.

It all came so fast, some years. It seemed like it had been just the day before that the swallows were swooping and diving in the clear blue vault of the morning sky, that it was just the evening before when we sat out on the back deck listening to the furious frenzy of a dozen rufous hummers competing for the plastic flowers filled with sugar nectar, carefully prepared on the gas stove. All this seemed like a mere second before. Where had the time gone? I suspected there was a time thief at work, a mysterious coalescence of energies that sucks time away into the black hole of memory, into the never-never dreamtime that only exists in the Outback. No matter, as in all things, there was a bittersweet tang in the taste of life, in the taste of transition, and in the inexorable slide into the future.

As for the hard hats? Squirrel was very busy throwing cones from the tops of the pines and firs. He had no particular aim; he simply cut 'em loose and they fell like stones. Bang! Bang! Hitting the red tin roof of the workshop with such force, the small explosions split the still morning air. Unless you made a quick dash to get under the roof, a hardhat was the way to go.

From hardhats to empty nests to returning winter friends, this was the rhythm of autumn, the solid, eternal march of the universal soul binding man and squirrel in the ritual of harvest before winter's dead hand closed the door.

THE POWER OF DREAMS

Toilet Paper Wars

Some of the world wants into your house in spring, too. No matter how tightly your home is built, mosquitos find a way in. Firhome was not as bad for them as the swamps up on the plateau, where I have seen walls of log cabins shimmer as clouds of mosquitos descended upon them, attracted by the warmth of sun-heated wood. Still, we did have an onslaught every June.

Slow, wet springs were the worst. I have been told that some varieties of mosquitos can lay their fertile eggs at high-water mark, where they dry out and wait up to seven years for another high water mark to come. They then happily hatch. A marvel of evolution, these flying blood-suckers can test the patience of any man or woman, especially at 4 a.m. on a June morning.

Several species of mosquito live in Precipice, but in all of them, only the females bite. They need a blood meal to develop and lay eggs. We distinguished between the several varieties in the Precipice by size. The smallest ones were the worst. Only about ¼-inch long, they were tiny, striped, yellow-green tigers on wings. Fresh from some puddle somewhere, they were hungry, fast and nasty. Not content with one bite, they often took two or three if they weren't yet full. They especially liked the early dawn light.

The first sound we'd hear was the high-pitched whine, like an over-revved chain saw about to explode. Then silence. We knew, in our half-drowsy state, that the beast had landed. But where? On whom?

Zing, a sharp little pain on my exposed shoulder told the story. Slap, roll, sigh, check the bedside clock, and try to head back to dreamland. But singles were rare. These little monsters came in threes, at least. By 4:30, sheet pulled over my head, concentrating on sleep so hard I was wide awake, it was time to get up, turn on the light, take a roll of toilet paper and go on the offensive. (Rosemary had her own solution—she wore ear plugs, figuring the suspense of waiting to be bitten was worse than the bite.)

When these little buggers settled, they could be very difficult to hit, but a roll of toilet paper gave better coverage and seemed to make the squashing process easier. It also soaked up the blood when I squished one of the full ones. Probably it was my own blood anyway, but you never know, it could have been the dog or some errant wild creature like a bear or a moose. Best not to get too involved with someone (or something) else's blood.

Thump, bump, swinging wildly, toe stubbed on the bedpost, air thick with purple prose, the naked human wielding the flying roll, this attack eventually won the first skirmish of the day. Finally, at 5 a.m., bloody roll sitting on the night table, wall splattered with blood to be cleaned at a more reasonable hour, finally, back to dreamland.

The next squadron (which must have been a different, sleep-in species) arrived about 7. At least this was a more reasonable hour, so instead of taking the roll and going on a full search-and-splat mission, we sighed, got up and put on the kettle, meanwhile promising ourselves to be more assiduous about mosquito search-and-kill patrol before going to bed at night.

This little routine lasted for most of June and often into July. Some years were worse than others, but I could always count on many mornings of toilet paper warfare just before the solstice.

Maybe that was it, the solstice, the ritual, the turning of the orb on its axis, soon to start the inevitable slide into winter, during the full-throated blast of spring morphing into summer. These squadrons of mosquitoes, zipping about so energetically, were trying to get it all done as fast as they could, before the puddles dried up and they could no longer lay their eggs, eggs which could lie in wait for years before they hatched into vicious little vampires, harbingers of the coming death in the height of life.

TAKING WING

Sandhill cranes flying over Precipice

Flockmind

Each spring we looked forward to the return of the swallows, both the tree swallows that use abandoned woodpecker nests and other tree cavities as nest sites and our favourite, barn swallows, which were especially adaptable when it came to nest building. Before Europeans arrived in North America, these birds used caves and other natural openings to raise their young. Now, they almost exclusively nest on human-built structures, so it was no surprise that Firhome qualified as a nest site.

I don't know if anyone rates these things, but if they do, swallows must be among the top 10 among all birds when it comes to flying. Their fluid motions as they catch mosquitoes and other insects on the fly are a marvelous aerial ballet. Yet, beautiful as their flight patterns are, swallows are remarkable in other ways as well. We had one pair nesting on the south eave of our house, just over the greenhouse. But as much as we enjoyed watching them, there was a downside. Not only would droppings block light coming through the Lexan on the greenhouse roof, they were also very unsanitary. When the rain washed them down and over the eaves, we didn't want that material on the ground where we would walk through it. So I built the sparrows a platform and screwed it to the underside of the exposed rafters, making a shelf for the nest, providing security of purchase and stopping the droppings from reaching the greenhouse roof.

This tidy arrangement did not happen overnight. For the first several years, the swallows tried to establish eight to 10 nests around the house, even over the narrow ledge above the front door. At first I used the jet spray from a hose to knock them down, but after we found dead fledglings in a destroyed nest we tried other tricks, such as tying ribbons of flagging tape on the eaves, putting up tin foil, hanging long strings of baling twine, even fixing tin pie plates and discarded CDs under the eaves. The house looked like the circus had come to town, but it was all to no avail.

THE POWER OF DREAMS

Barn swallows have a very precise ritual they follow when choosing a building site. A mated pair will fly to a location, perch and literally talk to each other. These warbling staccato conversations will go on for several minutes. Then they will fly to another site and repeat the process. Over a period of two or three days, a pair will eventually choose a spot and begin to build their summer home. If you knock this nest down they will scold you, dive-bomb your head, then return to the perch and have another long conversation. By the next day they will have started to rebuild in the same location, chattering away all the while. Not only are these birds very loyal to each other, they are determined to remain at the first site they choose. That is why I felt so cruel when I knocked down their nests, destroying their carefully-built homes, as well as chasing them away from the special spots they had so painstakingly selected.

Finally, in frustration, I simply knocked down *all* nests except for one on the south eave, just outside our dining room. Then I put a platform under it. This routine continued for three years: Knock down all nests except the one on the south eave and put a platform under it. Finally, on year four of my training program, an amazing thing happened. One pair built on the south eave and no other attempts were made.

By the fifth year, the flock was as large as ever, but just one pair was building on the house. They didn't usually select the platform from the year before. Sometimes they went to the rafter next to it, but they always stayed on that south eave. I waited until the nest was built, then moved the platform under it (I did this because one year their nest fell down and the babies in it were killed) and we were set for another season.

Even if this was the pair that built the year before, and remembered, what of the new pairs, not to mention the rest of the flock? How had they realized that there was one spot available on the house, and that no others were allowed? While a lot of the rest of the flock appeared to have relocated to the hay shed down on the valley bottom, somehow each spring the decision was made that one pair could use the south eave of Firhome.

Flock memory? Flock mind? Whatever the so-called explanation, we took pure and simple pleasure in watching them swoop and dive in front of our breakfast window, catching mosquitoes as we cheered them on. We continued to be bemused by the way they had accommodated both our wishes and their housing needs.

Or was it the other way around?

Killer Door

The upper floor of Firhome, our main living area, opened onto a deck which had a bridge-like walkway connecting it to a berm, where the solar panels were located. The deck was where we set up a variety of bird feeders. Some were simple platforms on poles, others were earthenware pots hung from large wrought-iron hooks screwed to the side of the house, and one was a movable, roofed platform hanging from a clothesline that stretched from the large fir by the deck to a tall young pine 40 feet away.

Unfortunately, that door was a killer. Not in the fashion sense, as in "It's a killer; stunningly beautiful." No, our door killed things. Well, maybe that's too harsh. After all, this was the door that provided endless hours of genuine pleasure for us, especially in the mornings, as we watched the birds tussle and jostle for position on the feeder hanging in the open air above the driveway to the woodshed.

Although it was simply a passive cedar door, fitted with full-sized double-paned glass, it had a dark side. Every so often, especially in the morning as we breakfasted, we would hear a dull *whump*, the kind of sound a snowball makes when it bounces off a cardboard box. If we heard this sickening sound, both of us, plus our cats, rushed to the door, where we all looked out onto the deck to survey the damage.

Sometimes it was a junco, sometimes a redwing blackbird or, one year, a varied thrush. That was a particular shame, because that was the first year we'd had them, and there had been only three. By May, two of them had met the fate of the Door. Occasionally, after flying into the glass at full speed, these birds would lie on the brown deck boards, stunned but still breathing. These we put up on the top of the planters, to let them revive away from predatory cats. Sometimes they might lie there for up to an hour before they recovered and flew away. At other times, as with the two varied thrushes, things did not work out. Those both broke their necks and died instantly.

We found this very sad and, as with the barn swallows attempting to nest, tried many things—putting up plastic cobwebs, owl images, fluttering flagging tape and so on—but unless we blocked the glass completely, an occasional accident still happened. For some strange reason, though, we never had a grey jay make that mistake.

Cat TV

But this was also the same door that enthralled our cats. They would sit behind the glass portal for endless moments, tails lashing as they watched birds. They sometimes became so excited watching Cat TV that they uttered a weird stutter-meow, sounding like a teenager whose voice was cracking.

Klaus' dog Kosmo came visiting our door on a regular basis, too. He thought Chilko was his big brother and tried to keep in close touch with him. Like all Komondors, he had a big shaggy white coat that formed dreadlocks, floppy ears, and size 14 feet. Standing 32 inches at the shoulder, he approached the door, his small eyes covered in long strings of hair, and pushed his nose onto the double-paned glass, trying to peer inside. If he saw no one, he knocked at the door with his big paw, making a scratching noise, alerting all who were at computer screens that he was there and wanted his (even taller) buddy, Chilko, to come out to play. The early morning sun backlit the squishy gray marks he nose left quite brightly, to show how many times he had been here in any week.

Chilko picked up Kosmo's routine. Although he didn't press his nose into the glass as much, he did the scratching thing, letting us know that he needed attention. If we didn't hear him, our large tabby Obi-Wan did and then came and got us, giving his special meow to let us know his canine buddy was at the door.

Not to be outdone, Obi-Wan used to sit outside the glass for long periods, waiting for someone to see him and let him into the house, probably hoping for Chilko to come along and scratch for him. This was especially needed when the snow was deep and he was loath to tread through it to get down the steep slope and into the woodshed to his cat door.

Every spring, we lived through a period when our killer door took its toll, but in the end we hoped the benefits of Cat TV far outweighed the occasional fatality. Maybe some kind of one-way glass would have solved the problem, but we couldn't figure out how to get it double-glazed in a size big enough to fit into that door frame. In the meantime, we continued to search for ways to watch wild TV on door channel one and make it safe at the same time,

THE POWER OF DREAMS

because as new energies emerged following the stillness of snow and frost, the return of the birds that had gone south for the winter was always a special reaffirmation of the cycle of birth following death: the miracle of spring.

Mid-Winter Thaw

One memorable year, the usual slight January thaw came late—about a month late—and was heartily welcomed by everybody, man, woman, dog and critter alike. While the winter hadn't been very cold, the daytime highs had not been in positive territory for months. Frost had gone deep and the snow had a crisp crust, which meant the ranchers were feeding more, the horses couldn't forage and the wild creatures were having to work harder to fill their bellies.

As I was snowmobiling to town one February day, I saw several sets of caribou tracks in the snow on the logging road. I figured they were moving down from the windswept slopes of Kappan and Trumpeter mountains, cratering for lichens in the patches of old growth squeezed between the logging slash and the alpine. Tough work.

Mid-winter thaws sometimes brought other surprises. For example, Rosemary had just come out of the shower one morning that winter when her eye was caught by a movement in the firs along the path that led to our front door, where we had a bush vehicle parked—snowed in for the winter then, of course. What Rosemary noticed was a large hawk-like bird sitting on the hood, slowly blinking its big yellow eyes, taking in the scene. Rosemary ran to the front door where she had a better view, and as she watched, the visitor waddled across the hood and jumped down to the snow-covered ground. Looking for all the world like a short-legged gnome, it carefully picked its way over to the edge of the ridge.

Still wet and clad in only a dressing gown, Rosemary shivered as she peered out at this unusual happenstance. Nevertheless she quickly ran upstairs, found her camera and came back down, stepped into her snow boots and slowly, gingerly, opened the door and crept onto the porch.

Goshawk on fir

The visitor eyed her without alarm, then casually flew up to one of the
low branches on a young fir that I call my teenager, since it is only about
a hundred years old. The bird was looking around, seeing if there was

THE POWER OF DREAMS

anything edible in the vicinity. At first, as Rosemary edged closer, it flew up a few branches, then as slowly and ponderously as a B52, this interloper from the cliffs and open spaces above us glided down and over the ridge, a silent predator looking for breakfast.

Rosemary later determined that her visitor was a northern goshawk, a truly magnificent creature with a two-foot wingspan and eagle-like disposition. Maybe he was there for the same reason the caribou were in the trees: the snow cover was not as deep and the thick, heavy crust did not form under the firs, so the chance of getting a mouse or a vole would be much better than in the open.

Chilko and the Owls

It was always a treat in late winter when the great horned owls, quiet for most of the winter, announced themselves. You'd rarely see them, but on those mid-March nights when the moon was large, they started their mating ritual. Part of their performance was to call to each other, the forest and anything else that cared to listen, with a series of deep hoots that sounded just like a dog woofing.

Chilko thought they sounded like a dog, too. So he answered, and answered, and answered, all night long. It didn't help that his voice echoed back from across the valley! I think the owls really got into it. It seemed that the more Chilko barked, the more the owls woofed in reply and the more the echoes reverberated.

The first time this happened, we let it go on for a few nights, thinking he would tire of this, but he didn't. So then, each time Chilko started the sequence we opened the door and told him "NO!" Poor dog, all that activity out there and he couldn't take part.

Well, almost couldn't. He figured he had developed a way to be in that action and still not upset us. He'd go up to a fir tree on the berm about 10 metres from the dining room door, where he would sit and give a swallowed sort of bumph non-bark. It was really hilarious. He'd sit there bumphing away, trying so hard to talk to the owls, while still obeying us.

But when the coyotes were calling, it was too much. He couldn't help himself, and he started to howl along with them. He couldn't really howl like a coyote—the song dog has it perfected—but Chilko sort of moaned and wailed, sounding for all the world like a nail being prised out of a 2x4. We got quite a kick out of it.

It was a different story when the big boys were on the block. When the wolves howled, Chilko sat and listened. He didn't even try to get into the act. I guess he knew better than to mess with the bikers.

Owls that woof, coyotes that sing, wolves that howl, and a dog that bumph barks, all were part of our night life at Firhome.

The Precipice Parade

Each year, one species in particular announced the impending spring. True, we had birds that wintered with us: grey jays, chickadees, Townsend's solitaire, nuthatches and nutcrackers and lots of LBJs, but sometime in late March the spring parade began, never exactly the same, as the participants, dressed in a spring finery of greens, reds, golds, blacks, oranges, throbbing scarlet and creamy beige, danced and twirled their way back into the Precipice.

The drum major, far ahead of the rest of the band, was a male redwing blackbird. He stayed for about three days in late March. His liquid "Chee er eee" was deliciously bountiful, full of vibrant, virile energy, telling the world that he was back and that all other blackbirds had better take notice. He then moved on to spread the word far and wide. Soon he returned with his flock, mysteriously rounded up from who knows where. Maybe they had been waiting down on the coast for him to report in re the new summer home, or maybe they were just dawdling along, spending lazy afternoons on the trip while he flew ahead, full of enthusiasm but then heading back into the safety of the flock after his lonely explorations.

In the days following, the parade picked up. Flocks of juncos swarmed the feeder, driving the older winter residents up into the big pines while they had their fill. By mid-April, a male rufous hummingbird arrived, but he was confused, because he was the only one at the nectar feeders. No other hummers around. Often he'd disappear for a day, but when he returned another male would follow and the sparring match would begin. One bird would sit on the tip of a fir branch, his head swivelling back and forth, flicking from side to side, doing a full scan of the surrounding air space to see if his rival was in view. Tiny eyes shining bright with anticipation, his scarlet gorget flashing in the clear spring air, he sat and waited for the challenge.

Suddenly he would be dive-bombed by the other male, moving so fast the eye could barely follow, and then the chase was on. Zoom ! Zoom! As they streaked by, one barely inches behind the other, they flew seemingly impossible patterns, high rolls followed by steep power dives, managing to scoop back up just before hitting the ground. Never did I see a mishap, a misjudgment of distance or space, never a collision with each other, a tree or, yes, the human standing in the flight path dead ahead. As they ripped by my face, just inches away, I got the feeling of the game, the eternal ritual. I wondered if this was really about defending territory or more about having a great time enjoying the thrill of a new season in the spring home. It wasn't so much a fight, really, as part of the boisterous spring energy. It must have felt so good to fly so fast, under such precise control, to be so alive, and to have a compatriot in these mock aerial battles.

We enjoyed sitting on the deck, marvelling at the dexterity and energy of these rufous hummingbirds. At times we had three feeders going and held great discussions about whether there were 20, 30 or more of the little guys as they sped dizzyingly from one to the other. The constant buzz was a song all its own, and the two cats never tired of their futile attempts to grab one out of the air. Our especially ineffectual (to our delight) little long-haired calico would partially hide behind a railing and bat the air as they flew past, all the time meowing loudly, evidently saying, "Here I am! Come to me!"

Hummingbirds are a constant source of entertainment and mystery. Even the date of their annual arrival can be a source of speculation and new questions. I read that new climate models show short-term cooling trends buried within the general upward climb of global temperatures, all to do with shifting ocean currents and their effect on rain and circulation patterns. Our springs in Precipice certainly confirmed that analysis. We had been recording the arrival of the first rufous hummingbird since we moved into the valley. Our second spring, while we were still building Firhome and living down at the Glad Cab, Rosemary was working in the garden and was strafed several times by an unexpectedly early arrival. The determined hummer then flew over to the tack shed, where the feeder had been hanging all winter, and circled it a few times. The bird actually waited until the feeder was filled and hung. After that, we always made sure we had the feeder up and hanging by the 18th of April, because he was bound to arrive between then and the 23rd. It was safer that way!

The process was the same each year, so when arrival times changed drastically, it was a surprise. One year the first rufous arrived on April 9, so we had to scramble to find the feeder, make the sugar solution and put out the food. In 2008, April was quite cold, dropping to -7 or 8 each night and the snow and ice taking forever to disappear. We put out the feeder on the usual date and waited. As the days went by, we started to become concerned. By April 30, we really began to worry. Maybe the whole flock of hummingbirds that know our feeding station, the only one at the time in the valley, had been wiped out.

Rosemary sent out a few emails to people in the Chilcotin, and yes, others had noticed late arrivals, but at least theirs had finally arrived. Each night, we brought the feeder in to stop it from freezing and put it out early in the morning, hoping to catch the first arrival.

I was in the office downstairs on the phone about 10 in the morning on May 1, when the first hummer flew at the window, attracted by my red sweatshirt. What a relief to see that little guy! I alerted Rosemary, and a few minutes later she reported that he'd arrived at the feeder, drinking and drinking and drinking.

A late, cold spring, as part of global climate change, caused our hummers to be more than a week late. I wondered where they had hung out for that extra week. Had they sat on the coast, checking the forecast on the web? Did they sniff the oncoming winds? What did they do?

Whatever it was, the very day it warmed up was the very day they arrived. A little bird with a big mystery!

Each day, different participants in the parade arrived to take up summer residence: golden crowned sparrows, white crowned sparrows, grosbeaks, savannah sparrows, wrens, kinglets, geese, ducks, woodpeckers, sapsuckers, hawks, everyone returning to their special place. All in all, over the years we listed more than 50 species.

Finally, those magnificent flying machines, the barn swallows, would come into view. They'd arrive early in the morning, swooping and diving with grace and dexterity. For me, swallows were the real, solid part of the spring parade. When they appeared, you knew this wasn't a rehearsal. It was the real thing.

Every year, something new happened. Once, we were treated to a flock of 11 trumpeter swans. They flew east every morning to their day pasture to feed and flew back west over us each night to their lower-elevation bedroom. A pair of loons did the same thing: they fed in the lake above the north side of the valley during the day, then flew back over us to sleep and nest in a different lake, perhaps with fewer food offerings but less wind, on the south side.

Once, our parade brought something different. We were awakened in the early morning grayness by the most unsettling cacophony: honking, choking, braying, gobbling and squawking, all mixed into one undulating sequence that was first heard as a distant rattle but soon grew to noise levels exceeded only by a garage band with the door closed.

Lumbering though the early morning mists, not so much flying as flailing, a group of huge, prehistoric-looking creatures were travelling home to their summer range. They were sandhill cranes, ancient beyond knowing, time travellers that have been making the annual trek for millions of years. Resembling their dinosaur ancestors more than present-day birds, these cranes connected my spirit with the eons.

The spring parade was timeless. We humans are barely aware of the rhythms and mysteries creating the spring festival. Part of the tides of life on this planet, our spring Mardi Gras was a humbling reminder that we were latecomers to the show, that we were not its creators but merely spectators who came late and were standing on the sidewalk.

Spring Dance of the Raven

From their raucous calls to their magnificent flying, ravens were a large presence all year round in the Precipice, especially in the spring. Spiralling across the spring sky in perfect unison, laughing at gravity, signalling their pleasure with a resonant "Pwok, Pwok," Raven and his mate leisurely glided in huge circles over the valley.

One morning, we were enjoying watching them when suddenly, with their slick black feathers gleaming in the morning sun, they snapped into a series of parallel barrel rolls that would have made any fighter pilot envious. They followed with an imperceptibly smooth transition into a power dive, broke into a side-by-side flare across the brilliant green of fresh spring grass mixed with last year's straw-coloured uncut hay and then, to regain altitude, flew loop-the-loops, climbing skyward until they were black specks against the white puffy clouds. Then came the grand finale. Slipping down through the air in a slow, shallow curve, one raven slid over onto its back, legs and claws stretched upwards, so the upper one could clasp hands, pulling skyward. Then the clench broke, followed by a short, smooth approach where the joining again took place. It looked like a 1960s jive dance, with partners joining hands, moving in close, then falling back, eventually unclasping fingers, each loosed for a moment but still paired in the rhythm. Three, four, five or more times the intricate handshake was performed in an undulating verticality: Clasp drop, clasp drop, clasp drop, switch top and bottom partner, clasp drop, clasp drop, clasp drop, slowly losing altitude, performing aerial magic.

Raven and his partner were having a wondrous time that day. There was no other way to describe it. Across the gulf of species, the feelings of energy and joy to be alive were unmistakably communicated by the lighthearted aura of this elegant couple, dancing the Spring Dance of the Raven.

Beavers, Redwings and Spring

My earliest memories of redwing blackbirds in the Precipice are of spring melodies floating over the wetlands behind our home. Whenever I heard their songs, time melted away and I was transported back to those magical times on the edge of an Ontario marsh, when I experienced the special wonder known to young children.

The redwings came back in April. Some people feel redwings are noisy, territorial birds that disrupt others, including those who want to lie abed on those spring mornings when they arrive with the dawn, but I grew up with redwings on the north shore of Lake Ontario. Each spring the redwings arrived in droves, and I listened for hours to their liquid silver songs, enchanted with them and the new life they seemed to be serenading.

I know now that the calls were really about territory, mating and all that practical stuff, but I still get a tingle at the base of my skull and a rush of pleasure when I hear these sopranos sing their hearts out. I don't believe it is *just* about practicality, either. If you have ever seen a male sitting on top of a small fir, overlooking the valley and giving full throat, then I think you would agree there is more going on than sheer mechanics.

Each year our little flock had increased, until we had 10 or 12 birds. Now, I know that for many of you, this is tiny. I had friends in Anahim Lake who boasted (or is that cursed?) groups of up to a hundred or more. But we were thrilled with our flock, because when we had first moved in there were no redwings at all. Since the valley bottom didn't have the marshy habitat they liked, we were out of luck.

Beaver Sculpture

THE POWER OF DREAMS

That is, until the beavers moved back. For years, the previous owner of the property had dynamited beaver dams on the Hotnarko River, just below the ridge that Firhome was on. He trapped the animals and burned their lodges. He felt that the dams were destroying meadows, causing flooding and otherwise interfering with his tiny ranching operation.

I must confess that, not knowing any better for the first few years, I dynamited the dams too, although I never trapped or burned lodges. It was how we were told we should manage the place. Beavers were up to no good and they had to go.

Soon, though, we decided that the beavers were as much a part of the valley as we were, so I stopped blowing up dams. About three years after that, there were two big dams in place and the ponds behind them began to develop marshy edges and swamp habitat, and eventually, a solitary redwing showed up. You can't image the pleasure it gave me to listen to its call. It peeled away half a century of life and took me straight back to my childhood. The bird stayed around for a few days, feasted on black oil sunflower seeds and went on his way.

The next year, he came back with a couple of others, and the rest is history. Yes, the flock was small, but the delight we got out of listening to them, seeing the scarlet slashes on wing shoulders as they flew, watching the young males and the females joust on the feeder as the flock made the place their home, was immense. And it was all thanks to the beavers, still out there, still repairing their dams and still providing a home for the redwings.

And I was in the middle of it all! And how had I done it? I left things alone, left them to interconnect the way wild things do. To get the miracle of redwings to serenade my Precipice spring, all I had to do was . . . nothing.

LBJs

One fall we had a friend visiting from back east. He was a city person and didn't really know much about birds. For him, there were big ones and little ones, which he called LBJs, Little Brown Jobs. The name stuck in my mind.

Juncos, chickadees, a large variety of sparrows, nuthatches, to name just a few, darting through the air, heading over the horizon into the gray morning mist: fish of the sky, schools of little brown birds twisting and turning in perfect unison as they gathered their energies for the long flight south.

Fall in the Precipice was the time when those who were unable to survive the coming winter prepared for their exit. This gathering-in was one of the markers of the season. Like the first spring swallows,or the hummingbirds that arrived within a few days of the same date each year, the gathering of many of the LBJs for their departure marked the beginning of the slow slide into deep winter. Tracks in the early morning frost, crunchy on the dry brown grass, told the tale of where a coyote had romped and yipped in the meadow at the early dawn light. The black gray mist curled around the ridges and hung along the tree tops, waiting for the brassy yellow sun to send it packing into the wild blue yonder. Aspens and then cottonwoods showed off their burnished gold dresses to the world, trembling in the light morning breezes. When the fog finally melted away, the sky was such a vibrant blue it seemed like the depths of the ocean. The lure of the abyss was so strong all you wanted to do was to dive deeper and deeper.

And the LBJs. The LBJs knew that feeling, I think. They wheeled higher and higher, their tight circles getting smaller and smaller, corkscrewing their way up and out of sight. Were they just having fun, exhilarating in the sheer joy of crisp, clean air and an ocean of space to flit and flirt in? Daredevils all, these LBJs ignored gravity and flaunted the laws of physics, unaware that they were the envy of many: the pinnacle of evolution navigating the thin air in a way I could only dream of. It was not only the flying, it was the whole package. All that energy, the subtle communication, the nonverbal links that bound the flock together. How did they do that? In one single motion, too fast to detect, the whole group moved instantaneously from an upward spiral to a swoop so fast that they must surely have broken the sound barrier, yet no sound emerged. What did their ears hear? The whistle of air past feathers? Sounds and impressions beyond even our imagination?

THE POWER OF DREAMS

Such energy, such talent, all contained in a little body a few inches long, weighing mere ounces yet containing the beauty, the elegance and wizardry of compact function far beyond our clumsy technology. LBJs were one of those daily miracles that surrounded us in the valley, a reminder that we were not alone in that place, that we had a moral and ethical responsibility to ensure that these marvels continued to have the space, the time and the habitat to exist. Without them, the place we lived in would have been lonely and dark. Without these LBJs and the things they manifested, this whole planet would be a dead world indeed.

Woodpeckers, Fir Snags and Hummingbirds

When you live in the wilderness, you never know what will spark a new level of understanding or a new view of the world around you. It is like being constantly in the moment of solving a mystery. You know the clues are there, sometimes subtle, sometimes so obvious you pass over them. To solve some of these mysteries is part of the attraction of living in wilderness, and to solve some of them, all you have to do is be aware and open to the sights and sounds around you. Like a tree connected to its unseen roots, ecosystems support and interact with each other in the most unexpected ways.

One February morning, as we sat down to our morning tea, we were greeted by bursts of the staccato tattoo of the pileated woodpecker. Rosemary and I went outside, tea in hand, and watched as a magnificent male with his scarlet red crest went about the business of announcing to the world that an old, half-dead fir was a corner of his territory and that he was open for courting.

In that marvellously intricate way that wild systems have, the old snag and the pileated outside my window were connected to the welfare of the hummingbirds that arrived, every year, long before there are any flowers for them to sip nectar from. The males staking out their territories, flashing their deep blood-red throat patches at each other, vigorously defending their turf as they waited for the ladies to arrive, burnt up huge amounts of energy in their jousts, not to mention that they had already flown thousands of kilometres back from their southern winter homes to reach these summer digs and, on top of that, required a prodigious amount of food to keep warm in the freezing nights of late April. So the question arose: Without humans and their feeders, how did they get the food they needed? There were no flowers out, snow was still on the ground in many places and it seemed like magic that the tropical guests survived.

One answer to the mystery was that they got the extra energy they needed by eating the sap and small insects trapped in it, oozing from, you guessed it, holes in the bark drilled by the pileated woodpecker when he made music on the snag or drilled for insect larvae. This smorgasbord of insects and half-dried, concentrated, sugar-filled sap provided both protein and glucose, a high-energy, balanced source of nutrition tailored to fit the hummer's needs. As in the well-known folk song about the knee bone and the shin bone, the old growth forest was connected to the fir snag, the fir snag was connected to the woodpecker, the woodpecker was connected to the holes in the bark, the holes in the bark were connected to the hummingbird and all were connected to the mysterious ritual of spring.

The next time you hear a woodpecker drumming, think of hummingbirds darting in the air. It's a natural connection.

ENDINGS

Annie after two weeks on the skidoo trail

A Time of Passage

There are times of arrival and there are times of passing, and in our time in Precipice, we learned them well.

One such passing was that of Mort Grass. He first lived in the Precipice in the late '80s, caretaking for Lee, then moved "up top," to the Chilcotin Plateau, where he took care of small ranch properties for several years, moving from one to the other. His last place had been called, rather ominously as it turned out, Trail's End. After a couple of years, his water source dried up, and Mort either had to melt snow water for his many animals and himself or haul it from town by Skidoo. He would have liked to move, but finding a place that could accommodate him and his animals was tough.

Rosemary, perhaps inadvertently, arranged for him to live in the Precipice again:

On his winter trips to town, Dave often made the 40-minute side trip to Mort's to make sure he had firewood and sometimes went to Anahim to fetch water for him. On one trip he mentioned that I needed to go to Bella Coola for some X-rays. Mort immediately said, "Oh, she shouldn't go on her own, I'll go with her." Dave interpreted this, probably accurately, as Mort needing to get away from his winter routine at Trail's End.

And so it was arranged for me to have company. I was ambivalent about this, as Dave and I had been living very much in each other's pockets and I'd been looking forward to having some time to myself. But on the day of my appointment I skidooed out to our SUV, then drove it along the back logging roads to Mort's place. We did a lot of catch-up chatting as I drove down the Highway 20 and the Big Hill to the Bella Coola Valley. At one point Mort said to me with a big sigh, "Rosemary, do you know how heavy a five-gallon pail of water is?" Well, of course I did, from hauling water from the river during our five years in the Glad Cab, but I was a lot younger. Without thinking it through, I said, "Come and live with us, Mort."

"Oh, no," he responded. "I don't want to live on Lee's property again; he has caretakers in that cabin now." "You would live in our Glad Cab," I replied. "No, I've too many animals," he responded. Silence for twenty minutes and I was thinking about other things completely. Then, "Could I bring my chickens?"

Uh-oh! What had I done, without consulting with Dave? But we were into it now. Things progressed, and by spring we were upgrading the Glad Cab, running solar power down from our house, reinstalling a phone, and upgrading fences and setting up a hen house for an elderly, sometimes cantankerous gentleman who had a very large menagerie. By then, he had many chickens, a pot-bellied escape-artist goat named Charlie, Nick the spitting llama, and two dogs—a three-legged sweetie called Cactus who was fast friends with Bones, a cadaverous redbone hound. The little cats, Thelma and Louise, were in contrast to his giant Belgians Jake and Jimmy, draft horses weighing in at a ton each. As you can imagine, this collection of creatures was a constant source of entertainment and untold adventures over the time he was with us.

Less fun were Mort's strokes, heart attacks, escaping animals, and coyote-challenged hen house. When he was 87, the snowmachine trips and the rigours of living in the Precipice so far from medical help got to him, and he decided that he needed to move into Anahim Lake. He was down to one dog and one cat by then, plus Charlie the goat, and he found a rancher to take his Belgians and llama. His chickens had all met their demise when he was in the hospital for three months, in spite of my daily visits. In his Anahim house he always had the coffee pot on, there was always a bed for the night if needed, and he kept his sharp wit to the end.

On a crunchy morning in March 2013, an inner voice warned me we should visit Mort. He hadn't been well and had a caregiver living with him. We knew he was dying. Suddenly it felt as if we needed to see him now. We alerted our neighbours, Fred and Monika, and we all made the trip out to Anahim.

When we visited Mort that Thursday, he was drifting in and out of this reality. For a few moments the old sparkle would blaze through the half-closed eyes, his sense of humour would rise, and he made comments like, "See what happens when you don't lock your doors? Guys like you can just walk right in!" At other moments, he engaged in brief conversations with people only he could see and hear. We are forever thankful we had that last day with him; he died a day later

Spring is a time of energy flows, vortices winding and unwinding, sliding and shifting, replacement of the old by the eternal new, itself a recycled reality from the stars. Spring is simultaneously old, young, new, transmuted and unknowable: all things at all times. So it had come to pass with Mort. He had had his last spring in this plane. That morning was his time of passage into the great Chilcotin in the sky, perhaps to collect yet another menagerie. May he ride in peace through the open spaces he loved. We still miss him. .

Mort and his team

THE POWER OF DREAMS

Another part of our life in Precipice was the horses. We'd seen the passing of several during our years there, but Annie is the one that stands out. Although Annie belonged to our neighbour Lee, she was part of the Precipice gang. In the early years we had four saddle horses, and Lee had a mixed bunch of ten. Feeding 14 horses from a stack or by snowmachine became an adventure as they crowded in for the hay. No matter, Annie always came galloping first across the meadow and used her size to maintain herd position, making sure she got her share and then some.

Now Annie was showing her age. Percherons start out black and then slowly turn white. Annie was pure white but still active. For a couple of days late one winter we hadn't seen much of the horses at feeding time, but I wasn't concerned; green grass was beginning to show in some places and I figured they were out rustling for the tasty greens. But then I found the herd—minus Annie. There were a lot of horse tracks leading out of the valley, an unusual occurrence in itself. Although they had never been fenced in, they were happy in our little oasis and never left.

I took the snowmachine and went out along the trail, following tracks. Then, as I rounded a corner, there was Annie, lying in the middle of the Skidoo trail, looking for all the world like a small brontosaurus, with a big distended body and a slender snakelike neck extended straight out. Instantly, I knew she was dead—the unnatural angle of the shoulders, the feet straight out, the tail curled over her back.

Annie was born in the Precipice in 1981, the last of the old-time Precipice horses. She was sired by one of the Three Circle studs that came from Lester Dorsey's bunch. She was a Percheron draft horse, a big, strong animal weighing over a ton and with a personality to match her size. Although she could pull with the best of them if she felt like it, she was not fond of dogs, geldings or too much work. Nasty at times, she was a biter, sometimes a kicker, and she definitely had a mind of her own.

She was already in harness and still a dappled grey when we moved into the Precipice in 1986. On those hot summer days, when the dust devils staggered across the meadow, she would be leading the team, pulling Lee's mower or rake across the field. In the last few years, pure white by then and retired by a 65-horsepower tractor and old age, she hung out around the feeder, gossiping with the new guys, telling stories and grabbing a little more than her fair share of grub. Old mares are like that.

She had never left the valley, never ventured up the road and into the great beyond. She was born there and never had any interest in the outside. That is why I was so surprised to see her, five kilometres out on the trail, dead as a beached whale. Well, at least finding her solved part of the mystery. But why had the horses left the valley in the first place?

When I found Annie, I could see where the other horses had been milling around her, then moved down the trail a hundred metres or so before yarding up again. It looked like they'd been there for a long time; the snow was really beaten down. Without Annie to lead them, they were confused, so they finally had turned around and travelled back home to the Precipice.

What had happened? Annie as the head mare had surely led them here, into new territory, far from home. But why? What had killed her?

After several conversations with long-time horse people, the best explanation seemed to be that horses tend to run away from pain, so perhaps Annie was looking for a pain-free place. The pain must have been bad for her to travel so far, to leave her birthplace, the only world she had ever known: the place where she had listened to the wolves' full-moon howls, tasted the beauty of tender spring grass, felt the bite of winter wind and chased all manner of bears, black or brown, mommas and cubs alike, across the big meadow and into the timber. Old, out of shape, not used to the heavy exercise of climbing up out of the valley, she probably had a heart attack, dropping dead on the trail.

I managed to get the Skidoo around her, through some shrubby bushes, and kept going to town that day for the mail. As I came over the rise on the way home again, there were at least a dozen eagles settled on the carcass.

Coyote tracks abounded, and it wouldn't be long before the wolves and the spring grizzlies would show up for their share.

Perhaps this was the most fitting epitaph for Annie. To return to the wild in which she was born, to be part of the eagles, wolves, coyotes and bears that she spent her life being aware of and entwined with as part of living here in this great free place.

The Last Time

Over the years we had four dogs in Precipice. The first one, an Irish Wolfhound, died of a twisted gut the year we moved in. His partner, Beardog, was shot by a sick hunter (who took his collar and the collars of other dogs he'd killed as souvenirs). Chilko was number four and left the Precipice with us. This story, though, is about Hobo, dog number three, a rescue dog from Bella Coola. All dogs are special, yet he was more than most. Trusted companion, never wavering in his affection, his loss hit us really hard. His liver failed when he was 14 and he was having seizures, so we took him to the vet in Williams Lake, were told there was nothing they could do, and sat with him as he was given the needle. To this day, tears well up as I vividly see that final scene in full colour and detail. His paws crossed, deep brown eyes looking up at us so trustingly, not afraid, happy to be with us. It was a tough time.

The year after he died, we were experiencing a beautiful second summer. The mornings were crisp, the air was sharp in the nostrils with the smells of earth and the rustle of dead leaves as they were pushed aside by our feet. As I stood out at the edge of the sidehill looking out over the valley into the distant mountains, I started to think of Hobo; this was one of his favourite spots. It was a strategic location. From here he could keep an eye on the house, the workshop and all in between. Standing in his place with the morning sun warming my face, I wrote his requiem.

The Last Time

When will the last time be? The last time I walk the trail, the last load of wood stacked in the woodshed, the last fire lit. The last time. To feel the sun on my face, to be pushed by the wind. The last time to hear a song, the last time to feel the beat, to drink a glass of whiskey, to sit by the fire. The last time. I'll never know the last time at the time. I always think there will be another time. Another time to make love, to wake up beside each other in the morning, to hold each other in our arms. The last time.

The last time to do, to experience, to feel, to become, to expand, to explore: the last time. Not morbid thoughts, but realizing thoughts, realizing the way of it, the dance of it; preparation. Preparation for the sure, instant knowledge that the last time has passed without knowing it was the last time at the time.

The last time for Hobo. The last time he went up the stairs, the last time he went rushing down the stairs to greet someone, the last floatplane flight, the last run in the meadow, the last horse nosed, the last canoe ride, the last bone chewed, the last deer chased away from the garden.

The last time. The last tree seen naked, the last ice walked on, the last anger, the last thought. The last time. Precious last time. Unknown last time. The last time.

There is a last time, and there *is* a time to leave. Leaving Firhome was the most difficult thing we have ever done. Sometimes you just have to put your head down, hunch your shoulders and go for it. Life is about process. Process takes time; it has its own rules and its own set of standards, which will be obeyed even if you tried to avoid them. The decision to leave Firhome was a process that unfolded over more than three years.

One spring I woke up on a particularly unpleasant early April morning, a late blizzard of snow attacking our windows, and said to Rosemary that I thought it was time to think about moving on. She responded in a very definite way that we were not leaving, and that was that.

Hobo, goodbye

The next spring, on a particularly unpleasant early April morning, Rosemary woke up, looked out the window and suggested that it was time for us to move on. I responded in a very definite way that we were not ready to leave, and that was that.

This dance went on for three springs, until on one particularly unpleasant early April morning we both woke up, looked out the window at the winter scene and agreed it was time to think about moving on.

The reasons were simple, in some ways: things like putting up five to six cords of firewood a year, doing biannual shopping trips lasting three or four days, coming and going on snowmachine five or six months of the year.

These were physical issues pressing on our bodies and our energies. There was also an increasing awareness that we had used up a lot of our mental resources and resilience over the past 27 or so years. I was 67 and Rosemary was 72, and we were experiencing a type of burnout regarding this remote lifestyle. It was time for a change.

Thus began the biggest roller coaster ride of our lives. The process unfolded in a series of decisions and actions, each leading inexorably into a new future. The simplest one, really, was to make the decision. Yes, it was a deeply soul-shaking idea, but it was just that, an idea, a new course of action to be plotted out, moved into, as we became entangled in a different life.

At each stop along the way we were faced anew with the reality of our decision. As the steps were taken, it became obvious that we were still conflicted. *When do we want to leave? In the spring? The summer?* We couldn't physically leave in winter, so at least that was easy to decide. There were drop-dead dates, such as the first of October, for example. We wouldn't be able to get moving vans in and out on the difficult, twisty road if there was any snow at all, so if we were not moved by then, it would be at least six months before the next window would appear.

Finally it became obvious that the timing would depend on the agreement made with the buyer. Then the next step was to advertise, to stand up and tell the world that our dream was on the block, and how much will you pay us for it?

That was the first real deep shaking of the inner jelly. What do you say? How do you advertise? We quickly found out, after talking to a couple of realtors, that they were not really interested. Precipice was too remote. There was no way to set a price, no ability show the property, and all in all it was not something they wanted take on. We realized that there was very little they could do anyway, except take a very large commission (they wanted 20%!). We decided to use the various eco-property websites for our listing.

And that led to the question: What was the asking price? What is a dream worth? What is nearly 30 years' investment of labour, energy, time and emotion going to fetch? When we added up the money we had put into the Precipice over the years, it quite quickly became a sum far beyond what we felt was reasonable. That process really ripped open the wound. All those years doing all those things. Putting in that first driveway, buying and hauling all the building materials, ongoing projects over the years, like fencing, building bridges, road maintenance, building garden soils—the list kept growing. Once we reached the top half of six figures, heading for seven, we stopped adding up the amount we had put in. That certainly was not going to make sense.

How to attack the problem? We decided to come at it from the other end, as in: Where did we want to go? In a sense, the world was our oyster at this point. Remembering how much we enjoyed New Zealand, we scoped it out, looking at property prices on the South and North Islands. No, that wouldn't work—Chilko would have to be in quarantine for six months. We checked out various provinces like New Brunswick, Nova Scotia . . . but realized, finally, that B.C.'s west coast was the only place for us. But where to go that didn't feel like a town or city?

As so often happens in life, the final direction came from a chance conversation, this one with Rosemary's nephew. He has a property on Gabriola and he suggested we give the island a look-see. The Gulf Islands? How could we possibly afford that? This was the dream land where the lotus eaters lived, but us? But—why not? All was still possible.

When we got off the ferry at Gabriola Island, the lushness of the forest reminded Rosemary of her childhood in North Vancouver. We both love the ocean and realized we would like to live beside it. There are a lot of other reasons, but the short of it is that we felt like this particular island was where we wanted to be. We did check out the other Gulf Islands, but none appealed to us the same way. And we discovered that the property prices on Gabriola had become extremely reasonable.

That decision made, another deep vibration shook the soul, a shock wave of leaving an ecosystem I dearly loved: the Interior dry forest. For me, that was, and still is, difficult. I have a soft spot for the ragged, sparse, hardscrabble land and an admiration for the sheer survival force evident there. No matter, we had decided where we wanted to go.

Based on the combination of what we felt needed to move to Gabriola and what we had the nerve to ask for, we established a selling price for Firhome. Putting a price tag on our dream like it was a chunk of beef on a marble slab was not easy. It was another realization driven home that this was for real, the reduction of all of it to so many shekels—again, another difficult emotion.

Each time we wrote and rewrote the listing information to go on the websites we had chosen to use, we wondered why and how we could bear to leave this paradise, this marvelous creation so carefully chosen and lovingly constructed over nearly three decades, this place that was so ideal. How could we possible leave?

Up one day, down the next. Waking in the night, the mind screaming *no, no, this can't be!* Bursting into spontaneous tears, even sobs, at the oddest moments, over little things, a garden bed here, a well-worn path there, the stones marking where "our best dogs ever" and all our cats were buried.

Slowly, slowly the acceptance began to settle in. The ability to envision a new life, and a new adventure, began to take hold, but it was not without effort and willpower. All we could do was to keep focused, to stay the course, to believe in our intuition, our bodies and our feelings, torn apart as they were.

It took nearly two years and three uncompleted offers before we eventually came to meet the people who purchased Firhome. Their vision is different than ours was, as they just wanted a vacation home, but then once you sell a property it is no longer yours in any sense of the term. On the positive side, they fell in love with Firhome itself. The buyer is an architect and marvelled at the big fir beams, the open cathedral ceiling, all the old-growth wood throughout, the mountain view, the sheer presence of nature in all its force in and around Firhome. The whole family was captivated.

Many images linger in my mind from that time. The trip to Bella Coola to sign the government papers relinquishing our title to Precipice still causes tearful emotions to well up in my chest. The area around the fire pit strewn with all our possessions, waiting to be crammed into the two small moving vans we had collected in Williams Lake, the bits and pieces covered with blue tarps and plastic shrouds, as if a thrift store had put its wares out on the lawn for all to see. It was so naked, so exposed, so vulnerable, and so uprooted. The empty house was naked too, looking so impersonal.

Leaving our friends, all gathered to help us with the packing and loading, and the farewell party, was another wrench. The spectre of having to form new friendships, moving from a truly tiny community of friends to a new, far busier one, was frightening and something we didn't dare dwell on.

Serendipitously, a place on Gabriola that we finally felt was right—we'd looked for 14 months, on and off—had come up at the same time as Firhome sold. So we had a place to move to before winter reached the Precipice. The new owners had said we could stay the winter, but that would be prolonging the misery of leaving.

 The moving experience itself was traumatic. It took three days in two fully loaded rental trucks, our suddenly sick Yukon on a flatdeck (full of stained glass), Rosemary in the camper van with the animals and some monster house plants, grinding up and down the hills from Precipice to Gabriola, arriving there in a pea soup fog so thick we could barely follow the truck our nephew was driving as he snaked along the oceanfront road and crept up the hill to our new place.

We are settled in now. Things have worked out for the best. Life is less physically demanding, services are handy and the climate is exotic; winters without much real snow, or if snow falls we can enjoy the beauty, knowing it will be gone in days rather than six months. Rosemary is able to pursue her passion for gardening in whole new ways, producing wondrous arrays of flowers and vegetables not possible before, and it's exciting to have access to the art, theatre and music that proliferates on our island. For me, not having the demands of maintaining machinery, keeping our route into the valley driveable, making my own boards and doing all the things necessary to keep Firhome functioning, has lifted a load larger than I realized.

The lifestyle we chose in the Precipice is not for everyone. You need to be fiercely independent and a good problem-solver, especially in difficult situations. Yes, it would have been helpful to have had basic skills for cutting firewood, fixing trucks, snowmachines and ATVs, managing electricity, and so on, but for me that was the interesting part: learning new skills and taking pride and satisfaction from figuring it out and completing the issue at hand. I'm very glad I'm not the one who will follow me doing any renovations to Firhome, though. They will see solutions and encounter designs not found in any book, that's for sure. I can only hope they smile and accept the new challenge of figuring out just what in blazes I did.

To follow a similar path, you're going to need what my mother used to call "sticktoitiveness." Giving up is not an option. But above all, you need to feel wild, untamed Gaia in your bones and be drawn to it like a moth to the flame. That is where the magic is, where the lifestyle makes sense and the energy comes from. Otherwise it becomes a battle, and that is one battle you cannot win, ever.

Over our 27 years in Precipice Valley, we encountered many challenges. Sometimes it seemed like a constant struggle: You get one thing done and something happens and you now have two more things to do, such as two metres of new fluffy snow closing the trail for weeks, freezing frost in August, forest fires on your doorstep with eviction notices (we never did obey them), plumbing that leaks, pumps that seize up, a machine breakdown miles out in the bush, swarms of blackflies so thick you can't take a breath without sucking them in, an aching tooth that needs to be put up with for several days because the dentist is a 13-hour round trip, trying to replace a starter motor on your truck while lying on your back 20 miles from home, cold snow blowing into your hood and down your back, fingers stiff with cold, dropping the bolts, cursing the gods and whoever else you can think of, having a small nut drop into the carb on your one-ton truck, then having to take the head off to get it out, only to bend a pushrod that takes two weeks to replace. As the years rolled by, there were many times it seemed an impossible journey, full of roadblocks and traps, but never once did we even consider throwing in the towel. You have to have that kind of personality.

I could not have done it alone. Rosemary and I are a team. We pulled in the same direction. Of course, we had times of discord and tension, inevitable when living in each other's pockets as we did, but because we felt the same underlying energies we had a base to fall back on. Without this basic connection, you really can't make it happen. In the years we were in the Precipice we observed many who tried the remote lifestyle, some in the Precipice and others up on the Chilcotin Plateau, and didn't make it.

Since we had no children, we could devote all our time to the life in that remote area. Having a family would have changed all that. Growing children need a more social environment, a community to grow up in, and the security of a steady income. Perhaps the downside of having no children was that there was nothing to cushion our own relationship. Often, we would be alone for weeks or months on end. This means you have to learn acceptance of each other and be good company. Precipice gave us both a different lens on life. There, the most important thing in the morning was to look out the window to see what the weather was, not to listen to the traffic update. Your centre changes. You take a longer view. We have become more tolerant of others and all the different ways of striving. Part of this is because we are in our seventies, yet there's no doubt that those years and experiences in Precipice Valley gave us humility and a huge dose of planetary reality.

Now, as I sit on a boulder-strewn beach, watching the ocean gnaw at the shore, I think of the Hotnarko River meandering through the Precipice, giving essence and energy to those who share its 10,000-year-old home, knowing that some of its molecules are splashing on the rocks here and wetting my feet. This gives me comfort and the understanding that such is life: Take it as it comes and let the river flow.

ABOUT THE AUTHORS

Dave was born in Ontario, but when he travelled across Canada to the Rockies he fell in love with the mountains and never wanted to leave. Instead, bored with a myriad of unsatisfying jobs, he went to university to study geography.

Rosemary was born in B.C. and went to university for similar reasons—she was tired of being in an urban business world. At UBC she studied psychology and education.

The Neads met there, and as the saying goes, that's all she wrote! They studied and hiked and scuba dove and shared their dreams of a wilderness life. When they graduated, they headed north and found the start of that life in Precipice Valley in the West Chilcotin of British Columbia's coast mountains. At this point they were in their 40's and, perhaps naively, decided to build their own home in the wilderness. Dave worked as a Park Ranger in Tweedsmuir Park in summers for several years and Rosemary learned ways to garden in a challenging, alpine influenced environment while keeping their home running efficiently. She also found time to develop a sideline with her stained-glass panels.

Concerned about the mismanagement of much of the land around them, they became deeply involved in local conservation issues. Over the next 25 years, Dave and Rosemary worked extensively on conservation and wilderness tourism issues, both locally and provincially. As an activist, Dave helped create several organizations to assist communities and First Nations in the creation of land use plans and protected areas.

They now live on Gabriola Island, BC— with slightly less snow.

Dave and Rosemary with Who Knows in Precipice Valley.

RELATED TITLES

Then & Now

This account, of the geography and history of some of the mountainous country drained by the South Nahanni River, is based on Lougheed's observations as a hiker and paddler, and on her thorough research — including interviews and correspondence with the people, and the descendants of the people, who made that history..

Nahanni

Lougheed, Vivien

978-0-88839-697-6 [paperback]
978-0-88839-697-6 [epub]
5½ x 8½, sc, 246pp

$24.95

Burnt Snow

Moore, Kieran

978-0-88839-100-1 [paperback]
978-0-88839-356-2 [hardcover]
978-0-88839-265-7 [epub]
6 x 9, sc, 272pp

$19.95

My years living & working with the Dene of the Northwest Territories

The reflections of the authors encounters with some of the leading figures of the North are quite humorous and consequential in the later development of the North. He describes the Indigenous Elders who would influence him in countless ways, and how their teachings are later, the source of northern survival in otherwise seemingly impossible situations. This book reflects the people of that time, and their lifestyle of living off the land in total independence and their incredible life-skills of survival.

A Home in the Kodiak Wilderness

At loose ends in his private life and at odds with society, the author persuades his wife, to join him in a new beginning. Before long, they and their children are living in a wilderness cabin on Alaska's Kodiak Island, outnumbered by the brown bears.

A celebration of nature and of the peculiarities of the Alaskan bush, this book builds from personal experience to a rounded and loving portrait of a place—Cottonwood Homestead—and a way of life. In these essays and sketches, by turns humorous, meditative and lyrical, the author goes beyond the challenges and triumphs of wilderness living to explore his environment, the relationships among the plants and animals and the people he meets. Along the way he wrestles with his doubts and reexamines his assumptions about life.

Land of Bear & Eagle
Ravicz, Tanyo

978-0-88839-722-5 [paperback]
978-0-88839-703-4 [epub]
5½ x 8½, sc, 176pp

$21.95

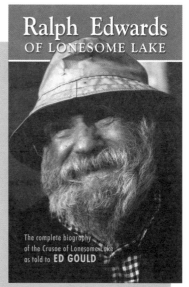

Ralph Edwards Lonesome Lake
Gould, Ed & Ralph Edwards

978-0-88839-100-1 [paperback]
5½ x 8½, sc, 296pp

$19.95

A trilogy of stories by the Edwards family about their fascinating life in the Bella Coola area.

Often called "The Crusoe of Lonesome Lake," because of a best-selling book written by the American journalist Leland Stowe, Edwards has gone on to live at least one more life and reveals himself to be a pioneer of a breed that no longer exists. Best known for his almost single-handed rescue of the trumpeter swans from extinction in North America, Edwards now related in his own words other aspects of his long, varied life, including experience with his missionary parents in India, as a telegraph operator under fire in World War I and his eventual return to Lonesome Lake.